FROM THE LIBRARY OF

_____

MARTHA STEWART WEDDINGS

MARTHA STEWART WEDDINGS IDEAS & INSPIRATION

Clarkson Potter/
Publishers
NEW YORK

Published in the United States by Clarkson Potter/Publishers,
an imprint of the Crown Publishing Group,
a division of Penguin Random House LLC, New York.
www.crownpublishing.com
www.clarksonpotter.com
www.marthastewart.com

CLARKSON POTTER is a trademark and POTTER with colophon is
a registered trademark of Penguin Random House LLC.

Library of Congress Cataloging-in-Publication Data is available.

ISBN 978-0-307-95465-7

Printed in Hong Kong

Some text and photographs have previously appeared in
Martha Stewart Living Omnimedia publications.

Book and jacket design by Michael McCormick
Photo credits appear on page 267.

10 9 8 7 6 5 4 3 2 1

First Edition

TO ALL OF OUR BRIDES—PAST, PRESENT,
AND FUTURE. MAY YOU
ENJOY THIS BOOK
AND LEARN FROM ITS PAGES.

CONTENTS

FOREWORD 8

CHAPTER ONE

YOU'RE ENGAGED!

10

CHAPTER TWO

DREAM UP YOUR THEME

22

CHAPTER THREE

JUST ADD COLOR

46

CHAPTER FOUR

STYLE YOUR LOOK

62

CHAPTER FIVE

SELECT YOUR STATIONERY

90

CHAPTER SIX

FIND YOUR FLOWERS

112

CHAPTER SEVEN

START TO CELEBRATE

146

CHAPTER EIGHT

WELCOME YOUR GUESTS

162

CHAPTER NINE

MASTER YOUR CEREMONY

172

CHAPTER TEN

DESIGN YOUR RECEPTION

200

CHAPTER ELEVEN

CREATE YOUR CAKE

222

CHAPTER TWELVE

PLAN YOUR SEND-OFF

248

ACKNOWLEDGMENTS 266   PHOTO CREDITS 267

INDEX 268

FOREWORD

I was married quite a while ago, but I remember every single moment of the day. Actually, I can clearly recall all the preparations prior to that lovely Saturday, July 1—a cool, sunny, summer day. I was just nineteen years old, madly in love, and I knew nothing about planning a wedding; but because I was an organized college student and very practical and economical, I was fearless about making arrangements with the chapel, the chaplain, the hotel, and the chef. My parents were not New Yorkers and not in a position to help me very much, with either the preparations or the finances. (My mother did help sew my dress and make my pillbox hat.) My parents-in-law-to-be were much more sophisticated and were able to guide me a bit, but ultimately I wanted to show that I could "make a wedding" we would all enjoy. I was so excited, so enthusiastic, and so motivated that our day did turn out absolutely fine (a few glitches, none serious). But if only I had had a real guide, who knows what I might have done differently.

Your wedding is one of life's most special "rites of passage." As such, much is written about its importance; huge amounts of time and energy are expended on planning the ceremony, reception, and dressing of the participants; and an impressive amount of money is spent. Martha Stewart Living has published the inspiring *Weddings* magazine for twenty years and has also created practical and beautiful books, planners, and well-designed online content to aid couples, and their helpers, with the myriad of issues that constitutes a "wedding day." Now, we have published what we hope is the most useful weddings guidebook ever. We aimed to answer all your questions and navigate your journey from dreaming to planning to celebrating. And we hope that you will be inspired to have the wedding you have thought about, the personal, lovely, evocative day you deserve. In other words, a day you will always remember.

YOU'RE
ENGAGED!

"

THERE IS SO MUCH JOY THAT GOES INTO THE PLANNING AND DREAMING OF YOUR WEDDING— IT IS THE HAPPIEST OF PROJECTS.

"

— Martha Stewart

CONGRATULATIONS! *Felicidades! Félicitations! Grattis! Mazel tov!* In all languages, the editors of Martha Stewart Weddings wish you the very best on the news of your engagement. We're also thrilled that you have looked to us to help plan your big day. Our goal is to inspire you to create a person-alized celebration that's fun, memorable, and everything you and your soon-to-be-spouse want it to be. You're entering one of the most exciting—and happy—times of your lives. The next few weeks will bring the exhilaration of sharing your news with friends and family, and then the whirlwind of putting together a once-in-a-lifetime event. Sound overwhelming? It can be. There are budgets to mind, parental expectations to navigate, and the sheer abundance of options available to you today: Will you get married on a tropical beach or in a ballroom? Mail letterpressed or engraved invites? Serve a towering cake or delicious pies? All these considerations can stump even the most decisive couples. The good news is that we're here to guide and support you every step of the way. Better yet, you'll see that our approach to planning a wedding is distinctive (after more than 20 years in the love business, we've learned a thing or two!). More than anything, we believe in enjoying—not stressing over—the process of designing your day. We also believe that just as no two couples are the same, no two celebrations should be alike. In this book, we'll share decades' worth of our wedding wisdom and time-trusted tips. So relax, consider yourself in capable hands, and relish this special time. The hardest part is over: You already made the decision to marry and spend the rest of your lives together. Now it's time to start celebrating that!

First Things First: Budget

As much as we would love to skip right ahead to the fun of cake tastings,
we'd be remiss not to steer you in the right direction, right away.
After you've said "Yes!" and slipped that pretty sparkler on your finger, it's time to
tackle a few tasks that will put you on the smoothest path toward the aisle.

WEDDIQUETTE
ANNOUNCING
YOUR NEWS

———

Changing
your status on
Facebook is one
way to spread
the engagement
word quickly.
But here's
another that
we're more fond
of: Go see or
call your parents
first (customarily,
that would be
the bride's
family, then
the groom's),
then pick up
the phone
and call your
closest friends to
let them know
you're getting
married—
yes, married!

We hear you, money talk can be deflating. But making plans without establishing a budget is like driving without a gas gauge: You never know when or where you'll run out of resources. And to us, the prospect of having to undo plans you've already set (or cut your guest list in half) is a lot more trouble—and heartache—than having the all-important money conversation in the beginning. So before picking a venue or putting down a deposit on a dress, do yourself the biggest favor and gather your fiancé and families together to discuss finances.

WHO PAYS FOR WHAT

Traditionally, the bride and her family cover the expense of the wedding, including the cost of the bride's attire, the flowers, day-of transportation, photo fees, travel and lodging for the officiant (if necessary), and all the reception expenditures. The bride then personally pays for gifts and flowers for her attendants, her groom's ring, and a present for him. The groom's parents host the rehearsal dinner, and the man of the hour pays for his clothing, groomsmen's gifts, the bride's ring, and a present for her.

These days, however, anything goes. Many couples fund their own celebration entirely themselves, while others get assistance from one or both sets of parents. The bottom line is that all parties should offer only what they feel comfortable contributing. If money is coming from a few sources, it's often more palatable for each party to pay for specific elements, such as the flowers or the band, instead of giving a lump sum. This tactic also helps offset costs from you (and defuses arguments) when a parent cares more about a detail than you do. If your mom and dad have strong feelings about the venue or guest list, for example, then it makes sense that they cover the expenses that come with procuring the location or having a larger fête, like catering or stationery costs. Or if your dad and mom (or groom) have their hearts set on serving filet mignon, let them pony up for it.

If you two are personally paying for the wedding, remember that this is just the beginning of your lives together; you will want to plan and save for vacations, a home, and maybe kids one day. So the less debt you can start your future with, the better. Ideally, you don't want to owe a penny postwedding, but since this isn't always realistic, here's a good rule of thumb: Avoid borrowing more money than you can afford to pay off within three to six months. To save up, create a separate bank account for the wedding. That way, you can see what you're both contributing together, and it's less stressful than writing a check from your personal account every time a whopper expense comes through.

WHERE THE MONEY (OFTEN) GOES

All weddings are different—some couples spring for a 16-piece band while others splurge on a breathtaking venue (or dress, for that matter), but usually most of your expenses will fall toward your reception even if you throw a low-key event (your ceremony should take up only about 3 percent of your budget, including the site cost, officiant fee, and printing programs, if you have them). It's vital to decide what is most important to you and set priorities before you arbitrarily assign numbers.

Divine Details You'll deliberate with care (and joy!) over every element—from your stationery and what you'll wear to the décor and menu. But you'll breathe easier while doing so if you know you're staying on budget. Remember to allocate for extras, including tips, fees, and wedding party gifts, from the start.

Breaking Down the Budget

No matter how much or how little you have to spend, take these general guidelines into account. Once you set your priorities, customize them as you see fit.

40%

FOOD

From hors d'oeuvres and drinks during cocktail hour to a delicious meal and big-finish cake, this will be your biggest expenditure.

10–15%

RECEPTION VENUE & RENTALS

This number can climb if you get hitched in an expensive city or place.

Cents and Sensibility Friends of this couple lent them their California property for their fall wedding. They redirected the savings on location to special touches. 1. A faux bois motif was introduced on invites and paper elements. 2. The happy couple. 3. Chocolate quail eggs graced the dessert table. 4. Linen napkins were embroidered with their initial. 5. Her bouquet included garden roses, bunny tails, and dogwood. 6. The tablecloth incorporated the faux bois motif. 7. Guests received the pair's favorite macarons. 8. A lavish dessert spread was served. 9. Bridesmaids' ballet flats matched their dresses.

12%

PHOTOGRAPHY AND VIDEOS

Great photos are a must, and we highly suggest hiring a videographer, too. While this is an additional expense couples often cut, we find many regret not having this amazing memento to watch or show their kids someday.

10%

FASHION

The bride's dress, veil, jewelry, shoes, and day-of primping and the groom's head-to-toe look fall within this budget.

6–12%

MUSIC

Give your ceremony and reception the ultimate soundtrack via a band or awesome deejay.

5–8%

FLOWERS

You'll need personal blooms (including bouquets and boutonnières) for your bridal party at the ceremony as well as centerpieces and arrangements for the reception.

3–5%

STATIONERY

Invitations come in a range of prices, depending on how you have them designed and printed. Include thank-you notes, and announcements or save-the-date cards if you choose to send them. And when you're allocating funds for paper goods, don't forget the cost of postage; it adds up quickly and often surprises couples.

2%

TRANSPORTATION

Shuttle services for guests are a nice touch, especially if your ceremony and reception are in different places, or you have lots of out-of-town guests. A cool ride from the event for the couple is a fun tradition, too.

1–5%

MISCELLANEOUS

Budget now for getting a marriage license and for paying tips, taxes, late fees, and for any unforeseen extras. Down the road, ask vendors to include the cost of taxes and late fees in their contracts. Consider buying wedding insurance as well; it can protect against sudden cancellations, damages, or vendor mishaps.

FACTS TO FACTOR IN

A lot of variables go into the overall cost of a wedding. As you strategize for yours, keep these in mind:

Prime season means premium costs. If you tie the knot during the high season of your chosen locale (summer for most places in the United States, winter for ski resort towns or tropical resorts), you'll pay more for your venue than you would during its off-season.

Holidays can hike things up. It may be tempting to wed over a holiday when you have more days off from work, but traveling during these times is usually more expensive. Your venue will likely be pricier, too, because of high demand and overtime pay for staff.

Weekends cost more. The most popular time to marry is on a Saturday, which puts places in high demand, especially if they can only accommodate one event at a time. If you wed on Sunday or a weekday–a Thursday or Friday night–you often save.

And it may seem obvious, but it bears repeating as it can be so tempting to invite everyone you've ever met to share in your joy: **More people equals more money.** The bigger your guest list, the bigger your budget.

Create a Guest List

*This may feel a little early, but trust us: You will want
a good idea of how many people you'll host as soon as possible.
The size of the list plays a major role in your budget and venue selection
(no need to pick a giant place if you don't have a big guest list).*

Over the years, we've seen the guest list become an issue when a couple wants a small wedding but their parents envision a big bash. Or, vice versa. So it's best to get on the same page right away. Plus, if you have an engagement party or shower, you'll need to know whom to invite; it's an etiquette no-no to include people who aren't also invited to the main event. (For more on that, see pages 150 to 152.)

Sit down with your betrothed and come up with a list together. In the meantime, ask both sets of your parents to draft up one of their own, including a list of must-have friends and a B-list of nice-to-haves. Then, review the combined list together. It's customary for each side of the family—yours and your fiancé's—to invite an equal number of people. However, today that allotment can shift depending on who is picking up the tab. When drawing up your list, consider our pointers:

REACHING OUT TO RELATIVES

Your immediate families are givens, and, usually, so are your aunts, uncles, first cousins, and grandparents. As you branch out on the family tree, remember that the more you invite from one limb, the farther you'll need to extend your list. (You can't invite your favorite second cousin without inviting her siblings.) The same goes for other close but nonfamilial groups: Say you're part of a book club. Once you invite a few members, it's hard not to include everyone. In both cases, you need to make an all-or-none call.

INVITING FRIENDS

Most people can't afford to extend invitations to every Facebook friend, so start by filling your list with your nearest and dearest. Then, as you work down your contact list, ask yourself if you can see having dinner with each person during the next year. If you can say you would, then put her on your A-list. But if you feel compelled to invite someone simply because you've known him since the second grade (or he invited you to his nuptials), place him on the B-list.

PICKING COWORKERS

The same rules apply here: The more people you include, the more you'll need to add. So extend the invitation to everyone in your department—or no one. One exception: people you actually spend time with outside of the office. As for the boss, if you work closely with her or feel that not including her would reflect poorly on you, mail that invite.

INCLUDING KIDS

Having children at your wedding is both a practical and personal choice. In some cases, an event isn't ideal for the wee ones. Perhaps you're going for a black-tie, late-night affair, or maybe you can't afford to host kids. Either is understandable. But if you want to include some children, it's important to know that this doesn't mean you have to invite them all. You just need clear parameters as to who makes the cut. Case in point: If you have nieces and nephews you would like to enlist as flower children or ring bearers (usually kids ages 4 to 8) or their slightly older siblings that you want to act as junior groomsmen, ushers, or petite bridesmaids (ages 9 to 16, traditionally), then do so; reasonable guests will understand that family is an exception. If you want a completely kids-free affair, bear in mind this can be a deal-breaker for some parents, especially if you have a destination wedding and don't provide childcare during the event. (Families that would tack a vacation onto it and take their kids may not come if finding a sitter proves too difficult.)

If you do opt for a bring-the-whole-family celebration, budget for and plan to extend the niceties that make it easy for everyone (including the parents!) to enjoy your wedding. A kids' table with fun games will keep them engaged at the reception. Another idea is to hire a few babysitters and book a room where they can wrangle and play with the children.

Whatever route you take, be sure to address your invitations only to the people invited in a household. For a childless affair, pen the envelope to the parents. Then, let your bridesmaids and family know to spread the word that yours is a child-free occasion.

PONDERING PLUS-ONES

Deciding whether to allow guests to bring dates is a gray area that all couples must walk, too. If an invitee won't know many people, it's nice to come with a companion. But it also means there will be people you've never met at your wedding—and you'll be paying for their dinner and drinks. If your budget allows it, go ahead. Otherwise, set parameters: If your friends are engaged or in a serious relationship (they live together), let them bring their partners. Instead of addressing the invite to your friend "and Guest," include the significant's name and post it to both of them.

A Sweet Size An American couple gathered 37 of their closest loved ones to celebrate at Longueville House, an 18th-century Georgian Mansion in County Cork, Ireland.

Consider a Planner

With your budget set and guest list in hand, it's time to have a heart-to-heart with yourself about how much time you (and your closest family members) can dedicate to planning the wedding—and whether you need to bring in a professional.

We're not going to lie: Putting together a celebration means work (of the best kind!), so if you have a full-time-and-then-some job and parents who are looking largely to you to pull this off, then explore the idea of hiring a professional consultant. This is important to do before you select your venue and start hiring vendors because a planner can help pick a great location and often pass on savings there. (Since they bring clients to venues, planners often can try to negotiate a deal and shave money off the price.) She'll also be able to suggest tried-and-true caterers, florists, stationers, bakers, and the like, which cuts down on research time for you. A pro can assemble a talented team fast and lower your stress levels just as quickly. The caveat? You pay for it (note: this shouldn't cost more than 10 to 15 percent of your total budget). But the time saved may balance the expenditure in the end. Here are some options:

THE CLASSIC PLANNER

This person is an orchestrator, devising timelines and managing all the moving parts and parties involved. She will help shape the look of your wedding and hire all the right people to carry out your vision. On the day of, she'll make sure everything runs smoothly. She acts as the point person for all vendors, and can be the heavy when problems arise so that you can remain the beaming bride.

One and Only A huge plus of hiring a planner? You narrow your contacts (for tent rental, flowers, catering, and everything else) to a single person who will handle the logistics, oversee setup, and troubleshoot.

THE EVENT DESIGNER

A professional who usually has a design background and focuses on the look of an affair is called an event designer. Many work with a planner, but some act as both. This person often enlists a team of vendors who she's worked with before to create a cohesive vision for the food, flowers, and décor. Each designer is different; ask exactly what she will bring to the table and how she prefers to work.

THE DAY-OF PLANNER

A newish option for couples, this person comes in toward the end of the process, making the cost less expensive than working with a full-service planner. You give her a download of all the details of the wedding, along with the contacts for each vendor, weeks in advance. Then, she creates a timeline and picks up as point person to make sure everything happens without a hitch. This is a great option if your mom or another relative can't act as manager come showtime (while you're busy being the bride!).

WEDDIQUETTE
TIPPING VENDORS

———

If he or she owns her own business, you aren't expected to tip your planner—or photographer, videographer, or florist. If they work for someone else, a gratuity is suggested. Allocate 15 to 25 percent of the catering cost to be given to the banquet manager, and split among the staff. Tip hair and makeup people as you would at an appointment (unless they, too, own their businesses). Assign a family member or attendant to distribute day-of tips, and remember to also reward great service with a glowing recommendation.

CHAPTER
TWO

DREAM UP YOUR THEME

THE MOST MEMORABLE WEDDINGS REFLECT THE COUPLE'S PERSONALITIES FROM START TO FINISH.

"

— Darcy Miller, *Editorial Director, Martha Stewart Weddings*

WEDDINGS ARE EQUAL PARTS reality and fantasy. Once you've got the budget set (your reality), it's time to focus on the fantasy: the style, mood, and environment you want to create for this most special of occasions. Where you wed is the key component to establishing that feeling, and it will also help inform all your subsequent decisions–from choosing a color palette and deciding what to wear on the big day to designing your invitations, picking music, and even making a menu. Consider the venue your springboard and then play off of all it has to offer. A Hawaiian beach, for example, could inspire a laid-back tropical bash. A historic mansion might beg for a glamorous Gatsby-worthy affair.

To get started, imagine what your ideal kind of celebration looks, feels, and tastes like to you as a couple. Maybe your mind immediately goes to a black-tie fête in a ballroom with chateaubriand, or perhaps a boot-stomping party in a barn with barbecue is more to your sensibility. Or it could be that an afternoon affair in a romantic garden is just your cup of tea. If, however, you're stumped for ideas (or torn between two different visions), never fear; this chapter is designed to give you a sketch of what a very personalized event might look like for you. You'll also learn about the benefits and limitations of different venues and how to secure one with your eyes wide open. The ideal place will give you that this-is-it shiver, and then you'll be able to start off your married life feeling right at home.

Let's Play 20 Questions...

Here's our approach to creating a personalized event: Begin at the beginning, with who you are—and look for inspiration in your histories. To kick-start the process, we ask couples these 20 questions to get a sense of them as individuals and together. The answers offer tons of ideas for wedding elements both big (when and where to wed) and small (signature drinks and even what to give as favors).

1
WHERE DID YOU MEET?
Maybe it makes for a meaningful spot to tie the knot or hold your reception.

2
WHAT DID YOU DO ON YOUR FIRST DATE?
You could wed at the restaurant where you ate (or have your rehearsal dinner there). Or, simply include a memorable detail from the night it all started: Play a song you heard, or serve a dish you shared there at your reception.

3
WHERE DID YOU GO AS KIDS (SUMMER CAMP, FAMILY TRIPS, STUDIES ABROAD)?
These could be great options for a destination affair.

4
WHERE WAS YOUR FIRST VACATION TOGETHER?
Even if you can't get back to Mexico for the wedding, you can serve margaritas at cocktail hour.

5
WHAT TIME OF YEAR DO YOU LOVE MOST?
If you live for summer, a garden or coastal wedding is fitting. If you cozy up to winter, try a ski chalet.

6
WHAT COLORS DO YOU GRAVITATE TOWARD?
Maybe your favorite shade is red—and his is blue. Or you adore the look of the sky at dusk or the hues of a particular painting. All of this can guide your setting and your color palette.

7
DO YOU LOVE A CERTAIN BLOOM?
In "Find Your Flowers" (see page 112), we'll address seasonal availability, cost, and hardiness, but thinking of your favorite flowers— or the varieties you like to give each other—is a good place to start when planning your style, color palette, and décor.

8
HOW WOULD YOU DESCRIBE YOUR DREAM DATE NIGHT?
If it involves line-dancing, then look to a rustic locale or barn for your nuptials and take to the floor to kick off your party. Should you favor a sunset sail or a bike ride, hire a schooner, or make your getaway in a canoe or on a tandem bicycle.

DREAM UP
YOUR THEME

9

WHAT POEM OR SONG LYRIC MOVES YOU?

Have a friend read it at your ceremony, dance to it at the reception, or add either to your program or invitations.

10

WHAT'S YOUR FAVORITE MOVIE?

Whether it's film noir, a Technicolor musical, or a Bollywood extravaganza, it can set the mood for your event. Or, just ask the band to learn a few tunes from its soundtrack.

11

WHAT'S YOUR GO-TO WATERING HOLE?

If you frequent a luxe lounge or fun pub, incorporate its house drink into your cocktail hour or host night-before welcome drinks there. Add your own "his" and "her" libations to your celebration—maybe it's spiked hot chocolate for you, and an old-fashioned for him.

12

DO YOU PLAY A SPORT OR ROOT FOR A TEAM?

Set up a friendly game of beach volleyball at the welcome party to a casual oceanside event. If your first date was a tennis game, go crazy using love match puns all over your paper goods. Or, if you're marrying an Aussie football fan, maybe the night wouldn't be complete without Fosters all around.

13

WHAT'S YOUR FAVORITE DISH?

Surely it deserves a place on your wedding menu, whether it's part of the main event or shrunken down to bite size (think mini tacos) for cocktail hour.

14

IF YOU COULD EAT AT ONLY ONE RESTAURANT, WHICH WOULD YOU PICK?

Fill your wedding with its attributes—maybe it's a great location for a rehearsal dinner, or you could ask for the coconut cake recipe for your baker. If the venue serves more casual fare, offer its signature sliders late night.

15

WHAT GUILTY PLEASURE DO YOU SHARE?

If it's a food, like gelato or saltwater taffy, it belongs on your dessert bar or in a favor. A massage at a heavenly spa? Gift a session to your maid of honor and best man—or better yet, make a day of it for a bridal shower or bachelor party.

16

WHAT ARE YOUR HOBBIES, AND DO YOU COLLECT ANYTHING?

Flamenco classes may lead your first dance or a cache of curios could add personality to your wedding-day décor. Look to your stable of paperweights, seashells, or books to personalize your centerpieces or guest book table.

17

WHAT FAMILY HEIRLOOM DO YOU CHERISH?

If you're close to your grandfather, borrow his cuff links and wire them into your bouquet for your walk down the aisle. Or carry your mom's brooch.

18

WHAT ARE YOUR NICKNAMES?

Use them as a motif for invites or in a hashtag, so guests can share photographs of your day on social media.

19

DO YOU HAVE A PET?

If she is well behaved, have her act as ring bearer or pose in photos. If she's cute but wild, place her image on printed materials or have it piped onto cookie favors.

20

DO YOU HAVE A FAVORITE BOOK?

Your shared childhood love of *Goodnight Moon* might inform your favors if you wrap star-shaped candy with tags that bid, "Goodnight Moon, Goodnight Guests, Goodnight Bride, and Goodnight Groom."

THE CLASSIC WEDDING

Elegant. Iconic. Traditional. If these are the words you use when you describe the dress you dream of, they likely apply to your desired venue and décor, too. Maybe you'll get married in your house of worship, then cut a rug at the country club, a landmark estate, or an ornate museum. Whatever you choose, it will be a place with an old-world vibe that you can give your own personal spin.

GOOD THINGS

A reception in a hotel or club's event space can be a grand experience, ballroom dancing and all. You may have to work with the venue's preferred vendors, but there's often a built-in rain plan and existing décor, and sometimes a ready-made motif or theme. (Love the fluting on the columns? Echo it on your invitations and cake. Or, if you're making it official in a historic building, send save-the-dates on vintage postcards of the area.) Some sites even provide their own in-house planner.

GOOD-TO-KNOWS

The drawbacks to marrying at a landmark or popular hotel or club is that there are often restrictions, whether regarding noise (no loud music after 10 p.m. so hotel guests aren't disturbed), food (no red wine to avoid staining antique carpets), or décor (no open-flame candles to avoid a repeat of the great fire of 1871). If the limitations stifle your style, keep looking. But if you're willing to play by the rules, then party on!

An Air of Elegance (this page, clockwise from top): A boys' choir sang "Ave Maria" during this duo's ceremony at Christ Church United Methodist in New York City. Botanical elements added an apothecary feel to a calligraphed suite. For a regal look, emulate European royalty and limit your wedding party to children. This lovely centerpiece was made up of fragrant gardenias and ferns. **Opposite:** A couple who met at Cambridge University in England held their luncheon reception in the College Hall, where they had often dined by candlelight as students.

THE COASTAL CELEBRATION

Maybe you met on the sailing team in college, or grew up going to Cape Cod or Sanibel island. Whatever the reason, if an oceanfront celebration floats your boat, a seaside hotel, yacht club, or private home on the water is likely to be smooth sailing. Anchors aweigh!

GOOD THINGS

A coastal or lakefront setting provides breathtaking views, meaning you can save on décor (and Mother Nature doesn't charge a fee for event design). Plus, the locale offers loads of inspiration for your menu, from raw bars to lobster rolls to freshwater fish. Even the drinks can get in on the thematic action (dark and stormy, anyone?). Ideas of coastal chic vary from captain to captain (maybe you're more sushi than clambake? Or you want to skip the piped buttercream seashells and cover your cake in nautical flags?), so there are plenty of ways to make the day one-of-a-kind.

GOOD-TO-KNOWS

If you want to say your vows on the beach (or bridge or boat), survey the area to see what annoyances you need to troubleshoot for guests. Some waterside spots can get buggy, and you'll want to spray them beforehand (great news, there are more eco-safe ways to do this now), or have natural bug repellents on hand. And when there isn't natural shade, you need to provide parasols or set up umbrellas. For hot locales, offer a serve-yourself lemonade station near the ceremony site. For cool ones? Make it a hot toddy!

For Shore (this page, clockwise from top): Pins pushed through inexpensive anchor charms affix calligraphed escort cards to a linen-covered corkboard. A buttercream frosted cake was adorned with white chocolate code flags. This alfresco ceremony was held on a cliff in Big Sur, California. A nautical-themed invitation suite set the tone for a Martha's Vineyard affair. **Opposite:** A New York couple tied the knot in Port Clyde, Maine, and posed for photos by the Marshall Point Lighthouse.

THE GARDEN AFFAIR

The world is full of flower fans, tree nymphs, and grown-up Boy Scouts who never lost their boundless love for the great outdoors. Your fantasy may be as lavish as the formal gardens of a storied estate, as vast as the grounds of a botanical garden, or as homespun as your own backyard, but it's sure to include lots of gorgeous foliage and fragrant blooms.

GOOD THINGS

If you're getting hitched at a scenic place en plein air, décor is already taken care of by the trees, flowers, and grass all around. Give the flora a supporting role in your wedding by making a tree or blossom a motif on your invitations and paper goods, or by topping your cake with buds. And who doesn't love looking at a sun-dappled day or staring at a starry night sky?

GOOD-TO-KNOWS

Hope for sun, plan for storms. Murphy's law and wedding planners agree: If you don't prepare for rain, it will pour. If you envision the event completely outdoors (as opposed to on a sunporch overlooking the garden, say), have an alternate space, or a tent and umbrellas, available. Another caveat: Remember that grass and stilettos do not get along. Think about laying down a floor, which is an added expense, but you (and yours) won't be sinking into the earth (or mud) all night. If you skip it, advise attendees about footwear in your invitations or on your wedding website.

Leafy Greats (this page, clockwise from top): Fishbowls filled with river stones and water plants adorned a guest-book table, with views of rolling Tennessee hills. A New York couple sent out leaf-filled invitations inspired by Aspen, Colorado, where they met. Twinkling lights added romance to an outdoor dinner in a Dallas sculpture garden. At a Michigan event, centerpieces included flowers and fruit to accent the Porthault tablecloths. **Opposite:** The bride's childhood home was a spectacular setting for this party in Santa Barbara, California.

DREAM UP
YOUR THEME

THE
RUSTIC
PARTY

If you feel at home on the range, or long for a little house on the prairie, consider a barn, farm, or even a quaint covered bridge as a place to get hitched. The rustic theme works in a variety of locales all over the country, from New England farmhouses to Rocky Mountain ranches, each of which comes with a heaping helping of atmosphere.

GOOD THINGS

Whether you define rustic as Western dude ranches, Midwestern farms, or a whitewashed Maine barn, the environment will undoubtedly influence the look of your invitations, the music and the food. Not to mention the décor: It turns out amber waves of grain and wildflowers make sensational centerpieces. The other personal touches will come from the two of you; choose a favorite song as a processional or create drink flags bearing your initials to keep the day about you and your partner.

GOOD-TO-KNOWS

Rustic shouldn't mean roughing it; make sure to provide enough creature comforts to please even the city slickers among your guests. In drier climes, offer refreshments before the vows so that no one is parched. Hand out fans or parasols to beat the heat, or shawls to ward off a chill. And make sure there's a place to take cover (beatific barn? spruced-up paddock?) just in case a shower rolls in.

Natural Beauties (this page, clockwise from top): The hay bales in the barn provided a picturesque photo backdrop for this Seattle-based duo, who wed on a friend's circa-1900 property in Lynden, Washington. Straws with foil-stamped flags dressed up cool drinks served in milk bottles. Stamps with woodland themes finished off these letterpressed invitations for a lakeside celebration. In lieu of a ring pillow, a couple used a nest found on the grounds of their 150-year-old Catskill, New York, barn. **Opposite:** Wheat-covered wire baskets made harvest-themed chandeliers, which were hung above a leather-covered table. Wildflowers in white-painted metal cans continued the Great Plains motif.

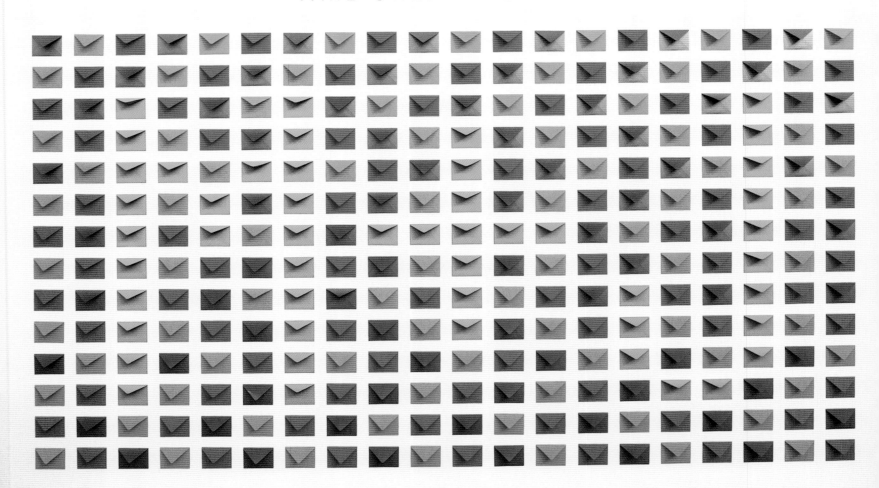

NEW YEAR'S RESOLUTIONS

TAKE ONE. MAKE ONE.

11.3.12

THE MODERN SOIRÉE

You love moving to the pulsing energy of a city, admiring the bold colors of contemporary art, and leaving your creative mark on everything you touch. If that's a fair description, a loft or rooftop high above the sparkling skyline of a metropolis, a vast industrial space that's been converted from factory to venue, or a contemporary art museum may be just right for your cosmopolitan celebration.

GOOD THINGS

A loft. A gallery. An airplane hangar. While traditional wedding venues tend to impose their style on the day, any unfinished space is an invitation for you to transform it into your exact vision. Set up backdrops, and splash your favorite colors everywhere. Hang fabrics to simulate the feeling of being inside a Moroccan market. Or keep things chic and simple with lots of candles and streamlined table settings. In a place like this, it's really up to you.

GOOD-TO-KNOWS

Because one-of-a-kind spaces are just that, each will have its own set of amenities—or lack thereof. A loft will likely have kitchen facilities. An art gallery or industrial space may not. Before you book anything, assess what you'll need to bring in and rent to get the place party-ready, taking into account how those basic necessities (chairs!) and extras (photo booth!) will impact your overall budget.

Mad for Mod (this page, clockwise from top): A punchy red and aqua invitation set the scene for a fun-filled Florida wedding catered by a food truck. The bottom tier of this cake was entirely covered in edible silver leaf, and adorned with a sugar magnolia. For a Broadway-themed celebration, gold decals added punch to a mirrored wall. A couple who met in New York City made it official in a Manhattan loft with a stunning roof terrace. **Opposite:** Guests at this New Year's Eve fête in a converted factory pulled whimsical resolutions out of this display of envelopes (which spelled out the couple's initials). In return, they left well-wishes for the newlyweds.

THE TROPICAL NUPTIAL

For serious sun-worshippers who are at their happiest with sand in between their toes, getting married on a beach isn't just ideal, it's inevitable. And if you love exotic flowers and the sound of the surf lapping at the shore, you can catch the waves at a far-flung resort–or capture the look of the islands at a seaside restaurant or public park.

GOOD THINGS
Many tropical weddings are destination affairs that the bride, groom, and their guests travel to attend. These can be amazing bonding experiences for all included; imagine being surrounded by everyone you love in a place you adore! Be sure to share what's special about your location with your guests: Favorite surf spot? Decorate it with colorful boards. If you come for the shell-seeking, fill the escort card table with prime specimens.

GOOD-TO-KNOWS
Before you plan a destination wedding, make sure that the must-have members of your guest list will be able to take the trip. If they can't, and you can't imagine getting married without them there, you may want to rethink your location. Beaches have their own individual laws and restrictions to be mindful of, and they can be windy, so if you're having your reception right on the sand, weigh down your tablecloths and centerpieces, secure your escort cards, and choose hardy flowers that are used to the wind and heat.

Tropic Wonder (this page, clockwise from top): A New Orleans couple held a seaside ceremony at a resort in the Bahamas. Orchids stand up to hot temperatures, making them ideal centerpieces for outdoor affairs in steamy climates. At their wedding on St. Barth's, this couple traveled from their ceremony to their reception in a rented Moke buggy, sporting a sign that read JUST MARRIED in French, the language of the Caribbean island. Tropical doesn't have to mean bright; for a wedding in Kauai, Hawaii, this pair chose a minimal suite with light gray lettering that looked breezy and inviting. **Opposite:** At an oceanfront wedding on Harbor Island, the escort card table was decorated in native pink sand and seashells.

Bev Martin

Harold & Judi Street

Arnold & Pat

Stephanie Linde

Margaret Reid

Bry Gwen Langley

David Luy

Tiffany Ly
Peter Knisley

Ann Moore

Ray Caroline Joiner

Brian & Denice Mock

Picking Your Place

It's a big decision, but once you find and book a venue (or two)
you are off and running! Here's what to consider as you look,
and everything you need to know before signing a contract.

VISIT SEVERAL LOCATIONS

Even if you have your heart set on marrying at the only lakefront church or restaurant in town, it's smart to research more than one option. That way, you know what the market is like in the area and you're already working on a backup plan if your first choice falls through. It's also time to decide whether you want (or need) to marry in a house of worship first, and then head to a (nearby) space to celebrate, or if you prefer to wed and party all in the same spot. The latter saves money and travel and gets the reception started at "I do."

NOTE WHAT'S INCLUDED

While you ponder reception places within your budget, be mindful of what each one comes with—and more important, what it doesn't. An all-inclusive locale, such as a restaurant or hotel ballroom, for instance, often provides catering, waitstaff, and all the amenities the space needs to do business every day (think: bathrooms, coat checks). And if you love the way it's decorated, you may not have to spend money bringing in lots of flowers or décor. A loft space, on the other hand, is often a blank canvas. You may be able to use any caterer you like and transform it to your heart's content, but you could also have to spring for renting chairs, tables, and everything that goes on top of them. Likewise, if you choose a backyard or remote outdoor spot, you might need to rent generators, portable toilets, and tents for a rain plan, too.

COMPARE SPACES

As you look at a variety of venues, make sure you're comparing apples to apples (the total cost of the reception, once rentals, if needed, are included). Then the rule of thumb is that you shouldn't spend more than 10 to 15

percent of your total budget on the locale. (If you're looking at all-inclusives that provide catering, however, add the percent earmarked for food and drink to that number, for a total of up to 55 percent.) Aside from cost, also compare distance and convenience: Will most of your loved ones be able to attend?

ASK THE RIGHT QUESTIONS

Even when a venue falls within your budget and is available on your date, there can be hidden deal-breakers that you should know about upfront (like if several other events will be going on at the same time). When you sit down with a location's manager, remember to ask the following important questions:

1. **What's the maximum head count?** Once you get an answer, reduce it by 10 percent—that's the ideal number of guests you can host without the place feeling like it's packed to the gills. Overcrowding inhibits dinner service, dancing, and guest comfort in general.

2. **Do you have any restrictions?** Chances are it's not the biggest deal if you can't use open-flame candles, and, depending on your taste, it may not be the end of the world if you can't serve red wine. But if a venue has a noise curfew that requires your party to end at an hour when most of your guests are used to just sitting down to dinner, or dictates the caterer, that might dampen your enthusiasm.

3. **Are there any fees I should be aware of?** Common I-wish-I'd-known-about-that-sooner costs include cake-cutting or corkage fees, setup and breakdown charges, hourly overtime rates, included gratuities, rental costs, even, at destination affairs, "resort fees," which mean guests who aren't staying on the property could be charged for coming on-site to attend the ceremony. Better to know all these upfront, so you aren't saddled with a pricey surprise on the day of.

THE
TIMELINE
VENUE

———

AS SOON AS YOU GET ENGAGED
After establishing your budget and guest list, start looking at venues.

10–12 MONTHS AHEAD
Book your place; at this point, you'll sign a contract and be expected to pay a 25 to 50 percent deposit.

4–6 MONTHS
Meet with vendors at your venue to go over inspiration, palette, and floral needs; if you can, do a walk-through of the space with the florist.

3 WEEKS
Confirm details and head count.

Having a Plan

When you're hosting an outdoor wedding, it's important to think of everyone's experience so that—rain or shine, cool or hot—they're happy and all set to celebrate.

Everyone loves the great outdoors, but the extremes—rain, wind, or even bright sunshine—can make it uncomfortable to stand outside for four or five hours. That's where tents come in: If you have one, you can hold your event in any venue. Even if you want an alfresco affair to be totally un-covered, you should still reserve a tent in case the weather acts up; you can cancel it the week before if blue skies are forecast. And while it's true you'll have to pay a fee (up to a 50 percent nonrefundable deposit), the peace of mind you'll have in the event of a downpour is well worth it.

FIGURE OUT THE RULES

First, ask if your location allows tents. If it does, learn what rules you must abide by and whether your tent company will need to get a permit from a government agency to erect one. Some sites have restrictions on the size; others, including many city parks, prohibit the use of stakes.

FIND A REPUTABLE COMPANY

Once you have established the location and approximate guest count, book the tent. Get recommendations on rental companies that have supplied tents for events similar to yours. When you contact companies, inquire about their clients and check references—since safety is such a priority with tents, this is not the place for a cut-rate vendor.

SURVEY THE SCENE

After you've chosen a company, schedule an on-site consul-tation to determine the right size of the tent and style. (Your tent will need to accommodate 10 to 15 square feet per per-son if you're having round tables that seat six to ten guests; for the dance floor, plan on approximately 4 to 5 square feet per person.) Discuss how the tent will be situated to take advantage of the view, as well as the placement of the dance floor, bar, food stations, and cooking tent if there are no indoor kitchen facilities nearby. Address when the tent will be set up, and tell your florist, caterer, and other vendors.

Amore Alfresco For their destination wedding on Italy's Lake Como, this couple chose a clear tent that let guests take in the scenery.

PICK A STYLE

All tents adhere to one of three basic types, with a few variations. The classic push-pole tent has a fabric roof over a straight line of high center poles that slope to a shorter set of poles, is a minimum of 30 feet wide, can be extended to almost any length, and requires about 8 additional feet of clearance on all sides for anchor ropes and stakes. With tension tents, soaring center poles create a "sculpted" exterior, with a roof of peaks and valleys. These have the same dimensions and clearance needs that pole tents do. Last, frame tents are ideal for small weddings or narrow spaces, as they tend to be slim (often less than 10 feet wide). They're supported by a framework of pipes, which is usually concealed with fabric, and don't use anchor ropes and stakes, so they do not require additional clearance.

THINK ABOUT CREATURE COMFORTS

You can add almost anything to a tent that you would to a house, from flooring (expensive, but it keeps feet dry and is easier for walking and rolling a wheelchair on) to sidewalls (some with decorative cathedral-window walls to protect guests from wind) to doors (for keeping warmth in), to fans, air-conditioning, or heating. Even if you're getting married indoors, in the case of inclement weather, guests will have to walk through the rain to get to the party; consider tenting the walkway from the end of the driveway to the door of the site, or equipping valets with golf umbrellas to shuttle guests back and forth in comfort.

GET IT IN WRITING

Before putting down a deposit, go over the contract with your rental company. Ask if there is a waiver in case any-thing is broken or damaged. Discuss the cancellation policy and find out if there's a penalty for a change in guest count. It's also smart to look at the company's insurance policy to see exactly what's covered should bad weather damage the tent, render the ground too muddy to stake, or force you to postpone the event. Finally, be sure your contract is fully itemized with all fees and services: time frames for tent setup and breakdown, deposit amount (usually 50 percent), balance-due date, and cancellation policy.

THE TIMELINE
TENT

7–12 MONTHS AHEAD
Hire a tent-rental company.

6 MONTHS AHEAD
Schedule a site inspection with the rental company.

4 DAYS AHEAD
If you've put down a deposit on a backup tent, notify the rental company whether, based on the forecast, you want to install it.

ONE DAY AHEAD
Tent company installs tent(s).

ONE DAY AFTER
Tent company breaks down tent(s).

DREAM UP
YOUR THEME

Spending Savvy: Venue

Whether your ideal venue is slightly out of your price range or you need to find a budget-friendly option, enlist these money-saving tips.

1

RETHINK YOUR DATE

Every locale has a high and low season, and most weddings are held on Saturday nights. If you're willing to get hitched in an off-month, or on a Thursday, Friday, or Sunday, you may save up to 20 percent off peak rates. If you are not offered a discount on an off-date, ask for one.

2

BE OPEN TO OTHER TIMES OF DAY

Find a restaurant that does a big brunch business to book a night-time affair, or vice versa. Businesses are always looking to be more profitable during their slower hours.

Dome Sweet Dome Lovebirds who met in Chicago returned to the Windy City to make it official. They celebrated under the mosaic-tiled ceiling and wrought-iron chandelier of the Chicago Cultural Center.

3

PLAN A ONE-STOP CELEBRATION

If you can host your ceremony and reception in the same spot, you'll save on both décor and transportation. And if you find a space that also handles catering (say, a restaurant or country club), you won't have to shell out for renting tables or kitchen equipment.

4

BOOK AS FAR AHEAD AS POSSIBLE

When you aim to secure your space a year in advance, you have a better chance of negotiating a good deal.

5

BENEFIT FROM EXISTING DÉCOR

While marrying on–or very close to–a big holiday may actually incur more charges due to overtime payments for the staff, many places decorate for the holidays far in advance (Christmas lights go up right after Thanksgiving), so there's often a window of time to take advantage of the flowers and décor without any added expense. Or look for restaurants that display beautiful seasonal arrangements year-round.

6

REJIGGER YOUR BUDGET IF NECESSARY

Can't get your ideal location to come down in price (or find another within your means) and all other money-saving measures have failed? Then move allowances from one area you care less about to your location budget. Maybe you go for a DJ rather than hiring a band, find a less expensive dress, or pass on the pricey engraved stationery. The sacrifice will be worth it to secure a stellar setting.

CHAPTER
THREE

JUST ADD COLOR

PEOPLE OFTEN ASK, 'WHAT'S THE SECRET TO ACHIEVING THE LOOK OF A MARTHA STEWART-STYLE WEDDING?' A BIG PART OF IT IS PICKING A COLOR PALETTE AND SIMPLY STICKING TO IT.

— Elizabeth Graves, *Editor in Chief, Martha Stewart Weddings*

ONCE YOU'VE SET YOUR BUDGET, made your guest list, and found your venue, there's a fourth piece of the puzzle that needs to be put in place before you get into the nitty-gritty of wedding details. It's one of the most important decisions you'll make in organizing your party, but we're happy to say that it's also one of the most fun. (And you might be ready for some of that after the budget discussion.) We're talking about picking a color palette for your celebration. At Martha Stewart Weddings, we never plan a party without one. It's the keystone to the entire look and feel of your event. A unified color scheme will make all the elements, no matter how many styles you love and want to include, appear cohesive. Beyond being pretty, a palette is practical, too. After you settle on one, every other choice you need to make will fall into place more easily—from deciding on the design of the invitations to what the bridesmaids and groomsmen will wear to the flowers and even the favor packaging. A color scheme essentially creates a magic domino effect. It's best to select just a few shades to decorate your day: the ones that establish the mood you desire, work well with your venue, and shine together. Neighbors on the color wheel, such as blue and green, or yellow, peach, and orange, are naturally beautiful combinations, especially if you vary the intensity of the shades. Complementary colors, which are opposite each other on the wheel, like lavender and yellow, make eye-catching pairs, too. In truth, the possibilities are endless! The good news is there's really no wrong combination, and choosing a personalized palette is simple if you follow our suggestions. Besides, you've already proven you're skilled at finding the perfect match.

Picking a Palette

Choosing your colors may feel high pressure, but you've been selecting clothes, accessories, even décor in the shades you love your whole life. Now it's time to determine which ones will work best for your wedding.

WEDDING WISDOM

When it comes to color, talk is, if not cheap, confusing; your idea of a dusty rose bridesmaid's dress might be someone else's mauve. And you don't want your vision of pink flowers to get lost in translation to your florist. To spare everyone headaches and disappointment, have physical examples, such as paint chips or photos, that make your colors crystal clear from the beginning.

The first step in homing in on a color scheme is identifying the hues you and your spouse-to-be reach for time and again. Then set about making sure those are the right ones for your day.

TAKE A COLOR INVENTORY

Review all those things you love to look at—the sea and the sky? Your lucky jade-and-gold necklace? Peaches and cream? All could lend themselves to a palette. Then, consider your groom's go-to shades, too. Open your closet, then your fiancé's, to see what colors pop out. Think of the flowers you buy to brighten up your home or your favorite ice cream flavors.

WORK TOGETHER

They say marriage is about compromise; so are colors. If your most beloved shades don't work well together (or you just can't see building a wedding palette around his treasured college sweatshirt's perfectly faded green), look to items you've liked as a pair. How did you decorate your home? What are each of you wearing in your favorite photo together? Where is your ideal place to vacation? Maybe a combination will spring from that spot, whether it's the muted earth tones of Santa Fe or the vibrant blues and white of a Caribbean beach.

GO FOR TWO

Most palettes start with two main shades, then bring in two or three accent hues. Black and white is a classic color scheme, for example, and it can create different moods if combined with a bright like red, a pastel like pink, or a metallic like gold.

TEST IT

You might love certain colors in theory, but in practice, you're getting married in a specific place, and they all need to be in sync. Once you've got a few palettes that excite both of you, take them to your wedding location to see if they shine or stumble. Bring paint chips, swatches, vessels, anything substantial, into the space. When shades clash with the carpets or fade into the scenery, move on to the next round. When they enhance and meld beautifully with the surroundings, you'll know you've found your palette. The next consideration: Do your colors work with the time as well as they do with the place? Silver and gold make sense at an evening wedding in winter, but might be too flashy for a morning ceremony in June. You can soften or amp up hues to make them work.

STICK TO IT

Once you've settled on a scheme, employ your palette from start (save-the-date cards) to finish (favor packaging) and your wedding will look chic and pulled together. Don't worry that your shades will seem repetitive if they're everywhere guests look; there's plenty of room to get creative. As long as the colors are on-palette, you can mix and match patterns throughout your event, scanning paper or fabric and printing it on programs, signs, escort cards, and just about anything else your heart desires. If you're still looking for your colors, read on for ideas on where to find inspiration.

Pulling From Prized Prints For their late-summer nuptials in California, this creative couple chose shades of mustard and rust inspired by her collection of vintage '60s and '70s fabrics. 1. Guests were given pine-filled sachets as fragrant favors. 2. Another on-palette takeaway: apricot jam topped in printed fabrics. 3. Attendees—even the four-legged ones—posed against cloth backdrops. 4. Dinner was served on flea market china in the same scheme. 5. Prompted by the invites, friends and family scoured thrift stores for appropriate outfits. 6. Golden lights strung from trees illuminated the celebration. 7. The happy couple got in on the action in a vintage dress and patterned tie.

1

2

3

4

5

6

7

Look to Your Venue

One of the easiest ways to add color to your space: Let the locale inform your palette. In some cases, its colors may even be what made you fall in love with the spot in the first place.

Do the resort's cabanas have the most cheerful yellow and white stripes? Is there a mosaic in the tiled floor of the reception hall whose black-and-gold fleur-de-lis details would look beautiful on invitations? Or is the view of the turquoise ocean and verdant palm trees the whole reason you're getting married on this particular beach? If there's a color–or pattern, or motif–in your venue that appeals to you, build a palette around that. If it's just one shade that jumps out (the pink marble walls or red-carpeted staircase), pair it with a complementary or pleasantly contrasting shade, a neutral, or other colors in the same range.

Embracing Aqua, White, and Chartreuse When two New Yorkers wed in the bride's Pennsylvania hometown, they took inspiration from the venue. 1. A ceiling in the reception space at Lauxmont Farms set the day's palette. 2. Tables were set with white-on-white–striped tablecloths that were topped with centerpieces of hydrangeas, dogwood, spirea, roses, and ferns on paper mats in the day's signature aqua. 3. Menus matched monogrammed napkins. 4. Guests showered the newlyweds with biodegradable confetti. 5. The bride carried a bouquet of dogwood and bleeding hearts. 6. On-palette pens were available for signing the guest book. 7. The invitation let guests in on the color scheme. 8. 'Maids wore aqua dresses with chartreuse sashes; groomsmen donned coordinating ties. 9. Even the getaway carriage wore the day's colors.

Celebrate the Season

As you home in on your colors, take into account the time of year— and the time of day—when you'll be saying "I do." Nature might have some suggestions for your palette; maybe it's the fiery orange of maple leaves in fall or the soothing pastel flowers of spring.

We immediately associate certain colors with specific seasons. In winter, deeper, richer shades are natural picks, whereas summer may inspire both bright and bold or soft and serene palettes. That said, know that you can make virtually any color work by varying its intensity and pairing it with the right mates. If you love pastels and are getting hitched in winter, steer clear of Easter egg brights and opt for more muted shades mixed with a neutral, like taupe or gray. Or, elevate any color for a formal evening wedding by adding a metallic into the mix. If you're marrying before noon, skip the high shine and use subtler finishes.

Playing up Pink and White Pink blooms looked beautiful in a spring wedding. 1. The Kwanzan cherry blossom trees in the Brooklyn Botanic Garden created a canopy for reception tables. 2. Bridesmaids were asked to pick a dress in a shade of coral or pink. 3. The Japanese floral motif appeared on favor boxes. 4. Flower-shaped punched paper, printed with names and table numbers and attached to quince branches, mimicked cherry blossoms for a memorable escort card display. 5. A sweet touch: mochi "cherry blossom" bites. 6. Rosé wine complemented centerpieces of peonies, ranunculus, sweet peas, and cherry blossoms. 7. For their late May nuptials, this couple sent out gray, pink, and white invitations based on Japanese floral textiles. 8. Layers of rosewater, ginger, lychee, and rosé Champagne gelée made for a lovely pink dessert. 9. Flower girls carried beribboned wands topped with punched paper.

Select a One and Only

If picking two main colors plus two or three accent hues proves tricky, settle on your single all-time favorite, and then invite every one of its shades to the party. You'll end up with an ombré effect that is out-of-sight beautiful.

When working with one color, you can use any number of shades within it as your palette (if it's blue, think powder blue, robin's egg, slate, cobalt, navy, midnight, and the like). Showcasing the gradations of one color will also simplify planning if your vows and party are in two different places, as a monochromatic palette can be easily adapted to both venues; and it makes dressing bridesmaids a breeze if you tell them to pick any blue dress (or pink or red or green, and so on). Here, we play with the celestial shade, which is one of the most popular wedding-day color choices; brides have been carrying something blue for luck since Biblical times. Like an idea here? Make it your something borrowed, too.

Mooning Over Blues This color can go nautical (navy and white), classic (think Wedgwood's baby blue and ivory), or modern (cobalt and fuchsia). Each shade is celebrated in these images. **This page, clockwise from top:** A vintage-looking invitation suite in light blue, robin's egg, and navy. Favors were presented in a foil-stamped cornflower bag. A festive tablescape featured mix-and-match china patterns and clusters of delphiniums, muscari, and dusty miller. Hand-painted flowers transformed an otherwise basic cake. Personalized guest books were simple cloth-covered unlined journals embossed with monograms. **Opposite:** Inexpensive Moroccan ceramic tiles did double duty as favors and escort cards when set on a board bearing table numbers (the digits were also written on the back of the tiles). Calligraphed with guests' names, they made pretty keepsake paperweights.

Tony Cohen

Katy Dablow

Mike Dablow

Micah Doreman

...leton

...leton

Bach

Beekes

Bree

R. ...

Nancy Ellison

Camp...

Lena...

Cora...

K.y...

Eloi...

2

Work In White

What if you've got one color you're crazy for, but aren't mad about ombré? Not a problem. Just pair your favorite with the undisputed bridal classic: white. The perfect partner, it looks right in every season and is an ideal match for any shade.

•

From white weddings to white Christmases, the most versatile hue has long been associated with love and hope, and cultivates a crisp ambience. We like the formality of black with white, the subtlety of gray and white that can go both modern or traditional, the classic beauty of blue and white, the romance of pink and white, and the fresh looks of green and white and yellow and white. However it's used, white is symbolic of a new beginning, which makes it just right for a wedding.

A Blanc Slate The ultimate crowd-pleaser, white adds elegance to any color. **This page, clockwise from top:** This petite posy paired white eucharis with pale green hellebores and leafy fritillaria. White daisies drifting down a yellow fondant-covered cake created a sweet, springtime dessert. Lucky guests got favor boxes tied with a knot and tagged with a horseshoe. A pristine packet—embossed with a "tea for two" stamp—holds sachets of Earl Gray for thoughtful takeaways. Citrus fruits combined with creamy gardenias, stephanotis, and orchids made sunny centerpieces for a winter wedding. **Opposite:** White tulips and tablesettings brought together tree peonies, garden roses, and ranunculus in a range of yellow tones from buttermilk to marigold.

Don't Over- look Neutrals

White's not the only color that goes with everything. Shades of brown, taupe, gray, and nude are just as versatile, equally gorgeous, and a bit unexpected. They also add a sophisticated air to any color, transforming your space into a soft sanctuary.

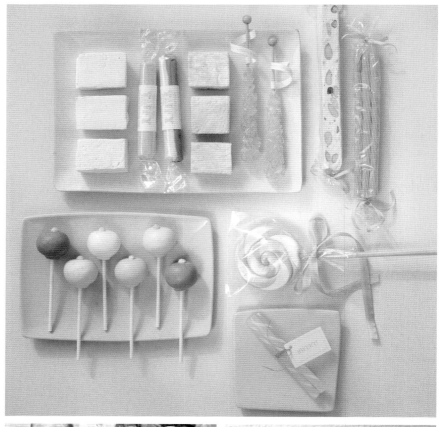

We love a romantic palette of powder blue and nude, which calls to mind the sky at daybreak. In fact, neutrals are everywhere in the outdoors, whether it's the ecru of a birch tree trunk against the green of the leaves or the sand against a blue sea. When you bring in natural elements, such as flowers and food, keep in mind you'll have some variation in tone (delphiniums, for example, are more periwinkle than powder). But those slight shifts just enhance the beauty of the composition. And if you want to up the shine quotient, remember metallics, like gold and silver, are simply a sparkly take on neutrals, and easy to partner with any other hue.

Subtle Distinctions Soft and sophisticated, taupes and soft browns lend a dreamy ambience to any affair. **This page, clockwise from top:** Pair latte-colored roses with something blue (like delphiniums and porcelain-vine berries) and your bouquet becomes as lucky as it is lovely; this one also featured ranunculus, dahlias, and pitcher-plant leaves. Display local cheeses during cocktail hour, each identified with an on-palette name flag. Postdinner, let guests walk down memory lane with a spread of childhood treats, from cake lollipops to rock candy. An invitation suite set the scene—and the color scheme. For a twist on place cards, wrap naturally neutral-hued baguettes in parchment paper and attach name tags with twine. **Opposite:** The wood head table got the royal treatment with a canopy of cloudlike fabric hung overhead and sky-blue linen runners draped across it.

STYLE YOUR LOOK

YOU'LL ALWAYS REMEMBER WHAT YOU WORE
ON YOUR WEDDING DAY, SO CHOOSE SOMETHING
YOU FEEL AMAZING IN. YOU'LL MAKE A
SPECTACULAR ENTRANCE—AND A LASTING MEMORY.

"

— Kate Berry, *Creative Director, Martha Stewart Weddings*

HERE COMES THE BRIDE, all dressed in . . . a breathtaking gown. Sure, the shoes, veil, jewelry, and hair and makeup play a role in the style of your wedding (as do the groom and attendants!). But the first step in looking—and feeling—like a bride is finding the dress of your dreams. This has been true since Roman times, when women wore a white tunic cinched at the waist by a knotted belt that was believed to ward off bad luck. Fast-forward a few millennia and a bride no longer donned white, just the best dress she could afford in any color. That all changed again in 1840 when Queen Victoria flouted convention (most royals wore silver at that time) and opted for a white dress, because it matched the spectacular lace she wanted the gown trimmed with on that day. Her image spread throughout the world, and the white wedding dress became the norm—for those who could afford it (as only the rich could invest in a gown that required laborious hand washing). Today most, but by no means all, wedding dresses are white or ivory. However, more brides are wearing color (and you certainly don't need to worry about wearing a knot at your waist). In fact, anything goes. There's only one style mandate you really need to commit to: Everything you wear—whether long or short, pricey or a steal—should reflect your personality and make you look and feel your best. The same goes for your party. Your groom doesn't have to wear a tuxedo if he doesn't want to. And your maids don't have to appear like satin-clad sextuplets in matching outfits. Stay true to your style, and you'll be the definition of a beautiful bride.

Finding Your Dress

*Before you embark on the shopping trip of a lifetime,
learn the smartest ways to search for that gorgeous gown.*

THE TIMELINE THE DRESS

---

12 MONTHS AHEAD
Begin shopping.

6–9 MONTHS
Order
your dress.

3 MONTHS
First fitting

1 MONTH
Second fitting

1 WEEK
Final fitting

SET A BUDGET

Expect to spend about 10 percent of your overall budget on your attire, but remember that this number is only a starting point. If fashion is more important to you than, say, flowers or music, you might splurge on the dress and scale back elsewhere. Or, you may choose to go easy on the gown and shell out for a great photographer, or five-star catering–whichever is your top priority.

START EARLY

If you, like most brides, are planning to order a dress from a bridal boutique, remember that once you've placed your order, it can take anywhere from six months to a year until it's aisle-ready; gowns are made to order, and many involve custom touches or details such as beading or lace trim that need to be applied by hand. So begin shopping soon after you get engaged (perusing websites and swooning over window displays counts!). That said, if you're having a short engagement, fear not; most dresses can be rush-ordered for a fee. The exceptions to that caveat: If there's a lot of handwork on a dress, or if you've got a really tight window (you need it in a month), a rush probably won't be an option. Many bridal salons can't fulfill orders in less than four months even with a rush charge. Luckily, it is possible to find your dream dress off the rack, be it in the eveningwear sections of a department store or boutique, from the samples of a bridal store (if you fit a sample size), or through a resale outlet or website. You'll have fewer options, but if you are open-minded about considering different styles and you know a speedy seamstress who can rush the alterations, you'll be wedding-ready in no time.

DO THE RESEARCH

Before stepping into a store, spend some time thinking about the kind of dress you want. This way, you won't be completely overwhelmed by the wealth of options. On the following pages, we offer a primer on silhouettes and lengths to consider. Also, along with a digital file, keep a physical folder where you can stash magazine clippings, plus anything and everything–fabric samples, ribbons, ephemera–that inspires you.

MAKE APPOINTMENTS

Once you have some idea of what you're looking for in a dress, it's time for the fun part: trying them on! You'll want to visit a variety of places, including bridal shops, department stores with full-service salons, and, if your budget allows, a couture house. Most stores that sell wedding gowns don't operate on a walk-in basis, so call for appointments at least two weeks in advance. If at all possible, pass over weekend time slots for weekday afternoons, when business is slower and service is better.

LIMIT YOUR ENTOURAGE

Less is more when it comes to opinions–everyone's got their own style, and you want your gown to reflect yours. Invite only one or two special people to your first few appointments to avoid the drama that comes with unwanted points of view, and focus on what *you* think looks great rather than the fact that, say, your college roommate hates lace. If you're set on letting your bridesmaids in on the fun, invite them to your final fitting where you can pop a bottle of bubbly and everyone will be able to ooh and aah over the pièce de résistance. Do make sure to have at least one friend or family member at your last fitting: Someone will need to know how to bustle your gown on the day of; she should come prepared to take notes or, even better, video.

PRIMP BEFOREHAND

One of the best things about bridal salons is that the in-store experience is top-notch–everything is designed to make you feel beautiful, from the salespeople to the lighting to the mirrors. Nevertheless, don't show up in leggings and a T-shirt. To help the consultant get a sense of your style and guide your search, arrive in an outfit that makes you feel confident and offers an idea of your sensibility. Also bring any items that you plan on wearing down the aisle, such as the shoes you love or your grandma's veil. Another great idea: Schedule a hair and

---

Divinely Draped Dresses need to be tried on your body (not summed up on the hanger) to get the full effect of their details—be it ruching, corsetry, or the flowing lines on this gauzy stunner.

makeup trial for the morning of one of your final fittings. When you slip on the dress, you'll be able to get a feel for the whole finished look, from head to toe.

LAY A GOOD FOUNDATION

While shopping, a strapless nude bra and seamless underwear are the most versatile underpinnings. But once you decide on a gown, it's the job of your salesperson and seamstress to suggest the right undergarments. Purchase all of these things as soon as you order your dress, and bring them with you to your fittings to make sure they work. (If they don't, you'll have time to try out other options.) Also keep in mind that, in some cases, your seamstress may want to sew your bra directly into the dress.

STEP OUT OF YOUR COMFORT ZONE

We're not suggesting you let a pushy salesperson talk you into a gown you don't absolutely love. But we do recommend that you shop with an open mind. A dress that looks like a paper bag on the hanger might just stop traffic on your body, so take advantage of the opportunity to try on a variety of styles—and prepare to be pleasantly surprised. Along with different silhouettes, consider a number of fabrics and shades to see which flatters you most (you may feel more radiant in ecru or candlelight than bright white, or vice versa). And if white doesn't suit you, don't feel pressured to pick a version of it. Pastels and metallics make gorgeous, and perfectly wedding-worthy, alternatives to a white gown, as do bold, bright hues or even classic black. The bottom line: Wear whatever makes you feel most like you!

IGNORE THE NUMBER

No two designer size charts are created equal, so if you're a size 6 in the ready-to-wear world, for example, you could be anywhere from a 2 to a 12 on Planet Bridal. It can be jarring to see a larger number on the order form, but resist the urge to get a smaller size. Remember, taking in a gown is easy, but letting it out (if even possible) is difficult and expensive.

TRACK THE MAIN CONTENDERS

Now that smartphones are ubiquitous, most shops allow snapping photos at appointments. Ask your shopping friend to take a few shots of you in your favorite dresses (request front, back, and side views, and make sure each gets your approval), then keep them organized by store

Asset Management Wear a dress that accentuates the positive. The inverted pleat "wings" on this strapless gown showcase a slim waist and disguise wider hips.

and name of designer so you can compare them later. Otherwise—trust us—it will all become a blur.

READ THE FINE PRINT

Repeat after us: No matter how excited I am about buying my dress, I hereby promise to read the purchase contract first. If you're shopping in traditional bridal salons, as opposed to buying off the rack, you'll try on samples and, once you fall in love with one, place an order for the gown to be produced in your size. At this point, a good consultant will walk you through all the nitty-gritty surrounding the order, including (but not limited to) the price, color, style number and name, delivery date, deposit, estimated alterations fee, and cancellation policy. About that deposit: Don't ever put down more than 50 percent. Otherwise you could be out hundreds or thousands of dollars if the gown isn't exactly what you expected. Also pay attention to sales tax, which can significantly add to the cost of the dress; ask what that will be—and budget for it—from the get-go.

SPENDING SAVVY: STYLE

A WEDDING DRESS IS A MAJOR INVESTMENT, BUT PURCHASING ONE SHOULDN'T PUT YOU INTO DEBT. HERE'S HOW TO GET A GREAT DEAL WITHOUT COMPROMISING ON QUALITY.

Keep It Simple

As a rule, the more embellishments a dress has (embroidery, appliqué, beading, corsetry), the more expensive it is. The extras themselves can be pricey, and applying them requires more work. To save cash, look for dresses with details that come from the fabric, such as ruffles, ruching, or a colorful ribbon belt.

Be Flexible

Love a designer but can't afford his or her work? See if he or she has a secondary, budget-friendly line, allowing you to score a designer gown for a fraction of the price. Also consider styles from high-quality mass retailers like J. Crew, Ann Taylor, and BHLDN, and peruse evening gowns at department stores.

Shop a Sample Sale

Bargains can be had here, with a potential savings of hundreds or even thousands of dollars. But there will be a few trade-offs. The selection will be limited, both in the styles and the sizes available (many samples come in only 6 or 8). And since the gowns will have been tried on by many women, they might need cleaning or repair, and alterations won't likely be included.

Try a Trunk Show

Unlike sample sales, these are previews of a designer's new collection. Though you can't always expect a bargain, many will offer an incentive to buy, such as 15 percent off. The catch? You'll have to purchase a gown on the spot, and it's generally final sale.

Buy Online

Yes, it is possible to score a designer dress for a great price online at a flash sale or consignment site. That said, not all sites are created equal (and if a deal seems too good to be true, it probably is). The Internet is rife with cheaply made designer knockoffs and bad business practices, including delayed shipping dates and sketchy return policies. Make sure the gown—and the site you're buying it from—is legitimate. Check that the business has a physical address, then head to the designer's website for a list of authorized retailers. If the site isn't included, move on. Finally, find a phone number, then call to see if you can speak to an actual human—always a positive sign.

MONARCH LENGTH

Reaches nine to twelve feet
from the waist

Learn the Lingo: Hemlines

You'll fall hard for the dress—but will you fall for long or short? Here are the terms to know for identifying the train (or lack thereof) that makes your heart race.

CATHEDRAL

Drops seven feet from
the waist

SEMICATHEDRAL

Extends five to six feet
from the waist

CHAPEL

Stretches four feet from
the waist

FLOOR LENGTH

Touches the
floor

TEA LENGTH

Skims
the shins

MIDCALF

Ends just below
the knees

KNEE LENGTH

Grazes
the knees

MINI

Hits above the
knees

The Primer: Dress Silhouettes

Brides come in all shapes and sizes–and luckily, so do wedding gowns.
Meet your potential match below.

BALL GOWN

Introduced by Queen Victoria, reimagined by Dior in the 1950s, and a longtime favorite of traditionally inclined princess brides, this shape features a full skirt and a fitted waist. It's excellent for hiding problem areas in the hips and thighs–and for making a grand entrance.

EMPIRE

Napoleon's wife Josephine introduced this high-waisted dress after the French Revolution, and it's still popular today. The cropped bodice complements smaller-breasted women, and the raised waist creates a long line, making it ideal for petite brides. As for the skirt, anything goes: It can be perfectly straight, slightly flared, or as wide as an A-line.

A-LINE

This classic '50s cut flatteringly cinches the smallest part of your natural waist before flaring out gradually to camouflage hips and balance wide shoulders. It's a great way to wear a full skirt without the drama of a ball gown, which is, for want of a better word, poufier right from the waist.

MERMAID

Got curves? Showcase them. This silhouette (also known as a fit-and-flare or trumpet) hugs the torso, but juts out into a fuller skirt somewhere below the knees. The gown should fit snugly in the hips and thighs while allowing enough room to sit, so go ahead and have a seat during your fittings.

SHEATH

Popularized in the 1950s by Marilyn Monroe, the slim, close-fitting shape encases the body like the sheath of a sword (hence the name). Its profile is sculpted with darts, tucks, and seams, making it a nice choice for women who are larger on top than on the bottom.

HALTER

This term refers to the neckline of a gown (most often a version of a sheath or mermaid), which loops around the neck and exposes the shoulders. Along with one-shoulder silhouettes, this style is especially lovely on brides with long torsos.

BATEAU

Modest but so chic, a bateau neckline spans across the collarbone from shoulder to shoulder. Also called a boatneck, it gets its name from the French word for boat, because it was traditionally seen on sailors' blouses and sweaters. Audrey Hepburn, most notably in the film *Sabrina* (which is yet another name for the retro style), was also a fan of this neckline, which makes shoulders look wider and waists smaller. A bateau neckline best complements pear-shaped and smaller-busted brides.

V-NECK

What's not to love about this neckline, which shows off a pretty décolletage and draws the eye right to the smallest part of the torso? It looks great on all but the slimmest brides and is adored by fuller-figured women because of its waist-whittling effect.

Completing the Picture

A dress without shoes, jewelry, and accessories is, well, just a dress.
Pair it with eye-catching accessories, and it becomes a beautiful ensemble.

GOOD TO KNOW

Customarily, the bride removes her engagement ring for the ceremony, to keep the focus on the wedding band (and make slipping it on easier). Swap yours to your right hand or give it to your maid of honor or mom before walking down the aisle. After the vows, your ring can be slipped on the outside of your band.

CHOOSING YOUR BANDS

By far the most meaningful accessories you'll select are your wedding bands. With no beginning and no end, rings symbolize endless love and unbroken marriage vows. And they've been doing so for eons: Ancient Egyptians wore reeds around their fingers, but modern couples opt for rings of precious metals.

Platinum: Commonly used in bands, it's one of the strongest metals in the world. It develops a rich patina over time, but its white-gray color will never, ever fade.

Gold: Softer than platinum yet still incredibly durable, gold is available in many variations, including white, yellow, or rose. If you're considering white gold, there's one caveat: Since it's actually yellow gold coated with a white metal like rhodium, it will need to be recoated by a jeweler every few years.

Other metals: Newer, trendier options like titanium and tungsten are much less expensive than other metals, but their chemical makeup prevents them from being sized or altered in any way, which makes it nearly impossible to wear one ring for a lifetime. As for silver, it's pretty but soft and prone to tarnishing.

OTHER JEWELRY

Whether you mix special heirloom pieces with inexpensive costume jewelry or buy something new you'll then wear for the rest of your life, your wedding day baubles should accentuate your gown—not distract from it. Here, what to wear with some of the most popular dress necklines.

Strapless: Bold, multistrand necklaces, bejeweled bibs, even classic pearls sync up exquisitely with this dress style; think of it as the ultimate blank canvas. Since the cut shows off your clavicle and shoulders, choose a necklace that's collarbone length. Follow the less-is-more mantra for earrings and bracelets: Studs and thin bangles hit all the right notes.

V-neck: A flattering style that draws attention to your face and neck, this works best when it's teamed up with long earrings and a delicate pendant. For an elegant twist, layer a few color-coordinating pieces together.

Bateau: This high, straight neckline practically begs for a necklace with a little length. Opt for translucent colored stones that let your dress stand out, or layer white, yellow, or rose gold pieces. Keep earrings and bracelets small and spare.

SHOES

If you're the kind of girl who can party all night in five-inch sandals, then by all means, rock them with that gown. That said, most women prefer something that mixes style with comfort, like a platform heel, which can make four inches feel more like three. Other options include a French or chunkier heel, which provides more support than a stiletto, or a modest kitten heel, which is especially sweet with a tea-length dress. Another idea: Wear heels to the ceremony and switch to a pair of wedges or flats for the reception. Also factor your location into the decision, as high heels don't make sense on the grass or in the sand, where they'll sink in, feel uncomfortable, and get destroyed. Whatever you wear, add a pair of gel insoles–you won't regret it. As for shoe color? Metallics, nudes, and whites always work, but the rainbow is at your fingertips; brightly hued shoes can be a fun way to add personality to your look–or sneak in your something blue!

EXTRAS

Consider an embellished belt to bring a little sparkle to a simple dress, or tie a pop of color around your waist with a length of ribbon. In cool weather you'll need a cover-up, whether it's a capelet, bolero, pashmina, shrug, or cropped jacket. Headpieces can be worn with or in lieu of a veil, and the options are endless, from headbands made of faux or real flowers to combs festooned with crystals and pearls. If you skip the veil completely, tuck an heirloom brooch into your hair for some sparkle. For a handbag, you can't go wrong with a classic clutch in a neutral or metallic for a timeless look, or a punchy color to go modern.

Lucky Charms Accessories are a great way to bring in your "somethings," whether it's a new clutch, an heirloom veil, borrowed jewelry, or blue gloves.

Today, I promise to love you,

THE
TRADITION
WEARING
A VEIL

———

Those delicate
wisps of fab-
ric originated
as a symbol
of purity, and
were thought to
protect the bride
from evil spirits
and the admiring
gazes of single
men. Custom-
arily, the veil is
only lifted after
the vows and
before the first
kiss, making the
marriage official.

Learn the Lingo: Veils

For some women, it's just the right finishing touch. Others consider a veil to be an extra their dress doesn't need. The decision to wear or not wear one is totally up to you. These are the most common options–from the longest length to the shortest.

CATHEDRAL

A popular choice of royals and A-listers, it dominates any setting and photographs smashingly. Extending between nine and twenty-five feet, it demands the wide aisles of a cathedral (hence its name), deft maneuvering on the part of the bride, and the assistance of at least one of her attendants.

MANTILLA

Long considered one of the most romantic choices, mantillas are defined by an intricate lace edge that's draped delicately over the head. The style (and the name) come from Spain, where mantillas were held up by upright combs called *peinetas*. Most brides these days skip the comb.

BLUSHER

Traditionally, for her walk down the aisle, the bride covers her face with a blusher, a short veil that extends just below the chin (so as not to interfere with the bouquet) but usually drops no farther than the waist in back.

THREE-PIECE

Defined by a short blusher, wrist-length drop, and sweeping chapel, this triple-layered veil creates a versatile, traditional look. Modern versions use Velcro to attach the longest piece, making it easy for a bride to remove it and kick her heels up on the dance floor.

FINGERTIP

This style gets its name because–you guessed it–it extends to the tips of the fingers. With its relatively modest length, a fingertip veil looks appropriate with virtually any dress silhouette.

BALLERINA

Especially striking with a sleek sheath dress, a ballerina veil hovers anywhere from knee to ankle. Since it's short enough for a bride to dance comfortably in, it's sometimes referred to as a waltz veil.

ELBOW

Often tiered for more volume, an elbow-length veil adds fullness to slim-fitting gowns. If you're getting married outside, have it piped with satin to weigh it down. A shorter version of this is the flyaway, a stiff froth of tulle (anchored by combs) that skims the tops of the shoulders, making it ideal for back-baring dresses.

BIRDCAGE

These cropped, face-framing veils, popularized in the 1930s, are made from tulle, mesh, or netting and appeal to brides seeking a vintage feel. They're often attached to a headpiece like a headband or fascinator (an accessory often made of feathers, flowers, or fabric). Birdcage veils work best with knee-length dresses.

Getting Wedding Ready

The quickest way to become a stressed-out bride? Putting tons of pressure on yourself to look your best and attempting a major makeover at the last minute. Instead, plan well ahead and you'll be rested and radiant.

Hire a Hairstylist

Ask pals and fellow brides for recommendations. Once you audition and select someone, he or she can help you come up with a look that suits both your wedding location and your dress. If you want to try something new, like highlights, book with a colorist well ahead of the big day.

Schedule a Makeup Artist

If you'd rather turn to a professional than do your own makeup (jitters can make for a shaky hand), many hair salons also offer makeup services and bridal packages. If yours doesn't, ask your hairstylist for a recommendation, seek the advice of friends who recently married, or visit your favorite cosmetics counter to see if any of the artists do weddings on the side (many do). Before you book a trial, look through a web gallery of recent work.

Elevate Your Skin

If you begin a regimen now, blemishes you've tolerated–acne, scars, sun damage–can be diminished through treatments, like retinol cream, lasers, or skin lighteners. To improve your complexion, consider monthly facials and at-home treatments like fruit-acid peels or microdermabrasion, which refresh skin's outer layer. It takes a few months to see improvements with skin, so start now.

3 MONTHS BEFORE

Shape Your Brows

If you're planning to reshape your brows or let overplucked arches grow in, put down the tweezers and see a specialist to come up with a game plan. To guarantee great results, book him or her for follow-ups every three weeks until the wedding–but not on the day of or day before, as shaping could leave your skin red and irritated for a few hours.

1 MONTH BEFORE

Brighten Your Smile

Pop into the dentist for a cleaning, even if you aren't due for one. Also consider a whitening treatment, which can fade stains significantly; results last six months to a year. Prefer to DIY? Drugstore whiteners, such as strips and gels, are also effective and less expensive. However, you won't see results for a week or two.

Hold a Beauty Rehearsal

Bring your veil and accessories to appointments with your hairstylist and makeup artist to create your wedding-day look. Then take pictures to make sure you love it. One fun idea: Schedule the trials the day of your bachelorette party or a special date night so all that gorgeousness has an appreciative audience!

Get Golden

Tan skin is a great look for most of us, but the sun damage that comes with it isn't. If you want a postvacation appearance, turn to sunless tanning options, including airbrushing, in which color is applied by an aesthetician; or spray tanning, in which tanner is misted on via jets. Do a trial run now, and book a second appointment for a few days before the wedding (color can take some time to set, and you don't want to smudge the dress).

2 WEEKS BEFORE

Cut and Color Your Hair

If you wait until closer to the wedding, a fresh cut will look too blunt, and color won't have settled in. This timing also allows room for troubleshooting, just in case you need it.

THE WEEK OF

Go for Your Final Appointments

Have your eyebrows shaped and other areas waxed (like your bikini line and legs), and book one final facial (if you've been getting them all along–otherwise skip it) and spray tan. Another great idea: a massage! If you've ever needed one, it's probably now.

THE DAY BEFORE

Banish Blemishes

Adrenaline can lead to breakouts. If this happens, don't panic–but do hightail it to the dermatologist for a cortisone injection. It will reduce a pimple's swelling and redness immediately, and nix it completely within twenty-four hours.

Put on Polish

Get a manicure and pedicure to allow your nails time to dry thoroughly. Plus, if you get a nick or smudge, you'll have time to revisit the salon for a touch-up.

Wash Your Hair

If you're getting an updo, sudsing up the day before is preferable to the day of. That's because the buildup of oils overnight makes hair easier to work with and helps hold the style in place. Wearing your hair down? Your stylist will likely cleanse it before blowing it out, so skip the at-home shampoo completely.

THE DAY OF

Just Relax

Easier said than done, we know. But if you're feeling frazzled, this works: Take slow, deep breaths, inhaling through the nose and exhaling through the mouth. If you practice yoga, a morning session also helps. And while a massage may be tempting, indulge in it the week before, as it can be dehydrating on the day of the wedding.

Pace Yourself

Give yourself ample time for hair and makeup. Hair should be first, at least three hours before you walk down the aisle, followed by makeup, which should take around an hour. Put on your gown only after hair, makeup, and perfume are set (oils in fragrance can discolor your dress).

Mirror, Mirror Aim for hair and makeup that has staying power. Think waterproof mascara and long-wearing lipstick.

Selecting Your Hairstyle

The look you choose for your wedding will live on in photos for years to come. Keep in mind that the most flattering options appear soft and natural, not beauty-pageant-perfect, and use these pointers to guarantee a gorgeous-hair day.

UPDATE THE UPDO

Buns, twists, and chignons will never go out of style—and with good reason. They're flattering, show off your profile, and keep your hair out of your face. There are a few ways to make them more modern: Work with, not against, your hair's natural texture, position the style at the nape of the neck (as opposed to the crown, which can appear dated), and secure it with pins and a gentle mist—not a gallon—of flexible-hold hairspray.

CONSIDER WEARING IT DOWN

Updos used to be synonymous with wedding hair due to their manageability and elegant effect, but they're hardly the only option. In fact, they can look stiff if you never, ever wear your hair up. Should you decide to go loose and flowy, whether half up or all down, the options are endless—from glamorous pressed waves to a supersleek blowout. That said, wearing your hair down requires some maintenance, and you may have to sneak away from the party to brush it back into place a few times—especially if you're really getting down on the dance floor.

KEEP YOUR LOCATION IN MIND

Getting married on the beach? A fresh blowout is no match for a stiff sea breeze; a ponytail with some height at the crown or a low, bohemian twist might be a better bet. On the flip side, at a formal, buttoned-up venue, a sleek bun is a more appropriate choice than a loose fishtail braid.

From Hair to Eternity Regardless of your hair length or texture, there's a style that will work for you. Seek out one that will photograph well, won't flop into your eyes (or get stuck in your lip gloss), and has a certain timelessness; years from now, you don't want people dating your wedding photos by your hairstyle.

FACTOR IN THE SEASON

If your hair has frizzed every summer you can remember, it's not going to act differently at your July Fourth weekend wedding, so reconsider the hair straightening and instead opt for an updo.

LET YOUR DRESS DECIDE

When a gown and a hairstyle don't complement each other, the whole look falls flat. A one-shoulder style practically begs for an updo that shows off the neck and shoulders, for example, while a sheath with a plunging neckline is fantastic nicely framed by long, loose waves. A great hairstylist will be able to guide you in the right direction; just show him or her pictures of your dress—and, ideally, you in it—when mulling over options.

AIM FOR SOMETHING TIMELESS

Twenty years later, wedding hair can look as tired as a supertrendy dress (case in point: the bouffant). Choose a style that's flattering but maybe not the braid-of-the-moment. When you gaze back, you want to look classic, not costume-y.

GO FOR A TRIAL RUN

Once you've got a stylist—and a possible style—in mind, make an appointment to have your hair done that way, and wear it for a night out to see how it holds up, and how it makes you feel. If you're planning to wear a veil, bring that along for your stylist to play with and figure out where to place it and how to remove it. Make sure it's easy to take off without completely destroying your do.

EMPLOY A SECRET WEAPON

Remember these two words: Elnett hairspray. The iconic gold bottle has been a favorite of top stylists, A-list celebrities, models, and beauty editors for decades, and for good reason: It provides soft, touchable hold that lasts for hours upon hours, making it the best mist on the market for sleek blowouts, elaborate updos, and everything in between.

WEDDIQUETTE
WEDDING PARTY HAIR

If you want your bridesmaids to look a certain way, it's perfectly fine to ask them to wear their hair up or to give each a specific lipstick for the big day. But if you prefer them to have their hair and makeup professionally done, then it's up to you to arrange for that to happen (whether at a salon or at the wedding locale itself)—and to foot the bill.

Choosing Your Makeup

On the big day, every feature deserves the white-carpet treatment. Whether you're booking a makeup artist or doing it yourself, here's how to create a timeless look that doesn't detract from your natural beauty.

GOOD TO KNOW

The key to well-blended makeup is applying it (or having it applied) in natural lighting. If you're near a window, face it head on—not in profile— to illuminate every inch of your face equally.

PLAY UP YOUR EYES

We recommend choosing one feature to enhance and letting the others play supporting roles. The beauty of an expertly lined eye is that it is always flattering and defines a captivating gaze that's visible in any photo. To get the look, dab cream shadow in a shimmery just-darker-than-your-skin-tone hue over your lids for a little sparkle, and brush on a matte powder shadow from lash to crease (it should be one tone darker than the base color you just applied). Curl your lashes, then apply two coats of mascara. Dip a liner brush into potted gel liner (choose a waterproof black or brown version for a smudge-proof look), then create small dashes from the inner to outer corner of your upper lash line, getting thicker as you go. Connect them, and voilà–perfectly applied liner! To avoid makeup overkill, keep your mouth neutral with a rosy lipstick that enhances your natural lip color.

. . . OR YOUR LIPS

If you prefer a bold mouth to defined eyes, pick your favorite lipstick and follow our guidelines for maximum staying power: First, smooth on color directly from the tube, blot, brush on translucent powder to set it into place, and repeat. Keep your eye makeup subtle to ensure a good balance–mascara, a little liner or shadow, and well-groomed brows are enough to have definition in photos but not compete with vibrant lips.

SCORE LUMINOUS SKIN

Regardless of the rest of your makeup, a glowing complexion will be key to looking your best. And even if you're a just-tinted-moisturizer girl in your daily life, you need some foundation on your wedding day to ensure that your skin stays shine-free in photos and throughout the celebration. The tricky part? There's a fine line between an enhanced complexion and one that appears heavily made up. To avoid the latter, consider both color and consistency. Getting the shade right is simple: Test a few on your jawline in natural lighting, and choose the one that disappears. To select the consistency for your skin type, head to the mirror first thing in the morning, before you wash your face. If your skin looks oily,

go with a sheer, oil-free non-comedogenic formula that won't clog pores. Spot some dry patches? Enlist a hydrating whip that won't settle into lines. If it's somewhere in between, a semi-matte version is your best bet. Apply and blend it with a sponge. To hide blemishes, dab on cover-up beforehand, choosing a shade that's a little lighter than your base.

ADD A FLUSH TO YOUR CHEEKS

Blush will give your skin a healthy glow in photos. Use a blush or bronzer that's close to your natural skin color. Apply it lightly under your cheekbones and on each side of the nose. Then put a brighter pink or peach blush on the apples of your cheeks for a slight flush. Choose sheer formulas, and go over the whole area with a large, clean, fluffy brush to blend any lines between the two blushes. Oily skin will benefit from a powder formula, while a dry complexion is a better match for cream or gel.

PACK A DAY-OF KIT

When a party lasts four to five hours (and that's just the reception), hair and makeup touch-ups are inevitable. Ask your planner or the bridesmaids to keep a pouch with the following essentials on hand:

· A custom makeup palette with empty compartments you can fill with a little of your lipstick, foundation, concealer, cream blush, balm, and gloss.
· Mini brushes to spot-touch makeup.
· Cotton swabs with precision tips to remove lipstick smears and neaten eye makeup.
· Cooling spray to set makeup and soothe hot skin.
· Sunscreen to protect exposed skin on the fly.
· Eyedrops to nix the redness of happy tears.
· Tooth wipes to polish your postdinner smile in a flash.
· Blotting papers to stop shine without ruining makeup.
· Hair spray to tamp down frizz.

Better Together Choose your hairstyle, makeup, and jewelry after settling on your dress (and any accessories such as capes or jackets). Your neckline will dictate the rest of your look.

Taking Care of Yourself

At your wedding, you want to look and feel fabulous—and that means happy and healthy, not hungry and irritable. Get into top shape by taking simple, sensible, gradual steps that will become healthy habits you'll hang on to for life.

Have Breakfast

You've heard it before, and we'll say it again: Never skip the first meal of the day. It wakes up your metabolism and seriously helps your mood. Plus, studies show that people who pass on breakfast tend to eat those calories—and more—later in the day.

Don't Go Hungry

To avoid overeating when you're ravenous, eat a little something every four hours for a total of three meals and two snacks a day.

Plan Ahead

At around 4 p.m., the office vending machine can start calling your name. To resist its temptation, stock your desk with small servings of nutritious goodies like fruit, all-natural granola bars, low-sugar protein bars, and nuts. The more you fill up on healthy snacks, the less you'll crave junk food.

Fill Up on Fiber

We're talking 25 to 30 grams per day. Fiber absorbs water and makes you feel fuller, so you'll eat less. The best sources are beans, greens, whole-grain cereals and breads, and colorful fruit such as blueberries.

Sip Green Tea, Not Coffee

You don't need to do it every day—even three days a week makes a difference. Hot or iced, green tea boosts your immune system and loads you up on catechins, an antioxidant that speeds up your metabolism.

Maximize Your Workouts

For an intense, calorie-blasting gym session, eat an energizing snack—like a nutrient-loaded apple with peanut butter—30 minutes to an hour before working out. After exercising, refuel your muscles with water, protein, and carbohydrates (think string cheese and crackers or nuts and dried fruit).

A Smart Start Starvation won't quiet the butterflies in your stomach, and it will make you more likely to faint (or get tipsy). Avoid that on your wedding day by eating a breakfast rich in protein and staying well hydrated.

Add Two Moves to Your Exercise Routine

Do push-ups (start with 10 per day, and work up to 30). Next, to strengthen and flatten your core, try "the swimmer": Lie on your belly with arms and legs extended in the air, fluttering your right arm and left leg simultaneously, then your left arm and right leg. Begin with 10 seconds every day, and slowly build to a full minute.

Double Up on the Stairs

Conquer those steps two at a time—it burns a few extra calories and provides a bigger metabolic boost than taking them one at a time. Also, skip valet parking, pick up your walking pace, and choose parking spots in the back of the lot to sneak in a stealth workout.

Banish Bloat

In the weeks leading up to the big day, reduce your intake of carbonated drinks, caffeine, artificial sweeteners, juices, and dairy products (especially if you're lactose intolerant). Refined flours and sugars—the kind found in high-carb items like white breads, cakes, and pastries—can also leave you puffy; steer clear of those, too.

Rethink Restaurant Food

Make it a point to order light, healthy options when eating out, choosing proteins that are grilled or steamed instead of fried; picking brown rice instead of white; and asking for all sauces and dressings on the side. Then—this is key—leave a third of your meal on the plate, and ask for it to go. When you order takeout at home, spoon a single helping onto a salad plate (rather than eating it straight from the container). Since a normal portion takes up more space on a small dish, you'll feel like you're getting more bang for your bite. And don't reach for seconds; pop the leftovers in the fridge and have them for lunch or dinner the next day.

Catch Your Zzzs

Aim for seven to eight hours of sleep per night (the amount most adults require). If that's a switch for you, getting used to the new schedule will take some slow-and-steady adjustments. Here's what we recommend: Set your alarm clock for a consistent time every morning, and move your bedtime 15 minutes earlier every few days until you reach your goal.

GOOD TO KNOW

Your heart will already be racing—and for good reason—come your wedding day. Throw warm weather into the mix and you could be approaching flop-sweat territory. To stay cool and calm and prevent overheating, do this right before walking down the aisle: Run cold water over your wrists, then press your chilled wrists to the nape of your neck.

Dressing the Guys

*What the groom—and his attendants—wear depends just as much on
the kind of ceremony you're having as on their personal style.*
Here, a gentleman's guide to a head-to-toe ensemble for every affair.

FORMAL

"White tie" is the most dressy, requiring that men wear a white tie or bow tie. "Black tie" comes next, and lives up to its name. And if you opt for "formal," that calls for a tuxedo (also traditionally expected if a ceremony starts after six p.m.). Look for one that's sleek and slim-fitting yet with a cut that's classic enough to be worn in five years. A good fit is everything—try a different style if the seams are pulling in the shoulders or thighs. And consider something unexpected but still formal for fall or winter: a fitted velvet jacket.

THE EXTRAS: Patent leather lace-ups or swanky velvet slippers would be equally appropriate. And don't forget the cuff links—you'll need them!

SEMIFORMAL

Many afternoon affairs are semiformal. Translation: A nice suit is appropriate. For a conservative look that works just as well in the boardroom as up at the altar, shop for a slim—but not skinny—suit in a rich, charcoal gray hue, paired with a slim black tie. In terms of versatility, gray is the new black.

THE EXTRAS: Look for timeless leather shoes with softly tapered soles and no ornate detailing, and a pocket square that complements the tie.

CASUAL

For an early-in-the day wedding, or one that takes place on the beach or in the backyard, you can have a more relaxed style; however, you still want to look sharp. Linen may seem right for an outdoor occasion, but it's also wrinkle-prone. Try a pale suit in a linen blend or lightweight silk-wool blend. One fashionable yet often overlooked option is a three-piece suit with a vest (a slimming piece). Feel free to play with patterns, but stick to a colorway: the suit, vest, and tie should have complementary shades.

THE EXTRAS: Add some sophistication to your ensemble with a textured tie that matches the suit (for a monochromatic look) or coordinates with the wedding colors (for a punch of personality), plus a leather belt in black or brown.

Dressing Your Bridesmaids

These days, there's more than one way to deck out your attendants—and it doesn't mean matching taffeta. Try these bride-tested, friend-approved ideas.

CHOOSE ONE COLOR IN A VARIETY OF SHADES

Rather than dressing everyone paper-doll style in the same exact dress, decide on a single hue, say, purple—and let your friends pick a shade from lavender to plum. Pair their frocks with nude or metallic shoes and simple jewelry, and voilà: looks that let your friends' personalities shine through and still have a cohesive feel.

OR ONE SHADE IN AN ARRAY OF STYLES

Along those lines, pick a specific color and have each friend choose a dress in that exact hue—but leave the style up to her. Give your attendants fabric swatches or paint chips so they know the shade you have in mind.

PICK A FEW COLORS

Select a handful of coordinating options (aqua, blush, lilac, and lemon, for example), and leave the rest up to your 'maids: who will wear which one, what the dresses will look like, and what they'll wear with them. If you want each dress to meet your approval, make it easy on your friends by creating a list or photo gallery with a number of options in every hue (and in a variety of price points). Ask them to let each other know which dress they claim to avoid any who-wore-it-best mishaps.

GO TO ANY LENGTH

Mixing hemlines lets everyone choose what they like. Plus, it makes the gang look more interesting as a whole. Change it up within the group, or keep the bridesmaids in short frocks and let your maid of honor stand out in a longer number—or vice versa.

MIX YOUR FABRICS

No need to be a one-material girl. A range of textures, from flowing tulle and sleek silk to boho chiffon, mingle nicely together when they're in the same shade.

USE NEUTRALS AS A BACKDROP

Black bridesmaids dresses are très chic, but there's a fine line between sophisticated and funereal. Likewise with neutrals—they're beautiful on their own, but can look a little blah in a group. To keep things on the bright side, mix in a punchy accent color (it should coordinate with the rest of your wedding hues) in clutches, shoes, wraps, and jewelry.

SPEAKING OF NEUTRALS. . .

Your bridesmaids absolutely can wear white. Just make sure their dresses are distinct from yours—maybe they're in knee-length styles, and you're wearing a floor-length gown, or they're sporting crisp whites and your dress is ivory. Add personality with accessories in saturated colors or gleaming gold.

EMBRACE LACE

Yes, lace has traditionally been reserved for the bride, but we love the way it adds romantic texture to your girls' gowns, too. Make it fun (and not so bridal) by incorporating color: Vibrant tones get noticed at an outdoor fête, and subtler shades fit a formal affair.

SHINE ON

There's no rule that says your entourage has to be understated. Sequins, beads, and studs can sparkle up your ceremony without being too flashy, as long as you keep dress shapes simple and necklines demure. Bonus: no major jewelry required.

DON'T IGNORE PRINTS

Solids are smashing, but prints—think florals, abstract watercolors, or even polka dots—can look surprisingly polished. Everyone can wear the same one (this works best for small parties), or you can choose a few that coordinate, both in colors and patterns (a group of florals, for example). Or, keep the bridesmaids in solids and distinguish your maid of honor with a pattern (or vice versa).

Bridesmaids Revisited You chose your friends for their unique personalities; find ways to celebrate their individuality, whether through different hemlines, patterns, shoes, jewelry, or even distinct flowers in their bouquets.

CHAPTER
FIVE

SELECT YOUR STATIONERY

> "
> YOU CAN CERTAINLY EMAIL INVITES, BUT
> THERE'S NOTHING LIKE RECEIVING A BEAUTIFUL
> WEDDING INVITATION IN THE MAIL. THEN IT
> BECOMES A KEEPSAKE YOU'LL ALWAYS HAVE.
> "
>
> —Shira Savada, *Real Weddings Editor, Martha Stewart Living*

PAPER DETAILS WILL BE WOVEN throughout your wedding celebration, from the moment family members and friends open their invitations until you mail your last thank-you note. A distinctive, personalized suite is also the first hint of the style of a wedding. As such, it can suggest the tone of your day, build anticipation among your guests, and offer a chic peek into your personalities and tastes. However, wedding stationery is more than just an expressive flourish; it does a great deal of work. Modern weddings can be complicated affairs, with multiple locations and various itineraries for different events, and guests need lots of information to get to the right places—and even to the correct seats—at the appropriate times. A cohesive suite ties everything together seamlessly to convey a well-thought-out event, whether that's a black-tie affair in a ballroom or a barefoot-on-the-beach shindig. Your paper goods create a visual language that you will use to communicate throughout your celebration. Maybe your vocabulary is based on a motif or monogram, conveyed through graphic pattern, or expressed by paper, ink color, or a certain typographical style. Whatever you choose, having a theme is powerful; it leaves a lasting impression, allowing the event to become engraved on guests' memories. And after the party's over, you'll continue to cherish all the elements of your suite.

kindly respond before
THE TWENTY-FIFTH OF APRIL

M _____

___ TO ATTEND

___ WITH REGRETS

MR. AND MRS. CHRISTOPHER RICHMON___
REQUEST THE PLEASURE OF YOUR COMP___
AT THE MARRIAGE OF THEIR DAUGHT___

Hillary Joy TO *Edgar Vinc___*

SATURDAY, THE TENTH OF M___
TWO THOUSAND AND FOUR___
AT SIX O'CLOCK

GRAND OAKS MANSI___
NEW ORLEANS

PLEASE SAVE THE DATE
FOR THE WEDDING OF

Hillary Joy &
Edgar Vince Ramsey

MAY 10, 2014
NEW ORLEANS

Invitation to follow

Mr. and Mrs. Andrew Nace
request the honour of your presence
at the marriage of their daughter

—————◆—————

Marie Nicole
to
Mr. Brian Michael Bridges

—————◆—————

Saturday, October fourth
two thousand and eight
at half past three o'clock

Saint Matthew's Lutheran Church
Hanover, Pennsylvania

The favour of a reply
is requested by
the sixth of September

Following the ceremony
please join us for
cocktails, dinner, and dancing

—————◆—————

The Pellington Estate
25 Alcott Road
Hanover, Pennsylvania

Menu

—————◆—————

Harvest Salad
Red and gold beets, fennel, and watercress
served with goat cheese and brioche croutons

Rack of Lamb Provençal
served with wild mushroom ragôut,
roasted garlic jus,
and a caramelized-onion tart

Roulade of Chicken
stuffed with Gruyére and spinach,
served with a creamy white-wine sauce

Fruit and Artisanal Cheese Plate

l-Apple Wedding Cake
d Petits Fours

Starting with Invitations

After you've booked your venue and decided on the style of your wedding, you can begin to think about your stationery. Here's your definitive guide to the who, what, when, and how of invites.

HIRING A STATIONER

There's a wealth of stationery inspiration online; look through the examples, and visit the websites of the stationers whose work you're drawn to. Once you've got a list of candidates, schedule consultations, and arrive prepared with some ideas of what you like. From the very first meeting, discuss pricing, including oft-overlooked expenses such as addressing and printing the envelopes and applying the correct postage. (Stationery should eat up only 2 to 5 percent of your overall wedding budget, but it can still add up.) Once you've settled on a stationer, you'll need to pay a deposit—usually 30 to 50 percent of the total costs—and sign a contract, which should outline the dates the work will be completed, the specific number of invitations to be issued, how many enclosures will be included in the suite, and who's responsible for correcting any errors in the finished product. Next, you'll collaborate to work out the design, which often requires reviewing PDFs several times. After you've inspected a physical proof, you can submit your order. Buy 10 percent more than you think you'll need, in case your list changes or you damage a few, and for keepsakes, too.

ELEMENTS OF A SUITE

The invite itself needs only to give the who, what, when, and where. It may include the following add-ons, but should never contain your registry info.

Inner envelope: An optional item, its primary purpose is to protect the suite from the wear and tear of mail delivery. (Similarly, tissue paper was originally used to prevent ink smears; today it's simply an elegant touch.) The inner envelope is where you write "and guest" or kids' names if they're invited.

Initial Here A gold-engraved monogram graces the invitation of this suite. Each piece is also distinguished by rounded corners and gold beveled edges. These touches signal a formal affair, and the colors and monogram reappear throughout the wedding, including on matchbooks and favor packaging.

Reception card: A small enclosure outlining the party details. If your ceremony and reception are taking place at the same venue, or you're having a less formal affair and like the look of including all the info on one piece of stationery, you can skip this add-on. Dress code info ("black tie optional") can be on the lower right hand corner.

Reply card: A card where guests can indicate whether they'll be attending your event. Usually these come with a separate stamped envelope for guests to mail.

Map: Often hand-illustrated, these give guests the lay of the land, which is useful for a destination wedding.

Accommodations card: This elective enclosure lists hotels in the area and might also include transportation info. It can direct guests to your wedding website (if you have one), too.

SAVE-THE-DATES

While you're not required to give your guests this heads-up, save-the-date cards are useful in helping them plan for your wedding—especially if they have to travel far. If you're sending these, drop them in the mail about six months in advance (or up to a year for a far-flung destination event). It's not necessary for your save-the-dates and invitations to match, although if you pick out your suite soon enough, you can tack on an order for them, too. Save-the-dates are almost always less formal than invitations, so they're a chance for couples to get creative; we've seen everything from flip-book versions to postcards of the wedding locale (which are cheaper than ordering custom stationery, and also more affordable to mail: postcard stamps cost 30 percent less than those for envelopes). Increasingly, couples are embracing electronic save-the-dates for more informal weddings, and online stationery companies have loads of charming designs that even "open" like envelopes in the recipient's inbox. That said, e-save-the-dates can get lost in an inbox, whereas guests can stick cards on a bulletin board as a visual reminder. Whatever route you take, whomever receives a save-the-date must receive an invitation to the wedding as well; we know you're excited to share your news, but don't send one to anyone who might not make the cut down the road.

THE TIMELINE STATIONERY

6 MONTHS AHEAD
Send save-the-dates, if desired.

4–6 MONTHS AHEAD
Order stationery, book calligrapher, if using.

2–4 MONTHS AHEAD
Mail invitations. Write thank-you notes as gifts arrive.

1–2 MONTHS AHEAD
Print programs.

2 WEEKS AHEAD
Create escort and place cards, menus, and favor tags.

Picking the Printing Process

The design of your invites helps set the tone for your wedding, but how they are printed—whether you go for classic engraving or artistic letterpress—is equally as impactful. It's also one of the first decisions you need to make.

LETTERPRESS

With roots in the 15th century, letterpress is the oldest print form in use. Blocks of metal or polymer plates with raised type are inked and pressed onto paper to indent letters onto the front and leave the back raised for a tactile, handcrafted appearance.

When to use it: You like an artisanal look with slight variations in each piece, and you chose a design with thin lines and fine type, which work best with letterpress. (Larger shapes can suffer from what printers call "salty color"—patchy ink placement that lets paper show through in spots.)

Timeline and costs: A letterpress order can take from two to four weeks. It's labor-intensive and done by hand, making it a pricier endeavor, with the cost of 100 invites ranging from $500 to $1,500. The more ink colors you use, the higher the cost, as each shade requires a separate plate to be made.

ENGRAVING

This process entails etching a design in reverse onto a copper or steel plate, depositing ink into the impressions, then pushing paper onto the template with a 3,000-pound weight. It creates raised lettering on the front of the card; you'll feel each character if you run your finger across the back, a telltale sign that a suite was engraved rather than thermographed.

When to use it: You want to signal that yours is a formal occasion. Unlike some other techniques, engraving also takes well to suites that pair light type and dark paper, which showcase the thick, matte ink that engravers use. One nice bonus: Some stationers give brides the plate used in their order as a graceful keepsake.

Timeline and costs: This painstaking process is the most involved—and can be the most expensive—of all of the printing methods, with the price of 100 cards ranging from about $550 to more than $2,500. If it's just your type, plan ahead: Completing an order can take six weeks.

THERMOGRAPHY

Thermography, like engraving, is a raised-print type, but no impression is made. That's because ink is applied directly to paper, then dusted with a resinous powder while still wet. The ink and powder are heated, and the letters rise, creating a 3-D effect.

When to use it: You want the appearance of engraving at a lower price point. Thermography offers an almost unlimited variety of typefaces, so get creative! Keep in mind, though, that thermographed letters are shinier than engraved ones, and their color is slightly less precise, since it's an ink-and-powder mix.

Timeline and costs: Thermography takes less work (and time) than engraving; an order can be filled in about a week (once you've completed the design). It costs around 50 percent less, too, with 100 pieces going for $250 to $500, but will still run you more than flat printing.

FLAT PRINTING

"Flat printing" is a catch-all term used for offset and digital techniques, both of which create stationery that's smooth to the touch. Offset involves transferring images from a metal plate to a rubber surface to paper with a lithographic press. Digital is a simpler process that prints right from a computer file. Used for commercial media like magazines and catalogs, flat printing is a low-cost way to get crisp, clean images.

When to use it: You want to save time or money. Which of the two should you choose? Know that while digital printing has come a long way, offset still offers the most luxurious options for paper selection, and its type is a tad sharper. But costs go up the more colors you use, while with digital, extra shades carry no additional charge.

Timeline and costs: Flat printing is a great option in a time crunch, with a turnaround of just a few days to a week. And it's the most economical of the major printing methods; both offset and digital will run you about $250 per 100 pieces.

Engraving

LETTERPRESS

THERMOGRAPHY

Flat Printing

Catherine Phillips

THE FAVOUR OF YOUR COMPANY IS REQUESTED
AT THE MARRIAGE UNITING

NAOMI JOUVIN & RICHARD SENDERS

OCTOBER 4, 2014 — EIGHT O'CLOCK IN THE EVENING
THE ACE HOTEL — NEW YORK CITY

DINNER TO FOLLOW AT THE BRESLIN

Choosing Your Design

Beyond the printing process and the colors, there are myriad ways to make your invitation wildly inviting. Pick an apropos motif, add some unexpected touches, and let the anticipation start building!

A few guests may skip the cake or miss the first dance, but every attendee will receive an invitation. Since it's so visible, and seen early in the wedding timeline, your stationery should capture the spirit of the event. Let your venue and palette inform your choices: If you're getting married by a lei-wearing officiant on a Hawaiian beach, opt for a colorful suite with a seaside motif. A religious ceremony at a house of worship, on the other hand, might call for the traditional wording expressed in ornate calligraphy, and an art-deco inspired fête in a former speakeasy would welcome some antiqued foil-stamped touches.

SUIT YOUR STYLE

Your suite should give your guests a sense of the ambience of your wedding, subtly cluing them in on the type of event to expect, and letting them know what to wear (whether implicitly, with formal calligraphy, or explicitly, with the words "black-tie" engraved at the bottom). Here are more ways to evoke a merrymaking mood based on your style:

Formal: You can't go wrong with classic black engraving on heavy ecru card stock. But you do have a million other options that still whisper "formal affair." Have the invitation—or just your names—calligraphed. Get a little gilty, with a gold foil emblem, like a wreath or tree. Or, have your first initials entwined in a monogram to adorn your invites. Chances are you'll want to include an elegant inner envelope, too.

Nature inspired: If you're getting married in a garden, go ahead and get floral, whether your motif is as tiny as a single bud or as bold as orange poppies splashed across a letterpressed suite. Don't be afraid to carry the motif over onto envelopes or address labels, and do look for coordinating botanical stamps. If your ceremony is by the shore, on the other hand, sail in a nautical direction (anchors,

compasses, sailboats, octopuses), or hit the tropics (palm trees, coconuts, orchids, hibiscus). Or, simply opt for scalloped edges on your invites to mimic the motion of the waves. Wherever you wed, you can hint at the seasons, with leaves in fall, and birch trees in winter.

Rustic: Letterpress imparts an arts-and-crafts feel, which might be right in line with your event. Pick a motif that signals your locale (a mountaintop for a ski lodge, or oars for a lakeside lodge), and, if you're planning a weekend-long affair, look for ways to pique guests' interest with fun extras, like a fishing lure (sans real hook) attached to a card inviting them to the day-before trout brunch.

Modern: For you, contemporary may mean minimalist: lowercase type in a sans-serif font and Bauhaus-inspired stamps on the envelopes. Or maybe it means emboldened: all caps letterpressed onto white paper, with a striped envelope liner, or your initials flatprinted on see-through vellum for an overlapping effect. Either way you'll want to keep things as clean and inspiring as a Frank Lloyd Wright–designed home.

Destination: Whether it's Brooklyn, Barbados, or Belgium, celebrating the location of your wedding on your suite always puts guests in the mood to travel—even if they're just hopping the bus to the venue. Print save-the-dates on sheets of paper created from an oversize map you've scanned. Use a compass as an icon, and find stamps that showcase a local landmark. Jetting off to India? Bring your favorite sari fabric to your stationer and ask her to design a suite in its spirit.

APPLY YOUR COLOR PALETTE

There are plenty of ways to communicate your wedding colors right from the get-go in your invitation. It can be as easy as picking colored ink and coordinating envelope liners (or striped or patterned liners in a few hues). Or, you could have, say, green card stock with white type. Or hot pink ink on cobalt paper. A calligrapher can work with ink in any shade as well.

Animal Magnetism If your fashion choices tend to be feline-inspired, your invitations can be, too. These bone-colored invites are calligraphed with each guest's name, then slipped into chic animal-print envelopes sealed with black tape and silver ink.

Believe it or not, the reply (or RSVP) card is a relatively new addition to an invitation suite. In decades past, it was proper to respond to a wedding invitation by sending a handwritten note on your own stationery to the bride and groom. Today, because of changing social etiquette, this tradition has disappeared. Now, most response cards are formatted with a space for guests to simply write in their name and check a box to accept or decline.

Style Inspiration: Stationery Suites

TROPICAL

MODERN

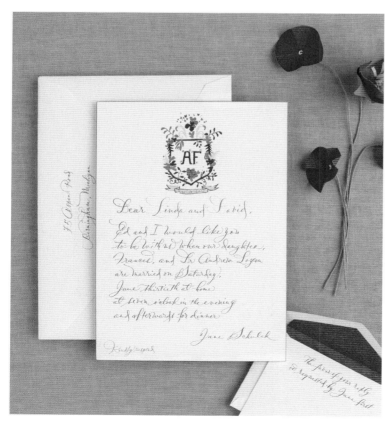

ROMANTIC

RUSTIC

NAUTICAL

NATURE INSPIRED

CLASSIC

MINIMALIST

Adding Special Elements

You've heard the saying: Little things mean a lot. When it comes to creating memorable wedding stationery, this holds especially true. Enlist any of these embellishments to take your invitation from simple to sensational.

While certainly not a "must," giving your suite a customized detail is a surefire way to make a statement—and the following options come in a range of price points.

Blind embossing: Ideal for adding crests or monograms, blind embossing creates a raised image without ink by squeezing paper between hot metal plates. It's also cost-effective to DIY: You can find a small at-home embosser for less than $50.

Deckled edges: These give card stock a feathery, intentionally unfinished effect that has a soft, antique look, as if it were torn from a vintage book. If Martha Washington were ordering invites for a fancy party, we bet she'd request them with deckled edges.

Die-cutting: It's a scary name, but a very cool technique. A sharp piece of metal (aka a "die") is used to slice letters or designs into a piece of stationery or to give standard paper shapes a more unique silhouette.

Edging: For an attention-getting accent, have a colored border hand-painted onto the sides of invites with a roller. It's most eye-catching when a highly saturated shade is used on stock that's at least 160 lb. cover weight.

Foil stamping: With shiny, matte, and even holographic finishes, foil stamping, which uses heat to adhere foil to paper, gives texture—and glamour—to flat-printed, engraved, or letterpressed pieces. (Note: It doesn't work well with thermography, as the heat involved will melt the raised letters.) Depending on your font, you could even have your entire invitation foil-stamped; the process is less pricey than letterpress and engraving but costlier than thermography and flat printing.

Liners: Don't overlook your envelopes! Use an apropos paper (think a pattern or solid in your color palette) to make opening them a delight. This is one job you can DIY to save money, or save time and leave it to a pro.

Thematic stamps: Search online stamp sources for on-theme postage in your color palette for an appropriate finishing touch.

Wax seal: Used to close an envelope and lend a rich, old-world look to any mailing, seals can come as pre-stamped and hardened stickers. Or you can create one the old-fashioned way by dripping hot wax onto the flap of an envelope and pressing a metal stamp into it.

CONSIDER CALLIGRAPHY

From paper and fabric to chalkboards and glass, there's almost nothing a calligrapher can't beautify. Many couples hire a professional to pen inner and outer invitation envelopes, which, along with the rest of the stationery, convey the style and tone of a wedding and get guests excited. Others have their names calligraphed on the invites themselves or commission calligraphy to call out the headings of card enclosures, like Accommodations or Activities, with the rest of the text printed. A calligrapher doesn't come cheap—most scribes charge by the piece—so you may need to use one sparingly, hiring him or her to make a special keepsake, such as handwriting the first page of your guest book. Or, have your names calligraphed, scanned, and printed on everything from napkins to programs.

If you decide to calligraph your envelopes, book your calligrapher after the stationery has been ordered and the guest list set, usually about four to six months ahead of time. A calligrapher needs about two weeks to complete the job, and you'll want to pop invitations in the mail four to six weeks before the wedding day. Other things to think of having calligraphed: the menu (whether on card stock at each table or on an oversize chalkboard), escort cards (on paper, mosaic tiles, seashells—the sky's the limit!), and table numbers (think placards, wine bottles, even calligraphed plants and leaves).

Dashing Dots This punchy letterpressed suite is full of surprises, from the party horn save the date to the packet of confetti printed with gold motifs on one side and useful information about transportation, accommodations, and pre- and post-parties on the other.

MARNIE & JAMIE

Miss Sophia Margaret Sterino
3512 Eleventh Street Southeast
Atlanta, Georgia
3 0 2 0 9

TOGETHER WITH THEIR FAMILIES

Marnie Elizabeth Hanel

AND

Dr. James Bordley, V

REQUEST THE HONOUR OF YOUR PRESENCE
AS THEY MAKE
a most romantic resolution
TO JOIN THEIR LIVES IN MARRIAGE

ON THE EVE OF THE NEW YEAR
SATURDAY, THE THIRTY-FIRST OF DECEMBER
TWO THOUSAND ELEVEN
AT SIX O'CLOCK IN THE EVENING

TRINITY PARISH
EIGHTH AVENUE & JAMES STREET
SEATTLE, WASHINGTON

Bubbles are Ballyhoo

FOLLOWING THE CEREMONY
SODO PARK
3200 FIRST AVENUE SOUTH

PLEASE REPLY
by the stroke of midnight
ON THANKSGIVING

_____ OH YES, WE'LL BE THERE!

_____ WE'LL BE TOASTING FROM AFAR.

LET THE
COUNTDOWN
BEGIN!

TOAST,
POP DOWNSTAIRS
FOR BREAKFAST ON
NEW YEAR'S DAY.

Getting the Wording Right

To compose the text of your invitations, don't sweat the etiquette.
Most invites introduce the host, name the bride and groom, tell everyone when and where to be
and ask for a response. Beyond that, the text is chock-full of hidden meaning,
and the placement of the names depends on who's
footing the bill. Here, the most common scenarios.

1

THE HOST LINE

Start with the names of those issuing the invitation—and, usually, paying for the shindig—. Traditionally, this meant the bride's parents. Evolving family structures and financial dynamics often make this the trickiest part of the process, so follow what fits your situation.

WHEN THE HOSTS ARE . . .

The bride's parents: Most married couples follow the standard format (top line below); if they have different surnames, an "and" joins them:

Mr. and Mrs. John Michael Williams
or
Ms. Jane Marie Parks
and
Mr. John Michael Williams

The bride's divorced parents: Names are listed on separate lines without an "and" between them, and remember that Mom always comes first. If Mom has remarried, use her married name; the oldest of etiquette omits all stepparents, though you can certainly add them if you'd like. If you do, and a remarried parent has a different surname from his or her spouse, put the birth parent first. If you must break the line, do it before the "and":

Mrs. Jane Marie Williams
Mr. John Michael Williams

Mrs. Paul Marcus Schott
Mr. John Michael Williams

Ms. Jane Marie Williams
and Mr. Paul Marcus Schott

Mr. John Michael Williams
and Ms. Stephanie Anne Johnson

Deceased parent: It's not traditional to include a deceased parent, but many people feel strongly about doing so. This wording should make it clear that the deceased parent is not issuing the invitation (courtesy titles such as Mr. or Mrs. would be awkward and are omitted):

The pleasure of your company is
requested at the marriage of
Elizabeth Marie Williams
daughter of John Williams and
the late Jane Williams
to
Douglas Arthur Sawyer

The groom's parents: If you'd like to mention them, do so after the groom's name. If they are cohosting the wedding, add them after the bride's parents' names:

Douglas Arthur Sawyer
the son of Mr. and Mrs. Robert Dean Sawyer

The couple: This format works well for delicate situations that involve some combination of divorced parents and stepparents. If the couple is hosting on their own, omit the first line:

Together with their families
Miss Elizabeth Marie Williams
and
Mr. Douglas Arthur Sawyer

2

THE REQUEST LINE

Two phrases are the most traditional; one indicates the ceremony will be in a house of worship, the other that it will not. But informal wording is becoming very common. Just be sure that whatever phrasing you choose indicates that guests are being invited to a wedding ceremony or the reception only.

IF YOU ARE MARRYING AT A . . .
Place of worship:
request the honour of your presence
Secular location:
request the pleasure of your company

Or, holding a reception only: Avoid phrases such as "celebrate their marriage," which could imply that guests will witness the vows. Instead, go for something like: "invite you to join them at the wedding reception of . . ."

3

THE BRIDE AND GROOM LINE

The bridal couple's names are set off, each on separate lines. The preposition linking them goes on its own line; traditional American formatting uses the word "to"; some Jewish formats use the word "and."

Traditional: If the bride's last name is the same as her parents' above, it is not repeated. No courtesy title (such as Miss or Ms.) is used:

at the marriage of their daughter
Elizabeth Marie
to
Mr. Douglas Arthur Sawyer

Contemporary: If the couple or both sets of parents are to host, treat the names equally:

Elizabeth Williams
and
Douglas Sawyer

4

THE DATE AND TIMELINE

Don't worry about using "a.m." or "p.m.," or a phrase such as "in the evening," unless the wedding will be held at eight, nine, or ten o'clock. The year is traditionally omitted as well, but it is sometimes included for the invitation's keepsake value.

Traditional: Spell out numbers and capitalize proper nouns only; you can begin the line with the preposition "on" if you'd like:

Saturday, the twenty-third of January
two thousand and ten
at half after six o'clock

Contemporary: Using numerals is more modern, but not necessarily more casual:

Saturday, January 22, 2010
at 6:30 p.m.

5

LOCATION

Classically, you do not include street addresses of houses of worship or well-known locations. Commas are not present at the ends of lines, and the state is always spelled out.

Traditional, religious:
Saint Paul's Lutheran Church
Walkersville, Maryland

Contemporary:
If you are using a street address, numerals are acceptable but no ZIP code is needed:

Ceresville Mansion
8529 Liberty Road
Frederick, Maryland

6

RECEPTION LINE OR CARD

If the ceremony and reception are in the same space, they can be on a single invitation. If not, a separate card might be helpful.

Same location, on the invite: This follows the location line:

and afterward at the reception

Different location: Note the capital "R"; the space before it should be a bit bigger:

Reception immediately following the ceremony
Ceresville Mansion

On a separate card: This approach keeps the main invitation from becoming too crowded. If the reception doesn't directly follow the ceremony, specify the time:

Reception
seven o'clock
Ceresville Mansion
8529 Liberty Road
Frederick, Maryland

7

RSVP LINE OR REPLY CARD

Brides today generally include a card with a stamped envelope to encourage guests to respond to their invitation in a timely manner, even though traditional etiquette doesn't actually call for them. It's not rude to omit these, but it might be risky to rely on guests to know to reply without one. Another option is to include RSVP info on the invitation itself.

On the invite: An RSVP goes in the lower left corner; you can also include mailing address, phone number, email address, or website.

On a separate card: This fill-in-the-blank version provides the first letter of Mr. or Ms.; or try a single line, such as "Please let us know whether you will join us," with space for writing:

Please respond before the first of January

Addressing the Envelopes

In this case, what's on the outside counts, too.
Learn how to annotate your envelopes to just about anyone.

———

It may sound easy—after all, you have addressed an envelope before! But sending wedding invitations is a little different and there are some rules to follow that will help separate this special delivery from all others. When you are addressing . . .

A Married Couple

Traditionally, you'd use the husband's name and both social titles of Mr. and Mrs., as in Mr. and Mrs. John Smith. No need to have the husband's middle name, but if you do, write it out in full rather than using an initial.

A Couple With Different Last Names

Whether they're living together or not, address the female first. If it's a married couple in which the wife has chosen to keep her maiden name, Ms. can be used, as with Ms. Jane Wilson and Mr. John Smith.

A Couple and the Wife Is a Doctor

We're about to get old-school on you: Technically, her degree "outranks" her husband's social title of Mr., so the wife should be listed first, with Doctor spelled out. If they're both doctors, you can either list them as The Doctors Johnson, or separate their names as such: Doctor Amy Johnson and Doctor Luke Johnson.

A Couple and One Spouse Is a Judge

Recognize a judge by using The Honorable, and list him or her first.

THE MRS. OR MS. QUESTION

It used to be that if a married woman kept her maiden name, she'd always be addressed as "Ms.," the idea being that Mrs. refers to a man's wife. Thus, you'd write Ms. Jane Wilson, not Mrs. Jane Wilson. These days, however, things have become much simpler, and the use of Ms. is acceptable, whether the female guest is married or divorced, or uses her maiden or married name. The one exception? Anyone under the age of 18 is addressed as Miss, and those older than that would take Ms.

THE QUESTION OF KIDS

When sending invites, it's not one per person, but one per household. Which brings up a question we hear often: How do I let guests know their kids aren't included? Technically, when a child's name is left off the envelope (inner and outer if your suite has both), he or she is not invited. But since many people aren't aware of this protocol, it's best to also let your guests know via old-fashioned word-of-mouth; have friends or relatives spread the news.

ADDING PLUS-ONES

Spouses of attendees should always be invited. When it comes to your pals' significant others or dates, to add or not add becomes a question. Use your discretion depending on your budget and how long the couple has been together (six months is a good gauge), and apply any rule you make across the board; if you say no significant others unless a couple is married or lives together, that goes for all invitees, meaning your friends as well as your groom's. If you are inviting someone with a plus-one, try to find out the name and address of his or her date and send two separate invitations. If that's not possible, address the outside envelope to the primary invitee, with the inside envelope reading Ms. Jane Doe and Guest.

———

The Write Stuff Every couple has their own personality, and there's a calligraphic style to suit their mood, from bold ornamental script to romantic flourishes to relaxed, all-lowercase writing in bright ink. Pick your penning, and keep in mind that calligraphers may charge extra for dark envelopes or multiple ink colors.

Going Beyond Invites

*While your invitation suite (deservedly) gets a lot of play, it's not the only paper element that will grace your day.
Consider a few options you may wish to include in your celebration.*

SIGNAGE

From oversize wayfinders to simple directional images, signs around your venue can direct guests to the ceremony and reception sites, bathrooms, dinner, dancing, and more.

PROGRAMS

These are not mandatory but can help engage guests who might not be familiar with the wedding rituals of your specific culture or know all your attendants by sight. Plus, they make nice keepsakes. A program details the components of your ceremony, including who's in your wedding party and the order of events. Though they're often bound and hand-tied like a booklet, programs can also take the form of single cards.

ESCORT CARDS

At seated lunch or dinner receptions, guests locate this card (often calligraphed) with their name on it to reveal which table they'll be sitting at for the meal. One fun idea that's also a money-saver: Add a name tag to your favors to let them do double duty. Mini frames, small potted plants or herbs, and calligraphed decorative tiles all work nicely.

PLACE CARDS

Found at each place setting at a seated meal, these cards direct attendees to their particular seat at the dinner table.

MENUS

Let your guests know what's for dinner by laying a menu card atop each place setting, propping one up in the center of each table, or designing an oversize sign to be displayed in one common and visible place.

FAVORS

The takeaway tokens you present to guests may include calligraphed tags or small adornments with your married monogram and wedding date and/or a sweet slogan thanking everyone for attending. For example, on a bow-tied packet of seeds, you could impart the message, "Love grows," or a bundle of local pistachios might have a tag reading, "We're nuts about you." For more favor ideas, see pages 252 to 263.

WEDDING ANNOUNCEMENTS

While they're not a necessary component of the stationery surrounding your wedding day, it's always a thoughtful gesture to mail cards announcing your good news to anyone among your acquaintances or in your extended family who wasn't at your wedding but would want to be informed of your marriage. These are posted immediately after the big day and in no way require the recipient to send a gift in return.

THE TRADITION
ESCORT CARDS

———

Typically, these diminutive cards include a guest's name and table number and are arranged in a special display near the entrance to the reception. Even though they serve a practical purpose of letting attendees know where to sit for dinner, they have a romantic past: In Edwardian times the cards didn't contain a table number; rather, they bore the handwritten name of the lady each gentleman present would escort to dinner.

Outside the Envelope (clockwise from top left):
A calligraphed menu was a feast for the eyes. Signage let attendees at a coastal affair know where to grab ice cream sandwiches. Escort cards slipped into folded hankies led guests to their seats at a rustic Montana wedding. A San Francisco couple had a banner printed to spread the news after their city hall ceremony.

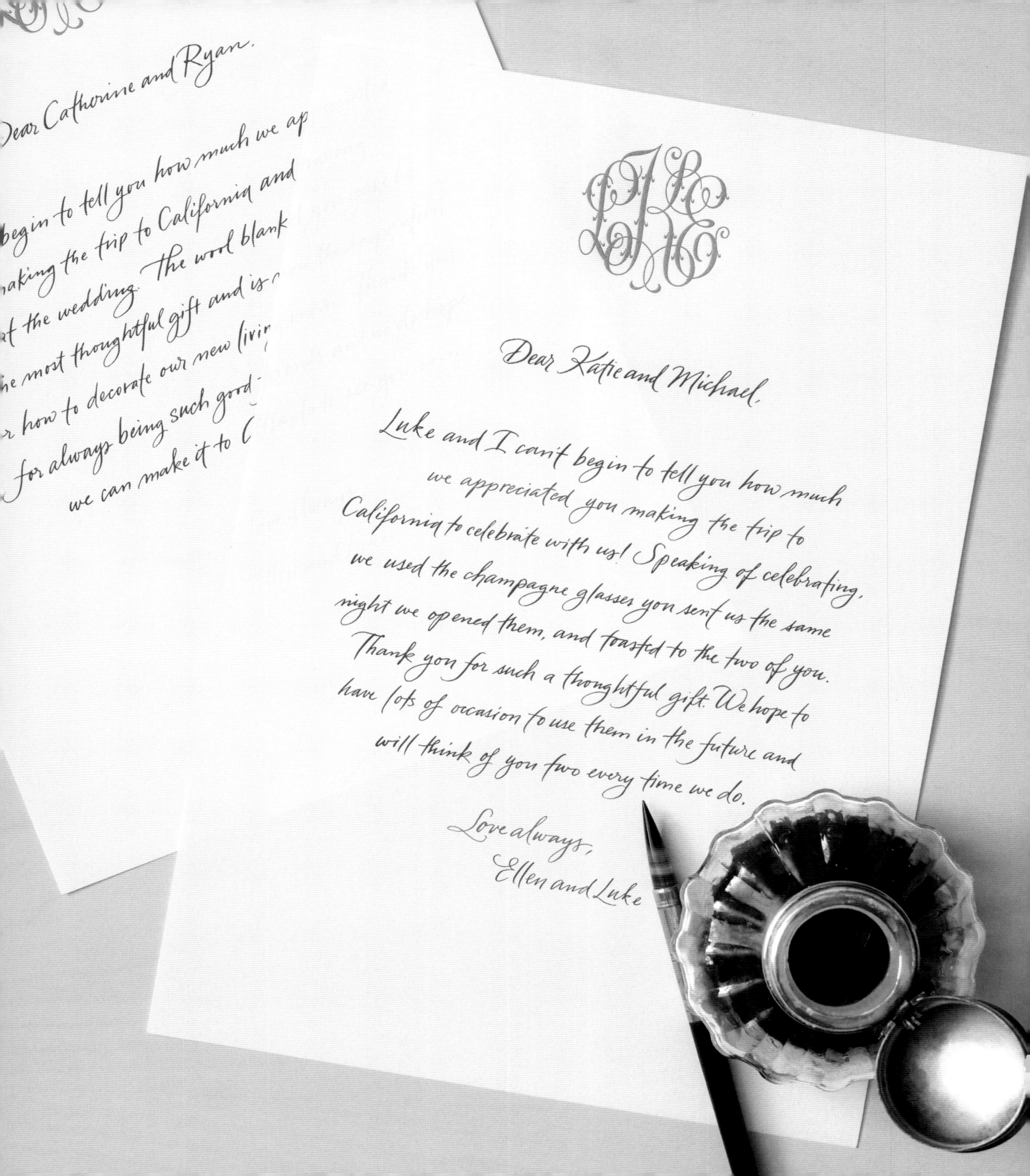

Dear Catherine and Ryan,

begin to tell you how much we ap

aking the trip to California and

t the wedding. The wool blank

he most thoughtful gift and is

r how to decorate our new livin

for always being such good

we can make it to C

Dear Katie and Michael,

Luke and I can't begin to tell you how much
we appreciated you making the trip to
California to celebrate with us! Speaking of celebrating,
we used the champagne glasses you sent us the same
night we opened them, and toasted to the two of you.
Thank you for such a thoughtful gift. We hope to
have lots of occasion to use them in the future and
will think of you two every time we do.

Love always,
Ellen and Luke

Saying Thank You

*In the afterglow of your wedding, you'll be primed
to express heartfelt gratitude for the gifts you've received.
Start the job as soon as presents begin to arrive, and you'll find this task
to be a breeze, and a nice way to relive all the wedding fun.*

PLAN AHEAD

Perhaps the only hard-and-fast rule we'll lay down in this entire book: Every gift you receive must be acknowledged by a handwritten thank-you note. To keep the task manageable, order thank-you notes when you do your suites; that way, you'll have them on hand to use as soon as you receive a gift. Ideally, you should acknowledge every present immediately, but sending a note within two weeks is also acceptable. If you fall behind, make every effort to send a thank-you as soon as you can—but within three months after the event.

SHOW YOUR STYLE

Many couples choose thank-you notes that reflect their invitation suites, whether they order them from the same stationer or buy packaged paper and stamp or emboss it with their motif. But that's just one option. If you want your cards to feature your new married monogram, they shouldn't be sent until after you're legally Mr. and Mrs. (both according to etiquette and to avoid bad luck!). Use different cards for thank-you notes that are sent out before the wedding date, or order some that combine the initials of your first names instead so you can begin sending notes right away. Similarly, don't wait for the photographer to get you proofs so you can have a shot of your wedding made into a photo card if it's going to delay your writing and sending your thank-yous; save the photo for your first holiday card as a married couple instead.

KEEP IT PERSONAL

As for what to say, you don't need to write a lot—four or five sentences will suffice—as long as what you express is sincere. According to etiquette, you shouldn't start off with the words "thank you" but with some pleasantry like, "It meant so much to us to have you at our wedding." If the person didn't attend, or sent the gift long beforehand, something like, "It's so sweet of you to think of us," or "It was such a delight to come home from work and find a package from one of our favorite people on our doorstep." Then you can get to the thanks, identify the gift, say why you appreciate it, why it has a personal meaning for you, and how you plan to use it. ("David and I adore the coffee-maker. As coffee lovers, we've used it every day since we got back from our honeymoon. Thanks so much.") For cash gifts, you don't have to mention the dollar amount, but it's a nice touch to say how you plan to spend the money.

An Attitude of Gratitude Thank-you notes needn't be formal, calligraphed letters. But they should be handwritten on nice stationery—whether it matches your suite, flaunts your new monogram, or comes from a store-bought box of pretty cards—and sent as promptly as possible.

GOOD TO KNOW

Add two extra columns to the spreadsheet you use to list invitees' addresses, and track their RSVPs. Use one to punch in the gift that they send and the next box to check off after you've mailed them a thank-you note. This keeps writing thank-yous easy (no digging for addresses) and ensures that you won't thank someone for the fondue pot when she gave you a soufflé dish.

CHAPTER
SIX

FIND YOUR
FLOWERS

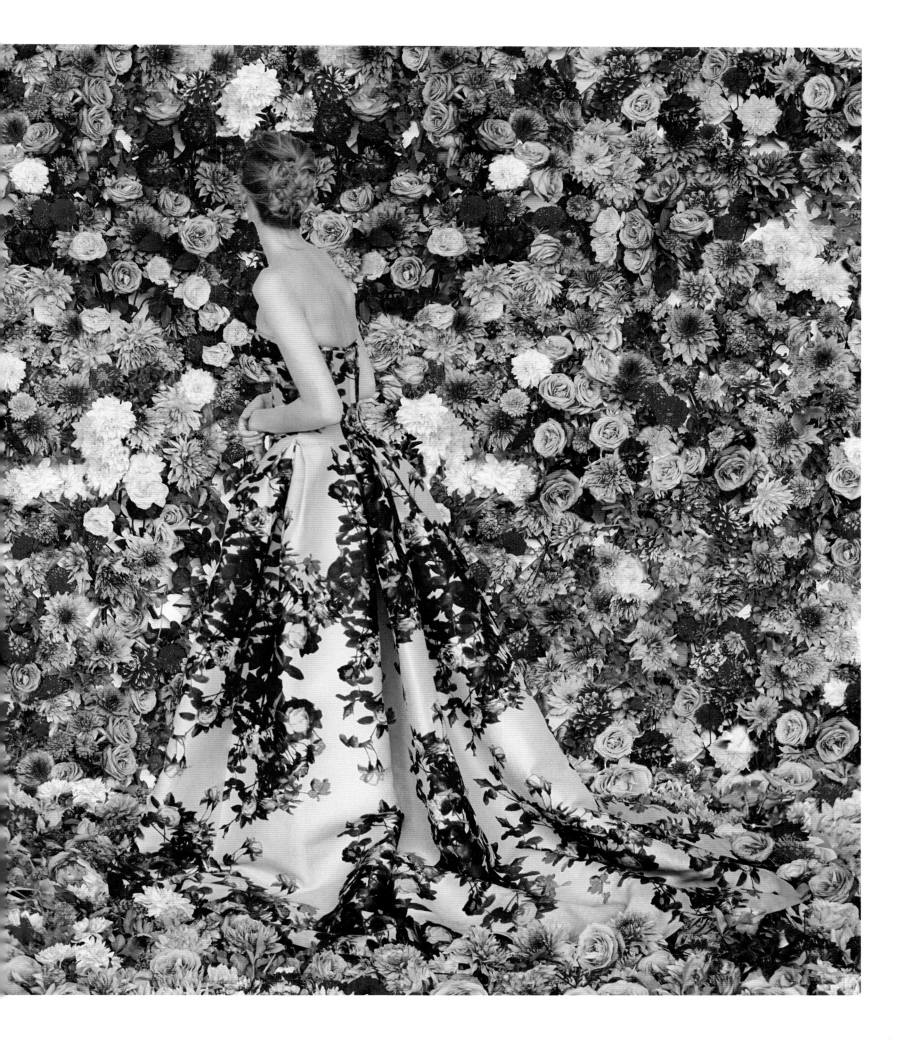

> "
>
> AT A WEDDING, FLOWERS AREN'T JUST DECORATIVE. THEY ALSO REMIND US TO ENJOY THE BEAUTY OF THE MOMENT.
>
> "
>
> —Naomi de Mañana, *Senior Style Editor, Martha Stewart Weddings*

ASIDE FROM THAT SPARKLING RING on your finger, flowers are one of the oldest and sweetest symbols of love and romance. They also have the innate power to delicately scent a space and instantly make it look ten times more special. Naturally, it's only fitting to fill your day in the most memorable way with them. But how to decide which ones? Gorgeous blooms come in hundreds of varieties and in dozens of shades, which means thousands of possible combinations. Fortunately, by setting a budget and then picking your location, date, color palette, and dress, you've already pared down your floral options tremendously. With those details in mind, you can also work with a florist to determine if your favorite flowers will be readily available then and there. (Hothouses and greenhouses–with a little help from overnight shipping–have made it possible to get virtually any type of bloom at any time; however, sticking with seasonal, locally grown flowers is the most eco option, and they can save you hundreds of dollars.) Next consider the style of your arrangements, including the shape of the bouquet that you'd like to carry down the aisle and how both of you envision the look and feel of the flowers at your ceremony and celebration. The following pages will lead you nimbly through this process. While flowers may not be as everlasting as that ring on your finger, long after your wedding has passed, the mere scent of your blooms will take you back to that extra-special day, and they'll remind you of the love and romance that came with them.

Taking the First Step

Your palette, theme, venue, and wedding date will inform the look of your arrangements, but inspiration can come from anywhere and everywhere. Brainstorming with a florist about your favorites in everything—blooms, art, colors, fashion—is a great way to start the floral design.

HIRING A FLORIST

There are professionals who only arrange flowers and there are florists who are more like jack-of-all-trades event planners, overseeing floral décor, lighting, and interior design. Know which type you want before you begin your search. You'll need to pick that person at least six months in advance of the date to make sure they're available; if you live in a big city, plan to book one year ahead of time. (An upside to hiring the vendor a year before the event: He or she will be able to show you in person exactly what's in season on your wedding day.) Getting recommendations from friends is the best way to come up with a list of good candidates—especially if those friends have similar taste. And don't just ask for the great experiences; ask for the bad ones, too, in order to weed out any unreliable or difficult vendors. Check with the manager at your venue as well: She may have a list of recommended florists who are familiar with the site.

Once you have two or three strong candidates, interview them, check out their portfolios, read online reviews, and contact past clients, if necessary, to get a full picture of their work and, just as important, their work ethic. Whomever you end up hiring will then offer you a written proposal that itemizes every cost and includes fees, such as sales tax and delivery charge. The final contract should specify setup information, spelling out who will oversee the process and the dates, times, and locations for delivery. It should also detail all the floral elements to be provided, and the payment schedule. Last, the contract should contain language about any unacceptable substitutes; for instance, if you loathe purple or blanch at the sight of roses, make sure that's noted. After all, when it comes to your wedding, you want only happy surprises.

CREATING THE LOOK

With your florist on board, it's time for the fun part: getting inspired! By all means, show her visuals—paint chips of your palette, swatches of the dresses, and tear-outs of arrangements that make your heart skip a beat. But don't forget to mine your personal histories for ideas as well. You might want to incorporate sweet peas in your bouquet because that's what your mom had in her wedding posy. Or, perhaps you think every centerpiece should have 12 roses because that's what your fiancé gave you when he proposed. And that ribbon you saved from his very first Valentine's Day gift to you? It could make for a gorgeous bouquet wrap. The more meaning you can inject into your wedding, the more memorable the day will feel.

DETERMINING WHAT YOU'LL NEED

Yes, you'll require a bouquet. But there are so many other ways in which you might want to enlist flowers, from creating a focal point at your ceremony to dressing up the reception space. You can also use flowers to honor special guests and top your cake, or give guests nosegays or small potted plants as favors. The number of blooms you decide on and the types you choose are entirely up to you. For all the ways you can work flowers into your ceremony and reception, simply turn the page.

Making the Gradiant This spill of flowers spans a number of shades, morphing from purple sweetpeas and anemones to pink garden roses, peonies, and double tulips, to cream dahlias, yellow ranunculus and tree peonies and orange ranunculus.

THE TIMELINE FLOWERS

———

9–12 MONTHS AHEAD
Begin researching florists.

6–12 MONTHS
Book your florist.

3–6 MONTHS
Meet to go over inspiration, palette, venue, and floral needs; if you can, do a walk-through of the venue with the florist.

3 WEEKS
Finalize flowers and confirm details.

Styling the Ceremony

*The flowers for your vows can be a mix of décor and personal blooms
that are carried or worn down the aisle. You don't need to have every type of floral
element listed below, but you certainly wouldn't go wrong if you did.*

1

CEREMONY DÉCOR

If your wedding site is naturally stunning (say, a cliff overlooking the ocean), you may not need to gussy it up much, if at all. But most couples will want to beautify in some way the spot where they'll commit to a life together. Hanging garlands or placing potted trees make for perfect altar markers, while pew swags brighten up plain seats in a house of worship, and wreaths can spruce up doors and welcome guests.

2

YOUR BOUQUET

This is something we don't recommend skipping. Yes, it's one decorative detail on a day made up of lots of them, but its dramatic impact can't be overstated. Plus, holding your bouquet gives you something to do with your hands as you walk down the aisle (and you'll want that). When choosing yours, be sure to factor in your dress style and body type (a petite bride can be overwhelmed by a large arrangement, and oversized flowers might hide the delicate details at the waist of your gown). Whatever the size and shape of your posy, it's always lovely to add a personal touch: A clutch wrapped in fabric from your mom's wedding veil or a palette that references a shared alma mater makes for a more memorable bouquet.

3

POSIES AND PETALS

After your bouquet has been designed, think about the bridal party's clutches. For their bouquets, consider a variation of yours; they could be smaller copies, or each maid could carry a single-flower bouquet starring one of the blooms in yours.

If you have a tiny attendant (or two), she'll need a vessel of petals to sprinkle down the aisle. And that vessel doesn't need to be a basket; there are more creative alternatives, such as a pocketed apron or paper cone. Moreover, she doesn't even need to toss petals—she could carry a small nosegay, hold a garland with another flower girl, or skip down the aisle waving a wand topped with blooms and wearing a floral crown. You decide!

4

BOUTONNIERES AND CORSAGES

Boutonnieres for the groom, groomsmen, and fathers of the couple aren't required, but they do add polish to men's suits. While a single bud from the bride's bouquet is classic, they can also comprise feathers, grasses, herbs, berries, or foliage. (A perk of nonfloral versions: They won't wilt.) And they don't have to be identical to each other. A grapevine sprig might be appropriate for your wine-loving brother, while nigella, the Alaskan state flower, will delight your pal from Anchorage.

Celebrate your mothers and grandmothers, as well as VIP guests like readers, with corsages. These can match your wedding party's blooms or be tailored to the wearer's preferences. Most are worn on the wrist or pinned to clothing, but you could have the recipient hold a single flower or nosegay instead, or pin the corsage to her clutch (if, say, your mother-in-law doesn't want to stick a pin in her new silk gown).

WEDDING WISDOM

———

Have your florist transfer your ceremony arrangements to the reception space after the vows, when guests are busy getting to the party or enjoying cocktail hour. This not only amps up the flowers at your event and saves you money, but also gives the two parts of your wedding a cohesive look.

Maid of Honor

Groom

Father

1

2

3

4

Prettying Up the Party

The function of venue flowers is to make the space look even more celebratory. Focus your energies (and funds) on areas that get a lot of attention, like table arrangements, but don't be afraid to use blooms strategically to surprise guests, whether topping the cake or floating in bowls in the powder room.

1

CENTERPIECES

These are the flowers your loved ones will be staring at for most of the night, so make them spectacular! Just ensure they're either lower than 14 inches or higher than 24 inches; anything in between restricts cross-table interaction between guests. Another alternative? Hanging blossoms overhead, which leaves the table clear for all that sparkling conversation.

2

DÉCOR

It's not just dining tables that need adornments. Think about all the areas at the venue that guests will have access to—from the buffet table to the escort-card display, the powder rooms to the bars—and get them wedding-ready as well. That could mean anything from setting a small arrangement in a visible corner to wrapping the cake table in garlands. Many florists swear by a large arrangement that acts as a focal point near the entrance of a venue. Then you can have fewer blooms elsewhere, and guests will still go home talking about the spectacular flowers at the reception.

3

CAKE

Topping your cake with real flowers is a standout way to bring in natural beauty and is more affordable than having sugar flowers crafted. But if you do choose to use fresh blossoms, make sure they are of the nonpoisonous variety (say, roses or chrysanthemums). There are also flowers that are completely edible, such as nasturtiums and pansies, which work well on individual desserts and can be sugared. (If using these, order only from a grower selling them as edible flowers.) Should you decide you absolutely can't have anything adorning your cake other than, say, lily of the valley (which can cause pain and nausea when ingested), don't let the flowers touch any of the slices that get served (there are "cake vase" devices that are made specifically to prevent this from happening), or better yet stick to a sugared rendition.

4

FAVORS

Send guests home with something botanical and beautiful. Mini terrariums and potted plants make wonderful living favors. And here's a great centerpiece alternative that's also a budget-savvy, two-in-one option: Consider decorating the tables with bud vases, either clustered in the center or placed in a row down the middle of table, then have guests take one each as favors at celebration's end.

WEDDING WISDOM

Guests not only spend a long time looking at centerpieces, they will end up smelling them all night as well. For that reason, avoid super-fragrant blooms—such as lilies and gardenias—in tabletop arrangements, and save them for stunning personal bouquets.

Thinking Seasonally

So much of wedding planning is about timing: Does the date work for your families and friends? Is your florist available? But you also need to consider Mother Nature's schedule. Choose your flowers based on what's in season, and you'll get the freshest blooms, the widest variety, and the biggest savings.

SPRING

WHAT'S IN SEASON:

BLOOMING FRUIT BRANCHES

DAFFODILS

IRISES

LILACS

LILIES OF THE VALLEY

PEONIES

RANUNCULUS

SWEET PEAS

TULIPS

Primavera Pretties (this page, clockwise from top): A sophisticated tablescape features a large arrangement of peonies, lilacs, bearded irises, and clematis flanked by sweet peas and peonies on the left and clematis and wild sweet peas on the right. This clutch is composed of tree peonies, cosmos, tulips, and delicate wire vine. A bouquet of sweet peas, ranunculus, parrot tulips, roses, and lily of the valley is wrapped in ribbon calligraphed with a line from the couple's vows. This bride wears a headpiece of sweet peas, wild sweet peas, lilacs and peonies. **Opposite:** A bridal bouquet brims with a mix of tree peonies, tulips, clematis, lilacs, and apple branches.

SUMMER

WHAT'S IN SEASON:
CLEMATIS
COSMOS
DAHLIAS (LATE SUMMER)
FREESIAS
GARDEN ROSES
HYDRANGEAS
QUEEN ANNE'S LACE (MIDSUMMER)
POPPIES

Fair Weather Friends (this page, from top): A wreath of hearty hydrangeas, garden roses, and silver millinery leaves adorns a sweetheart chair. Pink ranunculus have pride of place among poppies, corydalis, and sweet peas in this bridal bouquet. **Opposite:** White compotes burst with vines and branches laden with ripe peaches, viburnum berries, raspberries, and yellow plums, as well as "Sweet Autumn" clematis, red-orange dahlias, and garden roses.

FALL

WHAT'S IN SEASON:
AMARYLLISES
BITTERSWEET BRANCHES
CALLA LILIES
DAHLIAS
GARDENIAS
JAPANESE ANEMONES
OAK BRANCHES & LEAVES
ORNAMENTAL KALE
ROSE HIPS

Great Bloomers (this page, clockwise from top): Wispy clematis foliage, rattlesnake grass, and blueberries add an untamed feel to a centerpiece of garden roses, dahlias, and ranunculus. A wreath of curved driftwood and manzanita boughs is punctuated with fiery florals and fruit, including crimson amaryllis, inky privet berries, purply artichokes, and orange persimmons. Copper pipes form a striking tablescape when filled with miniature calla lilies and foliage, including ferns, verbena, and heuchera. Privet berries add dark beauty to a clutch of dahlias, roses, ranunculus, and andromeda. **Opposite:** A richly hued bouquet gets its colors from purple kale and salvia buds, black chervil, lavender garden roses, marbled coralbell leaves, chocolate cosmos, and gilded acorns and oak leaves.

WINTER

WHAT'S IN SEASON:
AMARYLLISES
ANEMONES
CAMELLIA
HELLEBORES
HYACINTHS
NARCISSUS
PAPERWHITES
QUINCE
SNOWDROPS

So Cool (this page, from top): Alabaster amaryllis is framed with parrot tulips, hellebores, snowberries, scabiosa pods, and round-leaf sage in this resplendent bouquet. Low, single-flower groupings of eucharis, hellebores, muscari, and amaryllis are accented with fruiting smilax vines and begonia leaves, and displayed in lichen-moss-covered vessels for a woodsy feel. **Opposite:** Two flowering branches—late-winter blooming quince and spirea—make a statement in this floral focal point, arranged in a large, paper-wrapped vessel with muscari and hellebores clustered at the base.

The Primer: Bouquet Shapes

*When it comes to posies, there's no one-size-fits-all approach. Below are the
most popular styles. You'll want to take into account your dress silhouette
as you're choosing, so the flowers will look harmonious with your gown.*

OVAL

These bouquets tend to be
large and dramatic (often more
than a foot long) and are well
suited to graphic- looking
flowers, such as ranunculus,
amaryllis, calla lilies, and
trumpet lilies. Because of their
size, pair oval bouquets with
streamlined dresses
(a body-hugging sheath,
say, rather than a
oluminous ball gown).

SHEATH

Also known as the
"presentation" or "pageant"
bouquet, a sheath is carried
in the crook of your arm
as if you were a beauty queen.
The sheath features flowers
with long stems that are
tied together with a wide ribbon
or wrap. Flowers for this type
of bouquet should have
stems that are strong, not flimsy,
so pick blossoms such as
tulips, lilies, cymbidium and
endrobium orchids, and
delphiniums. These bouquets
are usually very grand in size–
and thus the dress should
be suitably formal (but not with
a full skirt, as the cross-body
nature of these bouquets doesn't
enhance nipped waistlines to
their best advantage).

ROUND

If you're a no-frills type of bride,
then a round or dome bouquet may
be the shape for you. While this
versatile sphere is simple in design
(and thus suitable for nearly every
type of dress), it's still a chic choice
and by no means boring. With
this style, it's best to go with
blooms that are naturally circular
and have slender, flexible stems;
those that are wide and stiff
(like calla lilies) make it hard to
create the ball shape. For traditional
weddings, roses or hydrangeas
are a great choice, while anemones
or poppies will look more
contemporary.

130

CASCADE

Sometimes referred to as "shower bouquets," cascades feature an abundance of blossoms at the top, then taper off. The flowers are often wired to create a fanlike spray. Cascades tend to be loosely gathered, with the blossoms draping downward on their stems, and frequently incorporate trailing ribbons and greenery. Ideal varieties for this type include clematis, lilies, and dendrobium orchids, and any bloom or greenery that has trailing vines, such as ivy and stephanotis. With its long lines, a cascade works well for both sheath dresses and mermaid gowns. If you like this look but prefer something more compact (because you're petite or you want to show off a particular detail at your waist) go with a teardrop, which is rounded at the top with only a few trailing flowers to form a tip at the bottom. (As with cascades, each flower may be wired to create the shape.) Peonies, garden roses, lilies, and orchids are all good choices for this arrangement.

CRESCENT

If you've already booked a scenic and sprawling outdoor venue or want an ultra-romantic look, you may want to carry a crescent bouquet. The operatic arch that curves around your hands is perfect for an extravagant affair. (The only caveat: If your dress has gorgeous embellishments at the waist, you may want a clutch with less of a presence to better show off the details.) When thinking about flowers, select blooms with stems that aren't stiff and can be wired to create this distinctive shape. Poppies, cosmos, anemones, parrot tulips, mums, and bell-shaped nerines are all suitable options. Also try flowers that have tendrils, including sweet peas and fritillaria, to form the dangling ends.

ORGANIC

Free-form and asymmetrical, the organic style is perfect for the bohemian bride. With this type of clutch, there are no rules: The shape is created by the combination of flowers you choose– and you can pick any type. Mix big flowers with smaller buds, grasses, fruits, berries, leaves, or anything else you want to add. This style would go well with a flowing dress for a wedding that takes place in a natural outdoor setting.

WEDDING WISDOM

How you carry the bouquet depends on the shape and size of it. But in most cases, you should hold the handle securely in both hands, with arms extended downward so the clutch is just below your waist. Elbows should point out a little, away from your body, to reveal the curve of your torso. As you get nervous, you may notice the bouquet creeping up to your waist; if that happens, lower it below your belly button again so the V formed by your arms visually slims your middle, making for the most flattering photos.

Selecting Your Style

Flowers can appeal to most of the senses, delighting our sight, smell, and touch. No wonder they're such a powerful tool for setting a mood. There's an abundance of flowers (and fruit, leaves, grasses, and more) to match your theme.

CLASSIC

You'll never go wrong with perennial wedding shades of bridal whites and something blues. 1. A fragrant burst of eighty sweet peas is dotted by blue tweedia, and bound by a ribbon embroidered with the newlyweds' initial and wedding date. 2. Crisp white blossoms are like a long alabaster gown: They feel inherently special. (They tend to smell divine, too, as white flowers can't attract bees with their color and must rely on their scent.) This nostalgic cascade of calla lilies, gladiolus, sweet peas, and stephanotis vine hearkens back to the 1950s when creamy-and-green bouquets were de rigueur. 3. Light blue and green hydrangeas, tweedia, nigella, chinaberry, and maidenhair fern add color to a traditional low, round centerpiece spilling out from a compote. 4. White peonies and lilac make a beautiful, sweet-smelling sheath bouquet for the bride. 5. The quintessential wedding flower, lily of the valley goes contemporary when placed in clear glass bud vases lining a table. 6. This update on a round bouquet gets its organic shape from passion vine, carnations, anemones, and roses.

RUSTIC

Loosely tied stems in muted hues and free-form shapes lend a wildflower feel to any arrangement.
Clockwise from top left: A lightweight shell of birch bark filled with moss, silver lace fern, white hellebores, and African violets brings the outside in. Ranunculus, hellebores, and dogwood combine in this sweet clutch. A large sheath bouquet of chamomile, heather, white daisies, lysimachia, scabiosa, raspberries, and wild sweet peas has a fresh-picked feel. Don't overlook vines or fruit—Champagne grapes and porcelain vine fit right in at a vineyard wedding. In this organic bouquet, hellebores, green Japanese spray roses, apple blossoms, snowdrops, and double narcissus are tied together and allowed to fall every which way.

MODERN

To get a streamlined look, stick to a two-tone or monochromatic palette showcasing a range of shades in the same color. **Clockwise from left:** Less is more in a centerpiece displaying a single flower—"Showmaster" amaryllis. Fritallaria, hellebores, clematis, and "Green Goddess" calla lilies mixed in with large crocodile leaves form this sheath bouquet. A series of vases hold blooms both small (ranunculus and snowdrops) and spreading (Solomon's seal, spiraea branches, ferns, Japanese spray roses, and apple blossoms). This aisle is covered in ombré rose petals in four or five shades (guests are seated from the sides of the pews). Panicum flowers and white nerines join cymbidium and lady's slipper orchids in this bouquet.

TROPICAL

In heat and humidity, you need hardy flowers that will stand up to the elements (and stand out against cobalt seas and vibrant green trees). **Clockwise from top left:** A compote overflows with phalaenopsis orchids and stephanotis vine. Each of these silver vessels is filled with just one or two varietals, including, from front, yellow cattelya orchids, lemon phalaenopsis, calla lilies with apricot-tinged parrot tulips, lady's slipper orchids, and butterscotch ranunculus. A lush bouquet pairs fuchsia spotted orchids, magenta-veined mini phalaenopsis, violet clematis, and lilac double tulips with their opposites on the color wheel: orange ranunculus and peachy garden roses. Hot-pink and yellow sweet peas, tulips, and orchids, tied with a raspberry sash, make this eye-popping bouquet anything but traditional. Phalaenopsis, cattleya, and japhette orchids are set against begonia leaves and umbrella ferns in a cheery cascade.

GRAPHIC

Neutrals and brights work well for a look that's as fresh and fun as a game of croquet. **Clockwise from left:** Ruffly hydrangeas and viburnums resemble a Nantucket hedgerow on this green-and-white table; the weave of grosgrain ribbon echoes the colors in the centerpiece. Your bouquet can go black-tie, combining black privet berries with white peonies, tied with a striped ribbon. Chrysanthemums and anemones stand out when paired with silvery dusty miller in this bridal clutch. A mossy "ring pillow" is just the right touch for an outdoor affair.

ROMANTIC

Opt for lush varietals in colors both soft and strong, and tie clutches with rich satin ribbon. **Clockwise from top left:** A fragrant bouquet is composed of pastel blooms including bleeding hearts, lilies of the valley, grape hyacinths, forget-me-nots, and "Cécile Brünner" roses. Small vases overflowing with daisies, ranunculus, pink nerines, purple clematis, clover foliage, and muscari act as a table runner. A posy made of tiny flowers, including yellow pansies and purple columbine, makes a big impact. This bouquet, brimming with wildflowers, fritallaria, tweedia, sweet peas, chamomile, and maidenhair ferns was inspired by the fabric wrapped around the stems. These groups of pansies, ranunculus, and orchids in vases resemble a kaleidescope gone 3-D.

Deep hues in any number of shades bring drama to floral details. **Clockwise from top left:** Jewel-toned parrot tulips, hydrangeas, dahlias, and clematis complement the floral china on this elegant table. A bouquet that combines roses with seasonal blooms like clematis, hibiscus, and caladium leaves has a plucked-from-the-garden look. What's lush and lovely and red all over? A bouquet that pairs crimson garden roses, ranunculus, clematis, viburnum berries, and scabiosa with grayish-brown hellebores and a taupe silk bow. An abundant arrangement overflows with colorful flowers worthy of a Dutch masters painting, including lilacs, parrot tulips, tree peonies, ranunculus, bleeding hearts, coral bells, lilies, bearded irises, spirea, and mock orange.

139

FIND YOUR
FLOWERS

Adding Unexpected Elements

It seems counterintuitive, but the best floral designers know how to work nonfloral details into arrangements and tablescapes to boost visual interest and texture.

They're lovely to look at, but plants, beautiful objects, and ephemera aren't just a nice surprise when it comes to complementing your flowers. In many cases, they're more affordable and longer-lasting than fresh blooms, which means they can help you stretch your budget. Here, a few things to consider as welcome additions.

POTTED TOPIARIES AND TREES

Simple and elegant, these make great ceremony markers (and can be taken home at the end of the night or even planted outside your newlywed home). They're stunning even when they're small; use mini topiaries, for example, as escort-card holders or favors.

HERBS

A sprig of rosemary is fragrant and handsome enough to be a boutonniere; plus, it symbolizes remembrance, which is fitting for such a memorable day. If you're having a food-focused wedding, give potted herbs as parting gifts.

BERRIES

Hypericum berries, porcelain berries, snowberries, holly berries, and unripened blackberries or blueberries are just a few examples of varieties you could add to arrangements for a sweet, seasonal look.

PRODUCE

A bowl of, say, peaches at the center of each table is brilliantly easy and so charming for a summer wedding, while pomegranates would work their magic in winter. Whatever fruit (or produce!) you choose, just make sure there's a whole lot of it. You want the centerpiece to look abundant, not as if you grabbed it off your kitchen counter.

Special Guest Stars Flowers aren't the only way to make an arrangement impactful. **Clockwise from top left:** Hardy succulents, lotus pods, air plants, and moss are punctuated by hellebores, fritallaria, and lady slipper orchids (and the succulents can be potted later to be used in your home). A table evokes the feel of the sea with coral and shells. Vintage millinery trim swirls around lilies of the valley and hydrangea florets. Rich Japanese maple branches burst from a tall vase—and are echoed by a a single leaf next to each place card.

FERNS AND FOLIAGE

Supplement bouquets and centerpieces with greenery like ivy, boxwood, and dusty miller, all of which are generally less costly than flowers. Decorating with potted ferns is a smart way to create a lush garden look.

BRANCHES

Year-round, branches can enhance your décor with their graceful lines and architectural interest. Fruit branches like cherry blossoms flower in spring, evergreens are beautiful in winter, and branches with fruits or colored leaves are lovely come fall. Summer isn't prime time for branches (aside from mountain laurel or leaf-bearing types), but there's a wide range of flowers available.

GRASSES

Decorative varieties like foxtail, sorghum, and spray millet can add another layer of interest to floral arrangements.

SUCCULENTS

Cactuses and air plants lend a modern, unexpected feel to any celebration. Because they don't need much water, they'll look just as good at the end of a five-hour reception as at the beginning. And if you give them to guests to take away, they won't slosh around on the ride home.

MILLINERY DETAILS

Feathers, silk flowers, lace trimmings, pearl stamens, and other decorative elements look beautiful when woven into floral compositions. Added bonus: They never wilt.

COLLECTIONS OF OBJECTS

Augment (or even replace!) floral centerpieces with items like framed photos; groupings of shells, coral, or pinecones; your collection of vintage glass bottles; his hoard of vintage postcards—really, anything, as long as it's personal, pretty, or, ideally, both!

WEDDING WISDOM

When deciding on vessels for your flowers, look everywhere for inspiration. In the attic might be your grandmother's collection of teacups, perfect for floating buds. At the mall, you may find bamboo drawer organizers that could double as troughs for greenery and flowers. You can even get ideas at the hardware store: Brass mesh netting can embellish basic glass vases, and copper piping can be turned into gorgeous holders for your stems.

Speaking the Language of Flowers

Do as the Victorians did and say "I love you" without uttering a single word:
Let your flowers do the talking. Back then, a gentleman sending
red tulips to show he's smitten might get a bouquet of lilacs in return if his ardor was
reciprocated. While we no longer use blooms to converse, there's something
undeniably romantic about love that goes unspoken.

WEDDING
WISDOM

There are some
flowers we love—
lilacs and lily
of the valley, to
name a few—that
aren't the
longest-lasting
buds. If you are
set on a certain
variety that
may wilt before
the cake is cut
(because lilies of
the valley were
your grand-
mother's favorite,
for example),
use them in
bouquets, which
only need to look
good through
the vows. If
they're a little
wilted by the
time the
bouquet is
tossed, the
lucky recipient
won't care.

Add meaning to your bouquet with the following blooms, each of which carries a specific sentiment.

Baby's breath	Everlasting love		**Pink carnation**	Woman's love
Carnation	Pure love		**Pink jasmine**	Attachment
Crocus	Cheerfulness		**Ranunculus**	Radiant with charms
Daisy	Innocence		**Rosemary**	Remembrance
Dogwood	Duration		**Snowdrop**	Hope
Fern	Magic		**Stephanotis**	Happiness in marriage
Forget-me-not	Remembrance		**Sweet pea**	Delicate pleasures
Freesia	Innocence		**Tulip**	Declaration of love
Fuchsia	Confiding love		**White jasmine**	Amiability
Garden rose	Love		**White lilies**	Purity
Geranium	True friendship		**White rose**	Worth
Hellebore	Calming			
Hyacinth	Sport and play			
Ivy	Friendship			
Lady's mantle	Comfort			
Lilac	First emotions of love			
Lily of the valley	Return of happiness			
Mint	Virtue			
Orchid	Beauty			
Pansy	Thoughtfulness			
Peony	Bashful			

Say It With Flowers Corsages and boutonnieres can
be packed with meaning. If you plan on incorporating
symbolic blooms into your day, add a cheat sheet
in your program, on the backs of the menus, or as an
attractive display on a guest book table, so that guests
can understand the significance of your flowers.

everlasting
love

woman's love

confiding
love

THE LANGUAGE
AND SENTIMENT
OF FLOWERS

WARNE'S
BOUQUET
SERIES

LANGUAGE
OF
FLOWERS

Sport
and
play

FLORA'S
POCKET
DICTIONARY

THE
LANGUAGE OF F

FLORA'S

return of happiness
magic

friendship

Spending Savvy: Flowers

The average bride allocates anywhere from 5 to 15 percent of her wedding budget for the flowers. Consider these ways to save on blooms without sacrificing on style.

Ultimately, the amount you spend on flowers depends on you—specifically, the varieties you choose and how many you use. The good news: There are easy ways to prune your costs. The better news: Your guests won't even notice the difference, especially if you heed these tips.

STAY IN SEASON

The most cost-effective flowers are those that are naturally available locally during the time you wed. While somewhere in the world your favorite blooms are growing, you'll shell out a pretty penny (not to mention the carbon footprint) to have them flown to your locale.

SPLURGE IN MODERATION

If you're keen on incorporating a pricey variety (like peonies) at your wedding, go for it—but save money by using it only in the bridal bouquet, which everyone expects to be the loveliest (and the largest) in the wedding party.

THINK BIG

When comparing costs, keep in mind that you'll need fewer flowers if you stick to larger blooms like the anemones and chrysanthemums at left, even though some lush flowers (such as peonies and amaryllises) are among the more expensive varieties. Factor in the number of stems you'll need as well as the cost per stem.

BE OPEN-MINDED

Don't be a snob when it comes to varieties; carnations, mums, and baby's breath may seem pedestrian as single blooms, but gather a huge bunch of them en masse and you have an arresting display.

FILL THEM OUT

Use flowers sparingly and supplement with foliage, branches, and berries. The look is high-end, the cost is not.

CREATE A FEW FOCAL POINTS

Strategically place a couple of large, elaborate arrangements at the reception site—perhaps one at the bar and another at a centrally located table. Then you can get away with simpler centerpieces everywhere else.

REPURPOSE CEREMONY FLOWERS

Ask your florist to up-cycle the bouquets by placing them in vases after the ceremony. They can be used to decorate a cake table, the escort-card area, even the bridesmaid's table. Also, reuse the altar decorations for the escort-card table or reception entrance.

MAKE THEM MOONLIGHT

Enlist charming potted flowers, which are cheaper than floral arrangements, as centerpieces, then give them away as favors at the end of the night. Or, rather than having a huge centerpiece at each table, decorate with a grouping of bud vases, each filled with just one or two stems. Then, invite guests to take a bud vase home with them as a souvenir.

LET THERE BE LIGHT

Not all venues allow candles, but if yours does, take advantage of them. Nothing creates a romantic ambience like candlelight. And with a table already aglow and twinkling, you won't have to rely on superfancy floral centerpieces to do the mood-setting work. A few pretty blooms, or even none at all, will work.

Big Love Echoing the oversize Marimekko print on the table runner, the centerpieces at this mod affair were a few full blooms—chrysanthemums and anemones—floating in bowls. Large faux blooms on each plate doubled as place cards and favors.

GOOD TO KNOW

Farmer's markets aren't just good for locally grown food; they're great for fresh, affordable flowers. If you like surprises and have a game florist, ask her to create your wedding arrangements from whatever's available (and on-palette) at the market. Your florist may also have an in at local flower farms (or an abundant garden of her own). If she does, ask what they grow, and remember, a farm may be open to cultivating varieties just for you if you give them enough time (a year's notice).

CHAPTER
SEVEN

START TO
CELEBRATE

ENGAGEMENT PARTIES, SHOWERS, BACHELORETTE PARTIES, AND EVEN REHEARSAL DINNERS ARE INCREDIBLY FUN LEAD-UPS TO THE MAIN EVENT—AND EACH CAN BE PERSONALIZED.

— Darcy Miller, *Editorial Director, Martha Stewart Weddings*

WITH YOUR ENGAGEMENT ANNOUNCED, the celebrating can begin! Your wedding is unquestionably the most emotional and exciting event on your horizon, but those nearest and dearest to you will probably want to fête you well before the big day—and possibly more than once. Many couples start with an engagement party, and then, for brides, two of the most beloved events usually follow: the bridal shower and the bachelorette party. The first showers were held only for brides-to-be whose families couldn't afford to provide a dowry. To help the couple set up house, friends and family of the bride and groom would "shower" the newlyweds with household gifts to compensate. Nowadays showers are meant for all brides (and sometimes even grooms, if they're coed events), yet the purpose remains the same. Typically, the women closest to the bride throw a party in her honor and give gifts that she'll enjoy for years to come. The bachelorette party, on the other hand, is the less formal get-together of the two celebrations. Way back when, males-only bachelor parties came about as a way to celebrate a groom-to-be's last nights (or days) as a single man; now women get equal opportunity. However, a few tequila shots and a party-store veil aren't the only ways to make a bachelorette party memorable, nor does a raucous night in Vegas have to serve as a man's rite of passage. A singleton send-off can mean a weekend at a spa, a day of surfing, a night of barhopping, or all of the above. And the last party before the wedding is the rehearsal or welcome dinner the night before your nuptials. Read on for special ways to get the good times rolling.

PLEASE JOIN US

AT A BRIDAL SHOWER IN HONOR OF

SUMMER WATKINS

AS SHE KISSES HER SINGLE LIFE GOODBYE!

SATURDAY, JUNE 1 FROM 2-6 PM AT LAKE PARK CLUBHOUSE

1035 11TH STREET, HUNTINGTON BEACH, CA 92648

KINDLY RSVP TO MEGAN GONZALEZ BY MAY 25

XO

XO

PANTONE®
Warm Red C

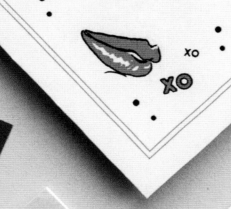

PUCKER UP,
buttercup

XO

OUR LOVELY BRIDE

IS WORKING ON COMPLETING

A HOME FIT FOR A MRS. AND HAS CAREFUL

CURATED A REGISTRY AT THESE FINE SHOPS:

BLOOMINGDALE'S, CRATE & BARREL,

BED BATH & BEYOND, AND

POTTERY BARN.

OX

KINDLY
DELVER

JOCELYN GIROUA

50 LINCOLN BLVD A

MARINA DL REY,

90299

The Engagement Party

It's certainly not a must, but being celebrated as a soon-to-be-wed couple is an undeniably wonderful way to observe your recent engagement. These events come in all sizes and styles—from the simple to the exquisite.

THE TIMELINE
PREWEDDING PARTIES

**1 WEEK–
3 MONTHS POST
PROPOSAL**
Engagement
parties

**4–6 MONTHS
AHEAD**
Complete registry
(unless an en-
gagement party or
bridal shower is being
thrown in your honor,
in which case the
bride should register
at least one month
before that event and
include gifts priced
appropriately)

**1–3 MONTHS
AHEAD**
Bridal showers

**2 MONTHS–
2 WEEKS AHEAD**
Bachelor and
bachelorette parties

WHO THROWS IT

Traditionally this celebration, which happens shortly after the question is popped, was thrown by the bride's parents and served to simultaneously announce the happy news and introduce the groom to the entire family. Today, anyone can host a cocktail party for a newly engaged couple, and it fulfills the same functions, acting as a nice prewedding icebreaker that lets both the bride's and groom's families and their guests get to know one another a bit before the big day.

If the bride's parents would like to throw an engagement party, it is still customary for them to hold the first one. Then, if the groom's parents would like to have another one, they may do so, followed by friends of the couple, if they so choose. Keep in mind it's also completely fine to host your own engagement party. You can have as many as you like—or forgo the tradition altogether.

WHO PAYS FOR IT

The host or hosts cover the cost of this event, and they can make it as casual or lavish as they like. Usually they will have you weigh in on what you would like. But before you ask for the moon, remember the time, energy, and money that is already being spent in your honor.

WHOM TO INVITE

To any engagement party, invite only people who will be included in the main event. Another tip: Gifts are not expected, but guests often want to give them, so it's not a bad idea to register for some things (more about that in a moment) in the weeks before this party. Your mothers or friends can let those details spread through word-of-mouth should people inquire (never put registry details on this or the wedding invitation, as it feels, well, tacky; the info is best relayed through friends and family or on your wedding website).

HOW TO CELEBRATE

There are no hard and fast rules as to what an engagement party should or shouldn't be. It's common for the host to have a cocktail party; however, an intimate dinner at a restaurant (or a home), a fun brunch, or even an afternoon open house or picnic could be festive, too. The bottom line is that it should feel comfortable for you as a couple. Whatever the hosts decide, be prepared to be the gracious couple. Your hosts will likely toast you both and your engagement, and it's fitting to say a few nice words back.

The Soon-to-Be-Weds Post-engagement party, send your host a thank-you note or small gift.

WEDDIQUETTE
RECEIVING GIFTS

Some guests will come to your engagement party bearing gifts, while others will not. To avoid the discomfort of those who don't (presents aren't required, after all), open gifts once you get home, and be sure to promptly write thank-you notes.

The Shower

Bridal showers are best thrown well in advance of the wedding, when the same attendees will likely be buying another present. Day or night, the shindigs usually last three to four hours and allow enough time for an activity, opening gifts, and a chance to eat something delicious.

GOOD TO KNOW

It's traditional to send shower invitations by mail—and it's fun; who doesn't love getting personal mail? The hostess should send them no later than one month before the celebration. But an emailed save-the-date is completely appropriate. Although your relatives and hostess can pass your registry information by word of mouth, mailed invitations may include it, too. Your mom may not agree with this, because it used to be considered bad form to do so, but that thinking has changed, since the point of a shower is to give presents.

WHO THROWS IT

In the days of yore, family members didn't host showers for fear of looking like gift-grubbers, but today anyone can take the lead. (Throwing your own shower is still a definite no-no, however.) These affairs are often hosted in groups, so bridesmaids may have one in the city where you live now, and relatives may have another in your hometown. If there is one event that most of your attendants will be able to make, use that weekend to accomplish other tasks, too, like trying on bridesmaid dresses.

WHO PAYS FOR IT

Anyone listed as a cohost on the invite, whether she's an attendant, a sister, a friend, or a relative, is expected to pitch in, cost-wise.

WHOM TO INVITE

While there is no limit on the number of showers thrown in a bride's honor, the guest lists must be different for each celebration so that people don't get partied out (or go broke buying presents). The exceptions to that rule: Your mom, future mother-in-law, sisters, sisters-in-law, and sometimes attendants are usually invited to every bridal shower. Just remind them that they needn't attend all of them, and that if they accept more than one invitation, they aren't expected to give more than one present. Also keep in mind that whether you're marrying for the first, second, or thirteenth time, your closest friends will still want to celebrate you, but etiquette calls for a smaller guest list if this isn't your first wedding. Above all, remember that invitees for all showers must be drawn only from the master wedding guest list.

HOW TO CELEBRATE

A shower is being thrown for you, not by you, so let the hostesses decide whether they want to give a brunch, a tea, cocktails, a sit-down-dinner, or, as is becoming more and more popular, a group activity, like a wine tasting. The party-givers may also pick a theme for the event or the presents—one popular option is the "Round-the-clock" shower, where everyone is assigned a time of day and gifts accordingly, choosing a coffeepot for 7 a.m. or a duvet for midnight, for example. Give input when it's asked for (and you should be consulted on the date that is convenient for you), but leave it at that. If your pals need ideas, refer them to this list of favorites:

For gourmets: Request gifts of cookbooks, family recipes, or kitchen equipment, and take a cooking or baking class.

For crafters: Go to a flower-arranging workshop, or make soap, ceramics, and more at a craft store.

For jet-setters: Have a travel-based shower inspired by your honeymoon location, serving champagne and cheeses for a trip to France, for example.

For fashionistas: Host a lingerie shower or plan a day of beauty at a spa or nail salon.

For game-night enthusiasts: Ask for board games as gifts, and engage in traditional shower activities, such as having guests compete in a multiple-choice quiz about the bride and groom with trivia sourced from friends and relatives.

Home-Baked Happiness A New York bride-to-be wanted to learn how to make the fixings for brunch; so she and her friends took a cooking class and then feasted together.

02|18
LAUREN'S
BRIDAL SHOWER

HAVEN'S KITCHEN · NEW YORK, NEW YORK 10011

THANKS!

THANKS!

LET'S *get* COOKING!

PLEASE JOIN US FOR A COOKING-CLASS & BRUNCH IN *honor*

of LAUREN RICH'S UPCOMING NUPTIALS

SATURDAY THE 18 OF *february*

AT 11:30 *in the* MORNING

AT *haven's* KITCHEN · 109 WEST 17TH STREET, NYC

R.S.V.P. AT 212-555-2012

GRANOLA · GRANOLA
HAVEN'S
H
KITCHEN
GRANOLA · GRANOLA

THANKS!

BE A GRACIOUS BRIDE-TO-BE

The one thing that's required of you is to show up, smile, and open presents. While the gift-opening aspect can make some brides uncomfortable, part of the fun for guests is watching you ooh and aah over the items they spent time picking out for you. (One exception: If you are painfully shy, you can pass up the custom.) As you open each gift, announce who it's from and, if the group doesn't all know one another, how you met the giver. "This blender is from Kathy, my college roommate and the ultimate fiesta-thrower. She taught me how to make margaritas. Thanks, Kathy!" It's a nice way to deflect the attention from yourself for a moment, and the recipient will appreciate the shout-out.

CONSIDER A FAVOR

While it's not required for the hostess to give small parting gifts to guests, it's becoming more and more common, especially when a shower has a theme or activity that the token can tie into. Invitees at a garden party brunch could receive a miniature potted herb, or those who attend a wine tasting can leave with a bottle of wine or a corkscrew.

INVITE THE GROOM

The traditional big finish of a shower is when the fiancé arrives (usually with flowers in tow), just after his bride opens gifts. This custom is the perfect opportunity for unacquainted guests to meet the lucky guy and makes a memorable photo op for the couple.

A Sweet Soiree When bride-to-be Dylan Lauren, the owner of Dylan's Candy Bar, was thrown a shower, the natural theme was to celebrate her favorite things: sweets! They appeared everywhere, from stunning candy rings on display to guests' well-wishing cards to drink stirrers with a confection motif.

GIVE THANKS

While it may seem obvious, pen-and-paper notes (not emails, texts, posts, or tweets!) are the only polite and socially acceptable way to communicate your appreciation. To ensure that no guest (or gift) is forgotten, ask the maid of honor or a family member to keep a thorough list of who gave what. Then, write and mail your notes as soon as possible. It's also customary to give a thank-you present to the hostess(es). If they've been consulting you about the theme, menu, and details of the shower, you can send a thank-you in advance that could be used on the day, like a flower arrangement that can serve as a centerpiece, or, if a friend is hosting in her home, a beautiful on-palette tablecloth, for example. It's also perfectly fine to send the thank-you gift after the fact, too!

THE COED SHOWER

If the groom would like to share in all the showering of love and attention headed your way, ask the party-givers if they'd be open to hosting a couples shower. These tend to be more of a cocktail party for the bride and groom's friends; presents may or may not be opened. Although a joint celebration is less traditional, it is no less special—just plan with coed alterations in mind (the lingerie theme can be rain-checked for your bachelorette party). Provide a multi-option bar, rather than one signature drink, and create an out-of-the-box game with a corresponding gift relevant to one of the couple's shared hobbies, such as a croquet match with each attendee giving a piece of a larger croquet set as a present. Remember: Because the guest list for a combined shower is bound to be large, it will require more coordination (and costs) for the hosts than a standard bridal shower.

Starting Your Registry

As you begin celebrating your upcoming nuptials, guests are going to be on the lookout for gift ideas. Make it easy on them by creating a thoughtful wish list. In turn, you'll receive things that you want and need.

THINK AHEAD

It can be difficult to imagine filling your newlywed nest with fine china in multiple settings (especially if your home is currently small), but it's important to look down the road for items you may require when it's your turn to host a holiday gathering, or if–rather, when–things break. This is the only time in your life when people will be lining up to give you these types of items.

GO HIGH-LOW

Before you get too trigger happy with that scanning gun, remember that some of your family members might want to shell out for an expensive gift, and younger friends (especially ones who will be coming in from out of town to your wedding) will want to spend less. Make sure you have options for both crowds, at two national department stores and some niche or local ones. Websites such as MyRegistry .com can aggregate items from any website in the world into one list for you and your groom.

DON'T ASK FOR CASH

Doing so is never appropriate. But, if you're comfortable with the idea, you can join an alternative registry site that allows you to attain the goals you'd put money toward. If you're saving for your honeymoon, for example, there are online sites that let guests allocate funds toward that trip. Or, if you're focused on helping others, register at sites that allow guests to give to a charity of your choosing. Keep in mind that many useful sites you already shop from have registry features; you can register on popular sites for everything from appliances to books, or if you're moving into a fixer-upper, sign up for paint, tools, and even lumber at a big-box home-improvement store.

SPREAD THE NEWS DISCREETLY

It's considered unseemly to send registry information with your wedding invites. Instead, post it on your wedding website, and let friends and family know where you're registered so they can pass on the info if asked. (If someone wants to know where you're registered, by all means, tell them!) Also share the info with the hosts of your showers; it is appropriate for them to include it on their shower invitations.

SAY THANKS

You don't need to wait for your marriage certificate to go into effect to write a note of gratitude for gifts. In fact, pick up pen and paper as soon as gifts start arriving. If you start the job then, the task will go quickly and enjoyably (and it won't be hanging over your head during your honeymoon). If possible, try to send notes within two weeks of arrival. One way to make it easier: Add two extra columns to the spreadsheet you'll create for addressing wedding invitations, and use the space to record the gifts guests give you and whether or not you've sent a note. And a writing tip: Keeping the sentiment meaningful from one note to the next is easier to do if you write three or four a day, rather than dozens.

START ENJOYING YOUR GIFTS

Break out your goods! Use the special stuff every day (rather than only at formal celebrations), whether it's decorating your vanity with trays and teacups to hold your jewelry, or placing a serving bowl on a living room table. Even takeout can feel elevated when you're using your favorite china and silverware.

The White Stuff Whatever your style, there's a china pattern (and silverware, and linens) to match. While registering is a venerable tradition, what you select can be anything but; look at the clean lines and contemporary shapes of this white everyday tableware.

THE TIMELINE REGISTRY

———

Register before your first celebration, whether it's a shower or engagement party, and at least three to four months before the wedding. It's fine (and smart!) to sign up for a few things you know you want early, then add to the registry gradually as you have time to browse and make selections, and as the items you chose earliest get snapped up.

The Bachelorette/Bachelor Party

The all-male festivity dates back to ancient Sparta, when on the night before a wedding, the groom and his comrades feasted while pledging their loyalty to one another. These days, women get in on the action, too. Hit the town for a night or let the celebration stretch out over several days.

WHO THROWS IT

Because these gatherings are more informal, they don't have the established rules of conduct that other wedding celebrations do. The maid of honor and best man often assume the job of planning the bachelorette and bachelor party, respectively, but anyone can pull it together. The group of attendees is usually small, including only guests the bride or groom is closest to: wedding party (but only those who are of-age; junior bridesmaids and groomsmen need not be included), intimate friends, and family members. The party-throwers should consult you before finalizing the list of invitees and then spread the word via email or phone, rather than by postage (formal invitations aren't necessary). And while surprises are fun, the hosts should keep the honoree's personality in mind. There's no need to plan a raucous escapade if the bride or groom would prefer a daytime activity or a quiet getaway.

WHO PAYS FOR IT

Attendees fund their own way, with whoever's in the driver's seat covering the bride's or groom's expenses (unless secondary hosts agree to split the VIP's tab). If the plan involves more than a simple party, the organizer should talk to the participants to get a sense of how much they are willing to spend. Because your friends will cover the costs, avoid sharing how you'd like to celebrate unless you're asked for input.

WHOM TO INVITE

Indulge whomever you want essentially, but this is a day or short trip with your closest girlfriends (or guy friends as the case may be). All of your of-age attendants should be invited, and it is wise to invite your future sister-in-law or brother-in-law if not including them would ultimately cast you in a poor light. It's best to start your marriage off on the right foot with his–or her–entire family.

HOW TO CELEBRATE

For a fresher way to approach these parties (that doesn't include a trip to Vegas), consider the following ideas:

Get pampered: Spend the afternoon at a nearby spa offering everything from full-body massages to pedicures and barber-style close shaves.

Get immersed: Head to the nearest waterfront for group surfing, snorkeling, or sailing lessons.

Get away: Book a weekend full of shopping sprees and movable feasts in the closest big city, like New York City, Chicago, or San Francisco. If you prefer rural charm to cosmopolitan chic, plan a mini road trip with breweries, distilleries, and wineries plotted along the journey, and brake at local haunts for regional bites and live music. Or, depending on what you love doing, go skiing, camping, or fishing. If you are a sun worshipper, pack up and hit Florida or the Caribbean for a few days in the sun.

All the Single Ladies No one knows you better than your close friends, so they're the perfect people to plan your last single celebration. The rules are, there are no rules. It can be low-key and sentimental, sharing memories and advice, or pure revelry, with drinks and dancing.

The Rehearsal Dinner

This party is far less traditional and etiquette-bound than the wedding itself. It has only one hard-and-fast rule: It shouldn't compete with the main event. Whether you choose a families-only evening or opt for a larger welcome gathering, here are the ins and outs.

WHO HOSTS IT

Traditionally, the groom's parents throw the rehearsal dinner on the eve of the wedding, because the bride's family customarily pays for the wedding. But given today's more relaxed standards, other relatives, close friends, or even the couple themselves can plan and foot the bill for the event. Whoever hosts should confer with the couple to avoid any conflict with the theme, menu, or décor of the wedding.

WHOM TO INVITE

The rehearsal dinner immediately follows the ceremony run-through, so the guest list should include everyone in your wedding party (even child attendants and readers could come for a bit), plus spouses or dates, and your immediate families. It's also customary to invite the officiant of the ceremony and his or her spouse, if he is close to the family. After that, the guest list is open, and extended family members and close friends may be added. Out-of-towners are often invited as a courtesy for traveling and to welcome them to the celebration. In most cases, the budget will determine how many places to set around the table, and no one will give it a second thought if that means only immediate family and the wedding party. Although it is not required to send invitations for the rehearsal dinner, it's best to do so if more than just family will attend. The invitations needn't be elaborate and should go out with your wedding ones or shortly after, so that travel arrangements coincide.

The Bright Stuff For their Fourth of July rehearsal dinner in Seattle, this couple invited all out-of-towners to a seated dinner in a museum, then to a nearby observation deck to watch the fireworks. The invitation let guests RSVP for any or all of the festivities, and the vibrant palette they chose tied all the elements together.

HOW TO CELEBRATE

Since this is a night when families and friends meet and socialize, sometimes for the first time, create a convivial atmosphere and help facilitate introductions. Rehearsal dinners are often held at restaurants or favorite spots that hold special meaning to the bride and groom. If Italy is the honeymoon destination, for example, an Italian restaurant would be fitting. Or, think locally and choose a venue that introduces invitees to the area and showcases it, like throwing a Kansas City barbecue or dishing up tamales and margaritas in San Antonio.

BE A GRACIOUS COUPLE

Your aim in seating guests should be the same as for any successful dinner party: to design tables with a nice mix of people. Seat guests according to convention: The bride and groom share a table with their bridesmaids and groomsmen at the rehearsal dinner (and find a moment to gift their attendants). The groom's father and the bride's mother head a second table, while the groom's mother and the bride's father head a third. If there are more tables, have at least one member of the groom's family, as representative of the hosts, seated at each.

PLAN FOR TOASTING

Unlike the wedding reception, where toasts are far more choreographed, anyone who's moved to can stand up and offer one. But to keep some semblance of order, there are a few guidelines: The first toast is made by the groom's father, to welcome the guests. After that, the best man can take over as emcee, ushering other well-wishers to share thoughts. Before the evening ends (which shouldn't be too late, or guests will be bleary-eyed at the wedding), the groom often toasts the bride, both sets of in-laws toast and thank each other, and the bride offers her own cheer to the groom.

Although it feels as traditional as any other part of the wedding, the rehearsal dinner is actually quite modern. It sprang from a very practical twentieth-century need to introduce families from all over the country, even the world, who would soon become in-laws but who might never have met the bride or groom.

CHAPTER
EIGHT

WELCOME YOUR
GUESTS

> "
> YOUR GUESTS ARE COMING TO SUPPORT
> YOU. FIND WAYS TO BOTH HELP AND DELIGHT
> THEM, SO THAT IT'S EASY AND
> FUN TO SHARE IN YOUR HAPPINESS.
> "

— Martha Stewart

EVERYONE ALWAYS INSISTS that this is "your day"—and rightfully so! But without guests, it wouldn't be a wedding celebration. It would be an elopement. And the people who attend are your nearest and dearest; their presence means so much to you that you've invited them to be a part of one of the biggest moments in your life. They will come from nearby and far away to support you and your spouse-to-be, and they're eager to shower the two of you with love and gifts. In return, you, as the gracious host, want to make coming to your event as enjoyable as possible. That means giving them all the information they need to plan for it well in advance, welcoming them warmly, and keeping them comfortable throughout the ceremony and reception (or weekend, as the case may be). To do so, it helps to change perspectives and look at your wedding through the eyes of your guests, minding their personal time, their own planning hurdles (will they need babysitters?), and even their budgets (not everyone can spring for a four-star hotel room). You'll also want to troubleshoot any problems that could arise at your locale to avoid them altogether. If you know, for example, your venue is very sunny and warm, or there is *any* chance of rain, you'll need to provide shade and shelter (cue the tent rental). You might also distribute shawls if you know it will be a brisk evening or fans if it will be a sweltering one. Getting hitched at the shore? Set out baskets of flip-flops and sunscreen. At a campsite? Organic bug spray. The bottom line: No matter how big or small the gesture, it will go a long way toward showing your guests that their happiness is a top priority. After all, it wouldn't be your day without them.

1

2

4

6

9

Managing the Logistics

You may be the ones walking down the aisle, but essentially you're bringing a lot of loved ones along with you. Here's how to keep them informed and in on the fun.

BE CORDIAL AND CLEAR

Without a doubt your guests are happy for you, and they're also ready to devote their time and, in many cases, a fair amount of money to attend your nuptials. The key to keeping them brimming with excitement is to equip them–from the very beginning–with all the pertinent details of your day, so that they can plan for it and make travel arrangements with ease. Plus, aside from not wanting to create unnecessary confusion, it pays to inform them fully the first time around so you and your family are not fielding countless queries during the busy weeks and days leading up to your celebration.

GIVE THE WHO, WHEN, WHERE

It may seem obvious to use your full name when inviting guests to your wedding, but we've seen people utterly stumped after receiving a "Bill & Jenny Are Getting Married!" save-the-date card. Lesson learned? There are other Bills and Jennys in the world! Likewise, state when and where you are marrying clearly (using the outline of New York state as a motif is nice, but there's a big difference between traveling to New York City and to Buffalo). If there are other events surrounding the day, a welcome party the night before, or brunch the day after, tell invitees as soon as possible (with the invite or soon after), so that they can also plan accordingly.

CREATE A WEDDING WEBSITE

This is not a must, but it is a valuable tool for both you and your guests–and it is the only place, with the exception of bridal shower invitations, where it is okay etiquette-wise to let people know where you are registered. If you'd like to skip the cost of sending additional cards with your invitations, a website is also the perfect place to share travel, lodging, and logistical information about your event, too. Make a site before you send out your invites so you can include its URL on your invitations.

PASS ON SAVINGS WHEN POSSIBLE

Given that weddings can be costly endeavors–for you and your loved ones–keep everyone's budget in mind. At least six months before your celebration, research and visit local hotels to find accommodations near your venue that aren't too expensive. Then inquire about group discounts. Depending on the size of your guest list, block out rooms at a few hotels with a range of rates. (You can also ask about complimentary services properties offer, like breakfast or guided tours.) Look into ways to save on air travel as well. If at least 10 people are flying to your wedding, some airlines will create a code (often for about 5 percent off) for your guests, even if they're not flying from the same airport.

WELCOME OUT-OF-TOWNERS WARMLY

Once guests who have traveled the farthest (and may be the most road-weary or jet lagged) arrive, greet them and show your gratitude. Not able to station yourself at their lodgings? Don't worry, no one expects you to. Instead, think about assembling them a small welcome bag of thoughtful items to help folks feel right at home and asking the hotels to distribute (keep in mind that many hotels charge a per-bag fee for this service). The best ones blend fun items (souvenirs) with practical ones (snacks or sunscreen), and encourage people to explore their surroundings (maps and recommendations). This hospitable gesture isn't required, but certainly is something that guests enjoy. If your budget doesn't allow it, simply providing helpful information, such as where to be and when, and giving it to guests when they check in (as well as having it on your website and/or in your invitation suite), is appreciated. Another idea: Write short heartfelt notes to traveling guests and leave them in their hotel rooms. It's a warm welcome in its own right, and it requires only ink and paper.

A Happy Hello Welcome bags keep your guests fed, happy, and informed. 1. Personalized provisions for a Big Sur wedding. 2. At a racetrack-themed party in Saratoga, New York, this satchel gets guests ready and set to go. 3. From citrus to shades, all you need for fun in the California sun. 4. Elegantly packaged essentials prep partiers for Costa Rica. 5. Irish brown bread and butter and other local fare greeted travelers at this destination event in Ireland. 6. Must-haves for a Montana ranch revel. 7. Nautical provisions welcome invitees aboard. 8. This sack stacks the deck in favor of attendees at a weekend in Vegas. 9. Bountiful bags warm up winter in Colorado.

THE TIMELINE GUESTS

12+ MONTHS AHEAD

Right after setting the budget, but before booking the venue, draw up the guest list (see page 18 in "You're Engaged").

Make a wedding website.

6+ MONTHS AHEAD

Send out save-the-date cards (optional, but a good idea for destination weddings).

Book room blocks at nearby hotels.

2 MONTHS AHEAD

Mail invitations.

Check if hotel delivers welcome bags and if there's a fee for it.

Buy packaging and bag contents.

1 MONTH– 2 WEEKS AHEAD

Assemble bags (omitting anything perishable).

1 WEEK– 3 DAYS AHEAD

Put together a distribution list for hotel, and put perishables in bags and drop off with hotel concierge.

1 DAY AHEAD

Double-check that hotel has delivered the bags or notes.

Getting Them Around

*Unless your ceremony and reception are at the same site
(and within walking distance of where guests are staying),
it's important to help get attendees from point A to point B without a hitch.*

THE TIMELINE
TRANSPORT-ATION

7–12 MONTHS AHEAD

Rough out a schedule of your wedding day's events, including how long it will take to get to the ceremony and from the ceremony to the reception.

6 MONTHS AHEAD

Book transportation for guests (if using), the wedding party, and yourselves.

1 WEEK AHEAD

Email the day's itinerary to the transport company, along with directions and any alternative routes in case there's a traffic jam.

DAY OF

Assign your maid of honor or a family member to confirm the exact pickup location and time, confirm driving directions, and provide emergency contact numbers to the drivers.

It may not be the most romantic element of organizing your day, but transportation is an essential, and its importance becomes very obvious if something goes wrong. If you want your wedding party and guests in the right place at the right time, it pays to plan for it.

ASSESS YOUR NEEDS

Are you expecting a large number of out-of-towners? How far apart are the venue and the hotel where guests are staying? Is walking difficult for some of them? These questions will help you decide if you need to book transportation. Also, check with your venue to see if they require that you provide shuttle services if they don't have ample room for parking. If you decide you need to arrange for vehicles, secure your ride at least six months before your wedding, but if your date is set for a peak time, like June, or is in a popular location, do it as soon as you're able–the earlier you book, the better the selection of vehicles, too. Note: If you choose not to book transportation, have the numbers of taxi companies on hand for guests should they want or need one at any point.

DO THE RESEARCH

Along with searching online for local companies, ask for referrals from your venue and hotel concierges, who have experience working with transportation companies.

GET IT IN WRITING

A contract–both for large vehicles such as buses or vans meant for guests and a limo or getaway car for you two–should include an itinerary, the number of vehicles needed, the make and color of any cars, the drivers' attire, the deposits required, overtime rates, and the arrival and departure locations and times. When agreeing on cost, don't forget to ask about tolls and parking fees. If you're hiring a shuttle bus for guests, clarify whether the fee is per drop-off (the number of times the bus goes back and forth) or per hour. Read the fine print: Some companies charge a base rate, to which administrative fees, a fuel surcharge, and a gratuity will be tacked on.

WORK OUT A DEAL

Don't be shy about asking for a discount. Small price cuts are often applied to large-scale services, and some companies offer complimentary honeymoon airport transfer the next day. Other ways to save: Booking one big vehicle, like a bus or van, usually costs less than getting multiple cars, as does designating one central pickup and drop-off location rather than having multiple stops at every hotel or inn.

SPREAD THE WORD

By the time invitations are sent, you should have worked out the day's transport details. If you're providing a shuttle or bus, add that info (along with other specifics, like hotel and travel info) to an enclosure card included in your suite. It's also a good idea to put any need-to-know news (include the addresses of the ceremony and reception sites) on your wedding website, and slip a separate card with the same info into welcome bags, if you're distributing them.

CONSIDER HIRING VALETS

If there is plenty of parking (say, in a church lot), you're having about 50 guests or fewer, or you're shuttling most guests in one vehicle, you probably will not need an attendant. But you will likely have to go to your town or city hall to find out whether you will need parking permits. (When using a valet service, many of them will do this for you.)

If guests are coming in individual cars, street parking is tricky, and the walk to the site may be long, you may want to hire valets. Beware of any company that simply asks how many guests there will be and does not care to see the site. Typically, every 25 cars require one valet, but if your venue has a long driveway or complex parking restrictions, you might need one for every seven cars. When you choose a company, request a certificate of insurance that includes contractor and garage liability, and workers' compensation. The host or hostess should be named as an insured party.

All Together Now An iconic British double-decker bus brought guests from the ceremony to the reception at a destination affair in Somerset, England.

WEDDING WISDOM

—

If you've got a several-hour gap between your ceremony and reception for logistical reasons (the church won't perform weddings after a certain time, say), turn transportation into entertainment. A sightseeing trolley or double-decker bus will keep guests amused and ensure they get to the cocktail hour on time. It will also make the day infinitely more fun.

Planning a Wedding Weekend

Whether you're getting married at home or far away, chances are some guests will be traveling to attend. Many couples opt to plan a weekend-long schedule of activities, allowing everyone to spend time together beyond the ceremony and reception.

SET A SCHEDULE

You want to have some structure to your weekend, but guests should be having fun, not following orders; so take care not to plan every second of their time (or feel offended if someone wants to take a nap rather than attend a picnic).

A typical wedding weekend might go something like this: guests arrive Friday afternoon or evening and are welcomed at a cocktail reception or rehearsal dinner (often paid for by the groom's family); the ceremony and reception take place on Saturday; then everyone departs on Sunday following a farewell brunch (which is often hosted by the bride's parents, but can be sponsored by anyone who has the inclination to do so). In addition to the larger events, there may be a mix of casual and scheduled activities, such as a group hike or an art gallery open house, inspired by the location. Those can be organized events arranged by the couple and their families or just listed as suggestions of things to do in a welcome packet.

Welcome drinks or opening dinner: Traditionally the rehearsal dinner was just for the wedding party and couple's family, but these days many couples invite all out-of-towners to the post-rehearsal meal, or to meet for drinks after a more intimate dinner. Whatever you choose, the first night should have open seating, so guests can meet new friends and visit with old ones. The goal is to leave everyone wanting more when it's over. If you're having a full dinner, begin on the early side and keep it casual. Ask your host (usually the groom's parents) to give a toast before opening up the floor to anyone else who wants to say a few words. And at the end of the night, it's your turn to thank everyone for coming.

Daily activities: Your friends and family are there to see you off into married bliss but also to vacation. Don't start

Great Getaway This California couple invited loved ones to three days of fun in the sun at a Carmel Valley campground. Activities included a pool party, crafts, Ping-Pong tournaments, and archery; bows and arrows and targets appeared throughout the paper goods.

activities before 9:30 a.m. and avoid scheduling anything too long or far away. Ideal activities are easy and don't leave anybody behind (say, a trolley tour of the city or a picnic at a scenic site). Also, let guests staying in or near the central hotel know where to find one another in your welcome packet, so they can make their own plans to hang by the pool.

Day-after brunch: Often held at the home of a relative or friend, a local restaurant, or the hotel where out-of-town guests are staying, this informal send-off allows guests to chat for an hour or two and exchange tales from the night's festivities before hitting the road. An open-house approach is ideal, letting people drop in anytime between 10 and noon, say, so they can sleep in and pack. Don't fuss over decorations; consider saving flowers from the wedding reception to kick up the décor. To smooth guests' departure, organize shuttle buses to the airport and offer on-the-go food options for invitees with early departures.

SPREAD THE WORD

Your entire guest list should feel welcome –but not obligated–to attend these ancillary parties, and you can expect any activities arranged on the eve of the wedding or on the same day to have the highest attendance. Invites for all events can be as informal or formal as you'd like: word-of-mouth, handwritten notes, or mailed invitations. Include all details in an itinerary placed in hotel rooms and on your wedding website–and notify guests well in advance. Keep invitees in the loop by updating your website to include hotel information, maps and directions, registry links, as well as details that won't make it onto your invitation, such as specifics about the dress code, a list of childcare options, and your personal guidebook to the area. Make an online RSVP for weekend activities, so you can plan accordingly and not overbook (or overspend!) on invitees who won't be there to join in. Keep the RSVP list visible; that way, guests can coordinate with other attendees planning to go. And remember not to list exclusive events online (like the ceremony rehearsal or bridesmaids luncheon), because more people than you planned for will join you.

CHAPTER
NINE

MASTER YOUR CEREMONY

> **THE CEREMONY IS THE MAIN REASON FOR THE DAY: YOU ARE THERE TO GET MARRIED, AFTER ALL. MAKE IT AS SPECIAL AND MEANINGFUL AS THE EVENT ITSELF.**
>
> — Eleni N. Gage, *Executive Editor, Martha Stewart Weddings*

YOU'LL SPEND HOURS AND HOURS obsessing over every detail of your reception, and with good reason—you want it to be the party of a lifetime. But it's also important to take a breather from all that to think about the other half of your day, the ceremony. That special moment when you and your fiancé make it official, the moment that your life changes, that makes your parents shed tears of joy, and that friends and family will remember long after the cake is cut and the bouquet is tossed. Every ceremony has the same monumental mission: to take two individuals and join them together to face the future. Each one, however, is as different as the people involved. In designing your day, think about who you are as individuals and as a couple, and about the kind of life you want to build together, and you'll find the answers to the questions that will make your wedding a ritual like no other. Will your ceremony celebrate one religion, two religions, or be nondenominational? Will you be married in a place of worship? Will you bring your respective cultures into the mix? Do you want to exchange traditional vows, write your own, or let your favorite poets do the talking through readings given by the people closest to you? Make these decisions thoughtfully, and your ceremony will be more than a ritual; it will be a moving example of who you are, an homage to the pasts that brought you here, and a symbol of how you want to live your new life together.

Hiring an Officiant

Every couple wants their vows to be meaningful, memorable, and legally binding. With the right person to marry you, and a little thoughtful planning, you can create a ceremony tailor-made for the two of you.

No matter what type of wedding you're going for, you can't make it official without an officiant. First, consider your options.

Priest, minister, rabbi, imam, or pandit: If you know you want a religious service, you've got this down. Now you can think specifically about who will do the job.

Unitarian minister: This is a good option if you'd like to combine, say, a Catholic prayer, Buddhist blessing, and Jewish observance; or if you don't practice any religion but want your day to feel spiritual.

Justice of the peace: When making it legal is all that matters, tap a JP or judge. While the service won't be religious, it will be special if you add readings and rituals.

Friend or family member: Being wed by a person who really, truly knows you calls for a couple of extra steps. Be sure whoever you pick is comfortable speaking in public, then triple-check with the county clerk's office to see that he or she has met all the requirements for getting ordained.

CONDUCT A SEARCH

Once you know the type of officiant you want, it's time to locate the right person. If you're not a member of a church or synagogue and want a clergyperson to marry you, call local houses of worship and your religion's national headquarters for referrals. If you're working with a planner, ask if she can pass along some names of officiants she's worked with. Take note of weddings you've enjoyed, and get references from friends as well. Last, there's also something to be said for an extensive internet search.

MEET TO FIND A GOOD MATCH

When talking to a candidate, gauge whether the person is genuinely interested in hearing all your details–the story of how you met, your family dynamics, what you love about each other. These are things she'll lean on to set your ceremony apart. It's also crucial for your officiant to establish intimacy among you and your guests, so observe her word choice and demeanor. And ask yourself how attentive she is to your needs. Is she sensitive to the delicate relationship you have with your stepmother, for instance? If you choose a religious leader, attend a service or two in his community if possible, to get a sense of his attitude toward God, love, and family, and observe his speaking style.

MAKE IT OFFICIAL

After you've chosen someone to officiate, it's time to put the paperwork into place. An ordained minister can perform a wedding in any state, but you'll have to call the county clerk's office where you'll be getting your marriage license to ask whether you need official documentation. That office will also be able to tell you when to get the license and if anything else (like a blood test) is required.

If a friend is marrying you, he can be legally ordained through an online ministry, which can be as easy as going online and filling out the forms. The process is quick, easy, and free, but further documentation, if required, may cost a small fee. For a more secular option, some counties, including most in California, will deputize an officiant to perform a ceremony on your day. In Maine, members of the Bar Association may legally marry couples. And in Florida, public notaries can. Each state has different laws; explore yours by calling the county clerk's office well in advance of your wedding.

Postceremony, your officiant will need to file your marriage license within a certain amount of time, and have it signed by you and two witnesses (again, look into the requirements of your specific county to make sure you're on the up and up). If the license isn't filed within the required time frame, your marriage may not be recognized by the state–and you may find yourselves getting married all over again at City Hall.

Last, if you're getting married abroad, check with the country's government bureau months in advance to see what you need to do–often a trip to City Hall to be legally wed in the United States is necessary.

From This Day Forward This New York couple were married in the terraced garden of the Ocean Club on Paradise Island in the Bahamas.

THE TIMELINE CEREMONY

———

9–12 MONTHS AHEAD
Book ceremony venue.

Book officiant.

Choose wedding party.

6 MONTHS AHEAD
Book ceremony musicians.

3 MONTHS AHEAD
Meet with officiant.

Choose readers and readings.

Finalize ceremony music.

Cement the ceremony order with officiant.

Design and print programs.

1 MONTH AHEAD
Get your marriage license.

Write vows.

10 DAYS AHEAD
Have final meeting with officiant.

1 WEEK AHEAD
Assemble programs.

Print readings.

Gather items for any rituals.

Composing Your Ceremony

Whatever your cultural background, your vows can be as traditional or idiosyncratic as you desire. Take a look at the following basic sketches of the five most common celebrations as starting points, then create the format that will mean the most to you.

CHRISTIAN CEREMONY

Typical Length
30 minutes for a Protestant ceremony

One hour for a Catholic mass

Note that Catholics may perform the wedding rite without the full mass (this cuts Communion and saves about 20 minutes).

———

Hymn

Opening Prayer

Readings
(In a Catholic ceremony, those would be an Old Testament Reading, Psalm, New Testament Reading, and Gospel; Protestants may choose any texts.)

Homily

Vows and Ring Ceremony

Lord's Prayer

Sign of Peace

Communion
(for Catholics only)

Blessing

———

Special Touch
Ask the priest to add the Prayer of the Faithful to honor family members who have passed.

JEWISH CEREMONY

Typical Length
30 minutes

Keep in mind this is a general overview; Orthodox, Conservative, and Reform Jewish weddings will differ from each other. To streamline this service, in many denominations, such as Reform Judaism, the only absolute requirement is the signing of the Ketubah, which means you can select what else you want to weave in; talk to your rabbi to get his or her point of view.

———

Ketubah: signing of the marriage contract

Bedeken: veiling of the bride

Huppa ceremony: The bride and groom move under the canopy, which represents the couple's new home and life together.

Kiddushin: circling and exchanging of rings

Sheva Brachot: seven blessings; breaking of the glass

Yichud: couple's alone time before the reception

———

Special Touch
Appoint a friend to collect the broken pieces of sheva brachot glass, which you can make or have made into a piece of art for your home.

MUSLIM CEREMONY

Typical Length
An hour and a half

Traditions will vary based on cultural, geographic, and religious differences between Muslim faithful. These celebrations can last up to three days; technically the only ritual you need to make it official is the nikah, the signing of the wedding contract, which can be done at home or in a mosque.

———

Al-Ijab wal-Qubul: offer and acceptance

Mahar: groom's gift to bride

Nikah: signing of the wedding contract

Recitation of the Fatihah: The first chapter of the Qur'an is read to conclude the ceremony.

Dua: prayers for the bride and groom

Salaam: wishes given by the groom to guests

Savaqu: showering the bride with coins

———

Special Touch
Plan a wedding weekend with some of the traditional prenikah parties, such as the *dholki* (which comes from the word for *drum*), in which guests sing, dance, and play drums; and the mehndi, when the bride and the women in her family have henna designs applied to their hands and feet.

HINDU CEREMONY

Typical Length
Three hours

This ritual will differ between communities, which may expand or contract this basic blueprint. To shorten the length, you can cut anything but the seven steps—without it, the marriage isn't valid.

———

Ganesh puja: prayer to dispel all evils

Baraat: arrival of the groom

Parchan: arrival of the bride

Kanyadaan: giving the daughter

Ganthibandahn: tying the knot

Mangalfera: walking around the fire

Saptapadi: seven steps

Saubhagya Chinha: blessing of the bride

Aashirvaad: blessings

Viddai: the bride's departure

———

Special Touch
Place a coconut under the wheel of your getaway car, a modern update on the tradition of a carriage driving over the fruit to test its strength.

NONDENOMINATIONAL SERVICE

Typical Length
30 minutes

You can tweak this as you see fit. If you are going for a very short ceremony—or guests are expected to stand during it (though we still suggest providing chairs for the elderly or those who need them), then you can go straight to the declaration of intent, vows, and exchange of rings.

———

Welcome

Readings

Officiant's address

Declaration of intent

Vows

Exchange of rings

Blessing or closing remarks

Pronouncement

———

Special Touch
Get creative by having loved ones (like your grandparents) stand up and give marriage advice.

———

Vows That Wow A New York City pair returned to the bride's ancestral homeland of Italy to wed in a Catholic ceremony at a 13th-century church in Positano.

Combining Religions & Cultures

*Even if you and your fiancé have two different backgrounds,
it's completely possible to create a service that intertwines your
individual beliefs and represents you both beautifully.*

BECOME YOUR OWN EXPERTS

Take some time to read about each other's religions in books and online. As you research, set aside readings and tips and make notes on the rituals that appeal to you. This way, you'll both be informed when it comes time to sit down with your families and officiant. Some religions are very tolerant of interfaith unions, while others are much less so. Rabbis in Judaism's Orthodox and Conservative movements have traditionally not performed interfaith ceremonies, for example, but some Reform-movement rabbis will marry interfaith couples–and some are even willing to co-officiate with a priest or minister. In Islam, it is permissible for Muslim men to marry Christian or Jewish women; however, intermarriage is not allowed for Muslim women. And in the Greek Orthodox Church, priests can only marry an interfaith couple if the non-Orthodox person is a baptized Christian.

INVOLVE YOUR FAMILIES

Since your marriage will ultimately blend two families together, it's a nice idea to sit down with both sets of your parents next. Listen to them about what's important to them, but remember that it's your wedding and what matters to you should come first. It might take a few conversations to settle it all, especially if either or both sets of

Two for the Road Immediately after model Chrissy Teigen's and singer John Legend's Pentecostal ceremony, the bride's mom performed a Thai water blessing. Twice-blessed, the newlyweds recessed wearing traditional jasmine leis around their necks and big smiles on their faces.

parents are paying for the big day. Go into the discussion with an open mind, and be willing to compromise. Don't be afraid to get creative; if one or both person's parents insist on a religious service in one faith, consider separate ceremonies on different days, for example. If they're concerned about having both sides equally represented, think about having co-officiants or an interfaith minister.

CHOOSE THE RIGHT OFFICIANT

Once you've decided what kind of wedding you want, the search for the right officiant begins. Religious celebrants often come with conditions. For example, a minister or priest might only marry you if the wedding is in a church, or a rabbi might request that you agree to raise your kids in the Jewish faith. If you're not comfortable with an officiant's requests, broaden your search to include interfaith ministers, who can "customize" a ceremony that incorporates both of your faiths.

CRAFT AN INCLUSIVE CELEBRATION

Regardless of whom you choose to perform the ceremony, you'll want to meet with him or her a few times before the wedding to establish a relationship and plan the ceremony. Tell the officiant which details you've worked out with your family, as well as any passages and rites you would like to include. Then ask for suggestions; he or she might recommend a universal adaptation of a prayer to make it more encompassing, for instance. If there are traditions you want to incorporate from both faiths, discuss those. The right officiant will be eager to create a ceremony that speaks to who you are as individuals and to the blended home you're going to build as a family.

WEDDING WISDOM

You don't want your grandpa to be confused when the groom steps on the glass or to leave Aunt Sadie mystified by your mehndi. Take the time to explain culturally specific rituals in your program so guests feel in the loop and can appreciate each custom.

Personalizing Your Ceremony

If you're having a classic religious ceremony, you may already know which special moments to plan. But if you're designing your own vows, it's up to you to choose the rituals that will resonate. Pick a custom that works for you.

Incorporating traditions from your heritage is a great way to honor family members and infuse your ceremony with personality. That said, every ritual you choose doesn't have to be laden with meaning, so if you find one that speaks to you–like creating an outdoor altar out of wheat stalks as Native Americans do–simply go with it! Just be sure to clue everyone in to what's going on with a brief explanation in your program. Here is a sampling of options, which run the gamut from very traditional to a little unusual.

UNITY CANDLE

In this Judeo-Christian custom, the bride and groom each use a lit taper to light a larger third candle that represents their union. This rite can also be performed by the bride and groom's parents to symbolize two families coming together. Another twist: Create a display of votives where each guest lights a candle and says a blessing as he or she enters the ceremony. As more friends and family arrive, the space will become brighter with the glow of candlelight.

BLESSING OF RINGS

Before the couple exchanges bands, the rings are passed among the guests (or, in larger weddings, just the first two rows) so friends and relatives can share their well-wishes for the marriage. (For style–and safety's sake–tie the rings to a pretty ribbon or attach them to a pillow.) Once they've made their way around the room, the bands are returned to the officiant, with everyone's love and support symbolically attached.

HANDFASTING

This ancient Celtic ceremony takes place just before the couple say their vows, when they join hands, making a figure eight to represent eternity (right hand to right hand, left hand to left hand). Their crossed hands are then tied together with ribbon to represent two individuals coming together. For a personal touch, use a swath of heirloom fabric in lieu of ribbon.

WATER CLEANSING

During this purifying ritual, the bride and groom stack their open palms together while the officiant pours a pitcher of water over their hands. This symbolizes the release of any past emotional blocks, letting both parties enter the marriage with open hearts. The cleansing ceremony works best at outdoor weddings where messiness is not a concern. Indoors, couples can hold their hands over a bowl or share a goblet of water to symbolize the purity of love.

FRIENDSHIP CIRCLE

A spin on a Quaker tradition, this ritual is ideal for a smaller wedding. Guests are invited to form a circle with the bride and groom, and are asked to share their thoughts on the couple (you may want to ask one or two guests to prepare a remark ahead of time, in order to break the ice). This is not only a great way for attendees to get to know one another, but it also gives the bride and groom a few moments to enjoy the presence of their loved ones.

TREE PLANTING

Planting a tree that commemorates your wedding and grows with your marriage is a thoughtful idea for ceremonies that take place at a family home. The tree should be almost completely planted prior to the ceremony, with soil reserved in two small containers. During the ceremony, the bride and groom place soil from the two containers on top of the planted roots, representing two people joining as one, or the beginning of a family tree.

A Far-Flung Fête Guests (and camels) watched on as a Texas couple exchanged vows poolside at the Jnane Tamsna resort in Marrakesh; colorful Moroccan rugs served as the aisle.

Writing Your Vows

Most ceremonies involve a declaration of love followed by an exchange of rings, but what's said in those vows varies widely. You can opt for the classic version or pen your very own.

THE TRADITIONAL ROUTE

Marriage vows date back to 1549 and the Anglican Communion's Book of Common Prayer. More than four centuries later, they're still the most popular choice among couples. You can use them as is, ask your clergyperson for your religion's version, or work these sentiments into promises you script yourself:

I, (bride/groom) take you, (groom/bride), to be my (wife/husband), to have and to hold from this day forward, for better or for worse, for richer, for poorer, in sickness and in health, to love and to cherish, from this day forward, till death do us part.

THE SELF-WRITTEN VOW

To create your own version, begin separately. Schedule alone time to write your vows before sharing them with each other. Doing this individually will help each of you reflect without the other's influence, making the results more interesting and personal. And start weeks, better yet months, in advance to avoid the pressure of trying to be poetic the night before your nuptials.

1. Ask yourself questions. Sit with a sheet of paper and ponder questions such as, "Why have I chosen this person to be my partner? What do I love most about him [or her]?" Take time to really think about the answers, and translate them into a vow.

2. Look for inspiration. Once you've gathered your own thoughts, scour books, poems, and other vows for words that express what you want to say. Mix old with new and classic with modern, and incorporate parts of traditional vows if you wish.

3. Write love letters. To get your feelings flowing, pen your thoughts in a private note to your fiancé that only the two of you will read. Don't worry about keeping it short or making it perfect. Set a date to sit down together to share your notes and read each other's thoughts. Decide which parts you would like to read aloud, and what aspects of traditional vows you plan on including, if any. Remember that it's best to keep vows as short and as simple as possible–a paragraph or two at most. Afterward, rather than throwing away these first-draft letters, file them as keepsakes to read on anniversaries.

4. Make promises. Focus on what marriage means to you by taking time to consider what you're saying yes to and what you intend to pledge to your partner. Reflect on and celebrate the good times, but troubleshoot the stumbling blocks in your relationship, too. For example, if you're working too much and not making time for each other, you may want to think about what you can promise to avoid falling into that trap again in the future.

5. Keep it serious. Naturally, it's fine to inject a bit of levity, but remember that a wedding vow is a solemn promise of love and commitment, not open-mike night. It's best to avoid sarcasm, as well as any references so cryptic that your guests will feel excluded.

6. Practice, practice, practice. Write your vows on index cards so you don't have to worry about memorizing them–and give a copy to your officiant as a backup. Rehearse with these flash cards prior to the wedding day. That way you'll know when to breathe, and you'll be prepared for the parts that may make you well up.

Mountain High These grooms exchanged tear-inducing vows in front of 51 guests outside the Figueroa Mountain Farmhouse in the Santa Ynez Valley of California.

Choosing the Readings & Music

Your selections for the ceremony not only elevate this incredibly romantic scene in your life, but your favorite songs also will provide a soundtrack that becomes only more meaningful afterward.

THE READINGS

Asking friends or family members to recite a special passage is a significant way to involve them in your ceremony. As a rule of thumb, choose no more than three selections that take no more than a few minutes each to read.

Invite favorite authors: If you love Hemingway, for example, this passage from *A Farewell to Arms* is appropriate: "At night, there was the feeling that we had come home, feeling no longer alone, waking in the night to find the other one there, and not gone away."

Think like a kid: Children's books are ripe with ideas: If you adore traveling, look to Dr. Seuss's *Oh, the Places You'll Go!* Or consider adorably appropriate passages from classics like *The Velveteen Rabbit, A Lovely Love Story, I Like You,* or *Winnie-the-Pooh.*

Reflect on your relationship: Go with a poem about the stars if your groom proposed under a night's sky, or look to your venue for inspiration. Shakespeare's *"Shall I Compare Thee to a Summer's Day?"* is perfect for a garden ceremony, whereas a beach wedding might call for lines from Anne Morrow Lindbergh's *Gift from the Sea.* Song lyrics can also be beautiful when read. Or, if your relationship started out long distance, go to your early correspondence to find something worth sharing.

THE MUSIC

You'll pick selections for the prelude, processional, bride's entrance, and recessional, and another hymn or song or two if you so choose. When vetting tunes, pay close attention to the lyrics, because breakup tunes can sound just like love songs! Also ask yourself if it fits the venue; the Rolling Stones might feel wrong in a church. Finally, ponder whether your tunes will stand the test of time. If in doubt, swap a top 40 hit with a classic.

Prelude
Welcome loved ones with about 30 minutes of music.

Classic Choices

"Arioso" (Cantata No. 156), Johann Sebastian Bach

"God Only Knows," Beach Boys

"One Hand, One Heart" (from West Side Story), Leonard Bernstein

"How Sweet It Is," James Taylor

Surprising Selections

"La Femme d'Argent," Air

"Love and Some Verses," Iron & Wine

"Méditation from Thaïs," Jules Massenet

"Knuddelmaus," Ulrich Schnauss

Processional
Pick one song—at least four minutes long—with a light but sincere tone to accompany your bridal party.

Classic Choices

"Gabriel's Oboe" (from the Mission soundtrack), Ennio Morricone

"Winter," Concerto No. 4 in F Minor, Antonio Vivaldi

Canon in D, Johann Pachelbel

"Maybe I'm Amazed," Paul McCartney

Surprising Selections

"Waiting on a Friend," Rolling Stones

Canon in F, The O'Neill Brothers

"Promenade" from Pictures at an Exhibition, Modest Mussorgsky

"Cinema Paradiso" (from the *Cinema Paradiso* soundtrack), Ennio Morricone

Bride's Entrance
Find a tune that takes its time and has apt lyrics, if any at all.

Classic Choices

"Bridal Chorus," Wagner

Canon in D, Johann Pachelbel

"Over the Rainbow," Israel Kamakawiwo'ole

"When a Man Loves a Woman," Percy Sledge

"Trumpet Voluntary," Henry Purcell

Surprising Selections

"Only You," Joshua Radin

"Heavenly Day," Patty Griffin

"Here Comes the Sun," The Beatles

"First Day of My Life," Bright Eyes

Recessional
Finish with a buoyant, gleeful piece that gears guests up for the festivities.

Classic Choices

"Signed, Sealed, Delivered, I'm Yours," Stevie Wonder

"Ode to Joy," Ludwig van Beethoven

"You're My Best Friend," Queen

"Wedding March," Felix Mendelssohn

Surprising Selections

"What a Wonderful World," Joey Ramone

"Could You Be Loved," Bob Marley & the Wailers

"Into the Great Wide Open," Tom Petty and the Heartbreakers

"You Are My Sunshine" (from the *O Brother, Where Art Thou?* soundtrack), Norman Blake

A Joyful Noise (clockwise from top): A bluegrass band played for an outdoor celebration in Santa Barbara. A friend of the newlyweds serenaded them on the ukulele. Keeping up the bride's family tradition, an alpenhorn played at a Rocky Mountain ceremony. A girl's choir sang carols for a New Year's Eve wedding in Seattle.

Including Family

They've known you from the beginning and they loved you first.
Without your families, neither of you would be here. Consider some of the following
elegant and easy ways to make them a part of your ceremony.

No one could exude more pride and happiness on the day of your wedding than the people who raised you. And all of them will likely want to play an active part from the time you get engaged until you say "I do." These days, the bride's and groom's parents, stepparents, and grandparents have important responsibilities to carry out during the planning period and on the day of the wedding. There are many traditional roles, such as the bride's parents acting as the official hosts for the celebration, as well as newer ones that serve the needs of blended families, like a bride sharing a special dance with her stepfather. If a parent has passed away, you might ask another close relative to assume some of these duties, or alter the customs in a way that celebrates everyone concerned. No two families are alike, so choose what feels right for you, and you can't go wrong.

HONORING YOUR PARENTS

Whether they're there for you in person or in spirit, your parents should be acknowledged. Here are ways to signal how special they are:

· Give your mothers special corsages or nosegays and your fathers unique boutonnieres.
· Have them light a unity candle during the ceremony.
· Use a page in your wedding program to express your gratitude.
· Thank them in a toast at the reception.
· Display photographs from their weddings on the escort-card table.
· Ask your officiant to mention them, or pay tribute to a deceased parent with a moment of silence during the ceremony.

INVOLVING YOUR STEPS

It's a nice gesture to include your stepmother (and/or the groom's stepmom) in the planning however you choose. Invite her to come to a dress fitting, or ask her to weigh in on something that might interest her, like the flowers if she's a gardener, for example. Along those same lines, it's completely appropriate for your stepfather to walk you down the aisle, particularly if your biological father has passed away. Having stepfather-daughter or stepmother-son dances at the reception is also a thoughtful touch.

CELEBRATING GRANDPARENTS

If they've been married for decades, acknowledging their union at your wedding can help illustrate the meaning of the occasion. One way to do this is by displaying photographs from their wedding at your reception, either on a wall or a seating-card table.

Your grandparents' wedding might even influence your own. Look at old photos, and talk to them or their siblings about that day. What song did they first dance to? What kinds of flowers did your grandma carry? You could re-create these as simple, sentimental touches at your celebration.

INCORPORATING KIDS

Little ones can be adorable additions to weddings. For a meltdown-free performance, remember these three words: *practice, practice, practice.* These are great ways to get nieces, nephews, sons, daughters, and friends' children involved.

Single flower girl: Generally aged 3 to 7, this little lady precedes the bride down the aisle, either scattering petals or carrying a mini bouquet or flower basket.

Multiple flower girls: The same duties can be performed by a larger group, which often includes slightly older girls who substitute for bridesmaids. If you have two or more flower girls, they often walk in together, carrying individual baskets or holding a garland between the two of them.

Ring bearer: This is usually a boy, aged 3 to 7, who walks the aisle before the flower girl, carrying stand-ins for the rings on a cushion.

Pages: Traditionally seen at very formal weddings (think British royalty), pages are boys aged 4 to 7 who hold the bride's train as she walks down the aisle.

Junior bridesmaids and groomsmen: These are children aged 8 through young teenagers who perform the same duties as their older counterparts (short of attending bachelor or bachelorette parties).

More options: Designate children to act as program distributors, ushers, readers, candle-lighters, or recessional bubble blowers.

A Family Affair At a South Carolina celebration, the groom visited with the female members of the wedding party on the first-floor veranda of the bride's parents' inn, while she welcomed male friends and relatives on the second.

WEDDIQUETTE
THE RECEIVING LINE

Greeting each guest is one ritual you won't want to skip. Some couples stop at each table during the party; others opt for a receiving line either just after the ceremony or at the reception. The shortest line comprises, in order, the bride's mom, groom's mom, bride, and groom. Dads often join or circulate among the crowd. (If one joins in, however, the other should, too; each follows the mom in line.) Though it's optional, bridesmaids and groomsmen may also line up, standing after the groom.

Picking Your Wedding Party

Standing by a couple's side on their wedding day is both an honor and a responsibility. Select your attendants wisely and treat them wonderfully, and you'll be surrounded by lots of love.

The custom of having attendants is about as old as marriage itself. As one story goes, a bride in early England surrounded herself with female friends dressed in outfits identical to her own to confuse evil spirits that might curse her happiness. Groomsmen were chosen to escort the bride–not the groom–to the wedding to protect her from dowry-seeking thieves. Though the tradition has evolved, your attendants (should you choose to include any) will play a prominent role in your special day. Today, some couples opt out of the tradition, while others have more than a dozen friends and relatives on each side. Still others take a cue from European royalty and have wedding parties entirely made of children. Whatever you decide, don't feel pressured to have an equal number of men and women. Loved ones don't come in boxed sets, and neither should your wedding party. Other than that, here's what to keep in mind when choosing your VIPs.

THE MAID OF HONOR

How to choose: Traditionally, the bride invites the sister closest to her in age to be maid or matron of honor, but these days she can ask any relative or friend–even a grandparent, parent, or adult child, or a brother or close male friend. If she can't choose between two people, there's no rule that says she can't have both. The maid of honor has varied responsibilities, so pick a good friend who will enjoy helping you.

Her responsibilities: As head bridesmaid, the MOH is in charge of delegating tasks and keeping the bridal party organized. She will usually help the bride shop for the gown and bridesmaid dresses, tell guests where the couple is registered, and host the shower and bachelorette party. On the wedding day, she'll tend to the bride's veil, train, and bustle, hold the bride's bouquet during the ceremony, and sign the marriage certificate as a witness. At the reception, she and the best man sometimes join the newlyweds for the first formal dance sequence and she may also offer a toast.

THE BEST MAN

How to choose: At one time, the best man was usually a brother. Now anyone is appropriate, provided he (or she) is close to the groom and is willing to assume this role.

His responsibilities: The best man helps the groom select the men's ensembles and reminds the groomsmen to get fitted. He may act as bachelor-party planner, and makes sure the groom arrives at the ceremony on time. Day-of, he stands at the groom's side during the vows, holds the bride's ring, and signs the marriage certificate. Afterward, he hands out payments for the officiant, and any other expenses that come up, offers the first toast, safeguards gift envelopes, and orchestrates a smooth departure for the newlyweds when the party is over.

THE BRIDESMAIDS

How to choose: Along with her family and friends, the bride's entourage may include the groom's sisters. Older girls and teens can join the party as junior bridesmaids.

Their responsibilities: The bridesmaids often help the MOH plan the shower and the bachelorette party or cohost these events. They attend prenuptial festivities and assist the bride or maid of honor with tasks such as securing hotel rooms and keeping a gift log at the shower. Bridesmaids purchase the dress the bride has picked and have it fitted in time for the wedding. If they're wearing dresses of their choosing, they need to be aware of any style or color specifications the bride requests. At the ceremony, they, with the groomsmen, precede the maid of honor in the procession.

THE GROOMSMEN

How to choose: Here, too, you want people you're comfortable with. A brother (or brothers) of the bride makes a nice addition.

Their responsibilities: Groomsmen pay for their own attire and might host prenuptial celebrations–especially the bachelor party. At the wedding, they often serve as ushers and should arrive early to roll out the runner, distribute programs, and escort guests to their seats. They walk in the procession alongside the bridesmaids and stand next to the best man during the ceremony.

MAN'S (OR WOMAN'S) BEST FRIEND

How to choose: Want to give your pooch the coveted position of ring bearer or flower dog? Fun idea–if your dog isn't skittish. If she's the nervous type, let her stay home.

Your responsibility: Keep Spot (and everyone else) as relaxed as possible. Give your attendants and vendors a heads-up that your pet will play a role, and notify your officiant, as some may refuse to preside over a ceremony with furry creatures. Consider hiring a handler whom the animal knows, or have a friend be responsible for him during the wedding. If your florist is adorning his collar, be sure she uses nontoxic flowers, and don't make him wear them for longer than necessary. Finally, keep your pet someplace safe during the reception so guests won't feed him.

The Gang's All Here This Kentucky bride got hitched with a little help from her friends, namely her 11 bridesmaids, a generous mix of friends and relatives.

1

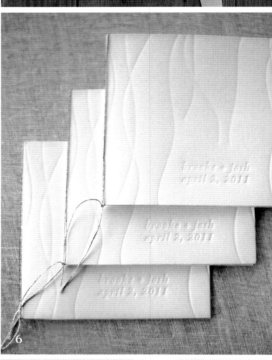

2

3

7

5

6

4

8

9

Creating the Program

Careful thought goes into each aspect of your ceremony, from the readings to the rituals you choose to observe. Share the significance of each with your guests through a booklet that will later become a keepsake.

This amazing little extra shows you and your groom have truly considered all the details. Programs aren't required, but they do serve to engage the guests in the wedding, especially if you're having a ritual-rich ceremony. Plus, they are a great place to communicate information, whether it's a request for no flash photos during the vows (to prevent interfering with the photographer's shots) or the names of loved ones you want to thank.

The most basic version is straightforward and purposeful: The bride's and groom's names act as a title and are typically followed by the date and location of the wedding. The order of the service, often including titles of readings and songs, lets attendees follow along. And listing the members of the bridal party, as well as others who have a role in the wedding, enables everybody to put faces to names. But that's just a starting point—you can absolutely get as ornate or creative as you like.

Get With the Program A ceremony booklet can come in any form or style to suit your wedding. 1. "Luggage tags" described the events of the day at a destination event in Bali. 2. A "playbill" for a Broadway-themed affair. 3. This fan set the scene for nuptials in a railroad museum in Georgia. 4. A letterpressed crest fit right in with a wedding in an Italian villa. 5. For beachfront vows, minibooklets were covered in canvas flags and tied with lovers' knots. 6. A blind-embossed handout for a white-on-white wedding in Washington State. 7. Bright-green–printed programs doubled as escort cards for a picnic nuptial at Martha Stewart's farm. 8. Fans kept attendees cool at an outdoor California fête. 9. A pair of photographers decorated their programs with a selection of their favorite images.

PUTTING THEM TOGETHER

Many brides opt to make their own programs, since that can be done well ahead. Even if you decide to have yours professionally designed, there are ways to limit costs. When you order your invitations, ask your stationer to print a program cover that includes the information you already know: your names, the date of your wedding, and the location. Then create, photocopy, and assemble the inside pages yourself later. Or, you can have the stationer make all the pages, then hand them off to you for assembly. Another great budget-friendly option is to have a single program professionally calligraphed, and simply photocopy it onto nice paper.

If you're feeling crafty, take a DIY approach from start to finish. Head to an art-supply store or stationer for quality paper with thick stock; next, design the template on your computer and print and organize the pages yourself. Chic note cards with a border or a small image make beautiful covers for computer-generated pages, and you can add names, monograms, or any other information with a custom-made rubber stamp.

HANDING THEM OUT

On the day of the wedding, have the ushers offer programs as they greet the guests, or assign the task to another friend or family member (children tend to love this responsibility). Alternatively, you can place a program on each seat, or stack them in a tray or basket near the entrance. Don't forget to save a few for the scrapbook. Years from now, this written record will stir as many memories as any photo.

WEDDING WISDOM

Before you make hundreds of copies, have your program carefully proofread by at least two people who didn't work on it.

Prepping Your People

*To get everyone settled into their seats with ease, and establish
a festive mood straightaway, have a preceremony powwow with
your wedding party at the rehearsal, sharing the following suggestions.*

WEDDING
WISDOM

———

If lots of kids
will be attending
the wedding as
guests, but you're
not the type who
thinks the sound
of a child crying
at a wedding
is good luck,
consider hiring
a babysitter or
two to set up
shop in a room
nearby (church
basements and
hotel suites are
great options).
Pop in a movie,
provide snacks,
and, most
important, let
parents know
this service is
available to them.

APPOINT A WELCOMING COMMITTEE

Ask your parents to greet people as they trickle in. From a guest's perspective, there's nothing lovelier than having the opportunity to talk to the hosts of the party before it begins. In addition, have ushers on hand to lead everyone to their seats; not knowing where to sit makes people uneasy. Ushers, who are often groomsmen (but don't have to be), can let guests know which is the bride's or groom's side of the aisle.

If you're having open seating and aren't choosing to appoint ushers to guide guests, have a greeter, a printed card, or a note on the back of the program to let people know to pick any seat on either side. It's always smart to save and mark off places for your closest family members. Brief your ushers about the most important people on your list, and ask them to escort only those guests to the designated area, usually the first few pews. If you don't have ushers, or you want a larger section reserved, block it off by draping a length of ribbon or garland across the opening of the rows in question, and let VIPs know they get front-row seats with an old-school note in your invitation. Historically, a stationer or calligrapher would create small cards that say "Within the ribbon" and then tuck them into the invitations going to close family members. When those guests arrived at the ceremony, they would present the cards to the ushers. Another traditional option is to send a pew card with your invitation that would say something along the lines of, "Please present this card at United Methodist Church, Saturday, the sixth of November," followed by a fill-in-the-blank "Pew number __."

KEEP EVERYONE COMFORTABLE

Consider your location–is it warm or cold? Is inclement weather on the way? Rather than just thinking, "The service is only 20 minutes, guests will be fine," do whatever you can to help them acclimate, like providing hot cider on a cool day or ice-cold lemonade for a warm-weather affair. Setting out baskets of items like pashminas or paper fans is a nice touch, too, but an extra, not a necessity. Speaking of necessities, if you'll be exchanging vows en plein air, a rain plan is an absolute must. Securing a backup indoor location is ideal, but not always possible. In that case, it's a good idea to reserve a tent, which often has to be done more than six months in advance. Keep in mind that for a Saturday wedding, the company will need to know if you plan to use the tent by the Wednesday before.

STAY CALM

The days before your ceremony can be nerve-racking; enlist these do's and don'ts and everyone should be relaxed and ready to go come showtime.

- **Do** have your greeters and ushers join the rehearsal so you can explain where you'd like the programs to be handed out and how people should be seated.
- **Do** plan to arrive at your venue ready to go half an hour before starting time. Make sure all you'll need is a little lip gloss and powder.
- **Don't** make guests stand if the ceremony is going to last more than 10 minutes. (Even then, there are people who need seats, so be sure to provide them for Grandma and Uncle Rick and his bad knee.) People might arrive early, and wind up on their feet for longer than you think.
- **Don't** keep your guests waiting. A few minutes is understandable, but more than 20, and they'll be tapping their feet (and likely frowning).
- **Do** let go. By the time you're walking down the aisle, what's done is done. Enjoy each moment: You've earned it!

Thoughtful Touches (clockwise from top): Fans and hats helped guests beat the heat at a summer wedding in the Berkshires. Blackberry lemonade was a refreshing sight at an at-home affair on Martha's Vineyard. At a celebration in Ireland, junior attendants directed revelers to the ceremony, dinner, and dancing. Preceremony sippers at this California fête included citrus-cucumber water and watermelon lemonade.

Assigning the Order

*Just like a memorable first dance, any ceremony requires
a fair amount of choreography in order to run smoothly. Consider these traditional
guidelines for the seating arrangements,
processions, and recessions, all of which can be adapted to suit your style.*

PROCESSIONAL ORDER

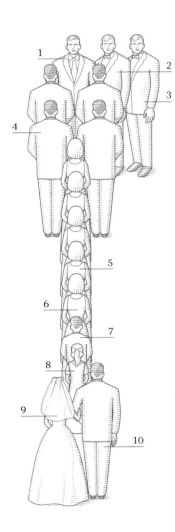

CHRISTIAN CEREMONY

The bride's family and friends are seated on the left, the groom's on the right. Ushers seat guests as they arrive, from front rows to back; the last to be seated are, in order: grandparents, mother of the groom (with father just behind), and mother of the bride. Just before the procession begins, the officiant takes his or her place, with the groom to the left, and the best man to the groom's left, facing guests. The ushers/groomsmen stand at the front, or start the procession as shown here, walking in pairs. Bridesmaids follow. The maid of honor enters next. Groomsmen and bridesmaids may also enter together, in pairs, with the best man and the maid of honor. The ring bearer and flower girl are the last down the aisle before the bride on her father's left arm.

1. Officiant

2. Groom

3. Best Man

4. Groomsmen

5. Bridesmaids

6. Maid of Honor

7. Ring Bearer

8. Flower Girl

9. Bride

10. Bride's Father

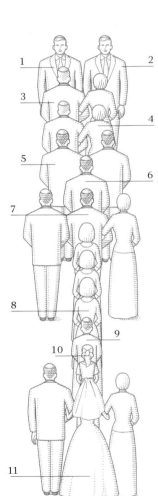

JEWISH CEREMONY

The bride's side is on the right, the groom's is on the left. Parents stand under the huppah during the ceremony; stepparents may sit in aisle seats in the second and third rows or stand under the huppah. The processional is the same as in a Christian service, except that grandparents, the groom's parents, and the bride's mother all join the processional, and both sets of parents walk the groom and the bride down the aisle. The rabbi and the cantor often lead the procession.

1. Rabbi

2. Cantor

3. Bride's Grandparents

4. Groom's Grandparents

5. Groomsmen in Pairs

6. Best Man

7. Groom with Parents

8. Bridesmaids

9. Ring Bearer

10. Flower Girl

11. Bride with Parents

RECESSIONAL ORDER

CHRISTIAN CEREMONY

As the musicians start the celebratory recessional music, the bride and groom turn to each other, link arms, and walk briskly back up the aisle. The rest of the wedding party follows them, also in pairs, with the women on the men's right arms. The flower girl and the ring bearer (if they remained at the altar during the ceremony) come first (if there's only one or the other, he or she can walk alone), then the maid of honor and the best man, then the bridesmaids and groomsmen. Ushers return to assist guests and direct them to the receiving line or reception site.

1. Bride
2. Groom
3. Flower Girl
4. Ring Bearer
5. Maid of Honor
6. Best Man
7. Bridesmaids
8. Groomsmen

JEWISH CEREMONY

The newlyweds lead, followed by the bride's parents, then the groom's parents, the flower girl and the ring bearer, the maid of honor and the best man, and the bridesmaids and groomsmen; all are arm in arm, with the women on the men's left arms. Immediately following the ceremony, the bride and groom often take 10 or 15 minutes to themselves in yichud, the symbolic consummation of the marriage. During this time they duck into a private room, where they have something to eat (breaking the wedding-day fast) and reflect on their marriage. When they join their guests, they are announced as husband and wife and are greeted joyously.

1. Groom
2. Bride
3. Bride's Parents
4. Groom's Parents
5. Ring Bearer
6. Flower Girl
7. Best Man/Groomsmen
8. Maid of Honor/Bridesmaids
9. Rabbi
10. Cantor

SAME-SEX WEDDINGS

Couples of every orientation are bending the rules to customize their ceremonies in unique and meaningful ways. Feel free to take a direct path to the altar that's a variation on one of the above, or follow a route less traveled. You can ask a person of mutual importance to escort the two of you on each arm, for example. Or, walk one behind the other with your respective parents, though you'll still have to figure out who goes first. If neither one of you is being "given away," proceed down the aisle together hand-in-hand. Or, try out an alternate floor plan by dividing the seating into three sections, separated by two aisles. This allows you each a path to the altar; you can walk in at the same time and meet in the middle. Just keep in mind that separate, simultaneous routes will require a second photographer (some photographers work with assistants who can document this; simply inquire).

Capturing the Moments

After all the care you put into your ceremony—and your entire event—
you want to make sure it's documented beautifully. The only thing
as magical as the day itself is reliving it for years to come.

**THE
TIMELINE
PHOTOGRAPHER
+ VIDEOGRAPHER**

———

**6–PLUS MONTHS
AHEAD**
Book
photographer and
videographer.

1 MONTH AHEAD
Introduce your two
hires (they'll have
to work with, and
around, each other)
and attend a
walk-through of
your ceremony and
reception venues
(if local) together.

1 WEEK AHEAD
Discuss shot list with
your photographer,
and let your videogra-
pher know (with
a list or pictures)
which VIP guests he
or she should target.

**2 WEEKS–
1 MONTH AFTER
THE WEDDING**
Receive the proofs
from photographer
and discuss post-
production details
with videographer.

**6–8 WEEKS
AFTER THE
WEDDING**
Receive the
photographs and
wedding video.

HIRING A PHOTOGRAPHER

Begin by thinking about the photographic style you want, whether that's formal images, narrative photos and candids inspired by photojournalism, or a mix. Then, survey friends and your event planner (if you're working with one) for recommendations. Narrow your list to three, and call to see if they're available on your date and gauge how you like their personalities. Before you meet, the photographer will send you a portfolio of images, either as prints or digital files. Be sure the group includes pictures from recent weddings, ideally at a similar venue and time of day as yours. Look at a nuptial they shot from start to finish, not just a collection of highlights from several events.

When it comes to pricing, most photographers offer multiple options. A major factor influencing the cost is the number of hours of coverage, usually ranging from six to ten. (One way to save: Ask for an hourly rate instead of a set fee, have a friend document the prewedding prep, and keep the professional for the ceremony through the cake-cutting.) Other variables that influence price are whether they shoot digitally or with film (a very nice but more expensive option) and if an album or prints are included. If you're on a budget, see how your photos (and wallet) look after the fact, and then order extras such as albums à la carte, or make your own scrapbook. If you fall hard for a photographer you can't afford, try to negotiate, letting her know you love her work but can't cover her fee. Or, ask her to suggest a less-pricey colleague.

Before you settle on a shooter, discuss what will be shot in color and in black and white; the quality of the processing and prints; how many images you'll see; how the proofs will be delivered (a formal album, loose in a box, on contact sheets, or as digital files); how many sets of proofs are included; and whether the proofs need to be returned to the photographer. Typically, you'll need to put down a deposit of roughly one-third of the total fee to secure your date. The photographer will draft a contract that includes the deposit paid, the due date for remaining payments (usually, one is expected the week before; the next on the day of the event), plus the refund or cancellation policy. The contract will note all of this plus the logistics: the addresses of the locations, the start and end times, any extra expenses you agree on (such as travel), and the number of proofs and enlargements included, if any. Finally, make sure you will own the personal-use rights to the images after the party; otherwise, you may have to pay twice the price every time you reorder.

HIRING A VIDEOGRAPHER

It's not essential to have a videographer, but couples who don't often regret not having a video record of their day. To find one, ask friends, your photographer, and other vendors for referrals, or contact a professional organization, such as the Wedding & Event Videographers Association.

When considering videographers, view complete events, not just selections. Meet with the person you like and let him know what attracted you to his work, such as the blend of candid moments and still photos. Pay attention to the editing, which sets the pace for the film and is just as important as the way it's shot. You should also discuss sound, including your choice of background songs and whether any of the original audio will accompany the final product, as well as what you want him to deliver as a finished video; most videographers offer options, from a five-minute music-video–like montage to a two-hour documentary. Once you settle on your choice, tell him if there are special guests or moments that you want to capture.

A contract signed by you and the videographer should stipulate what the total cost covers, including method of editing and any special effects; the hours of coverage; arrival times; videographer's attire; amount of deposit and payment schedule; overtime fees; schedule for delivery; length of the video; and cancellation policy. It should also specify who will work your wedding; some companies have several videographers, and you want the one who makes you smile.

A Cheer-full Exit At this autumnal affair, guests tossed mini-pom-poms, both handmade and store-bought, as the couple exited the church postceremony to head to their backyard reception in New Jersey.

CHAPTER
TEN

DESIGN YOUR RECEPTION

> "
>
> GONE ARE THE DAYS OF COOKIE-CUTTER OR FORMULAIC WEDDING RECEPTIONS. THE ONLY BOUNDARY IS YOUR IMAGINATION, AND THE SOLE REQUIREMENT IS THAT GUESTS HAVE THE TIME OF THEIR LIVES—AND LEAVE WELL FED!
>
> "
>
> — Peter Callahan, *Caterer and Contributing Editor, Martha Stewart Weddings*

FIRST COMES LOVE, then comes marriage, and we all know what happens next—one amazing party! But before you start clinking glasses of bubbly, there are a few things to keep in mind. After all, even the most relaxed affairs require a fair amount of foresight and planning, from organizing the flow of the fête to picking cocktails, and, of course, devising the menu (which, thankfully, no longer just means choosing chicken or beef). And while you may not be event planners, gourmands, or wine aficionados, you are the world's top experts in what will make your reception the best reflection of the two of you. All of your choices, from the music played to the food served, should represent who you are as a couple. If brunch is your all-time favorite meal, there's no need to throw an evening dinner reception at the country club when you could have eggs Benedict and a spectacularly reimagined pancake buffet at a great restaurant. The second most important element of the reception is your guests' comfort and enjoyment. Aim to pamper, surprise, and delight attendees, while staying true to your vision, and you can't go wrong. Then let go and get ready to celebrate. While the details of planning require careful consideration, the most important thing about your reception is that when it finally happens, you're relaxed and ready to enjoy your ideal party, surrounded by the people you love.

Getting Ready to Celebrate

*Are you going for an elegant party, a high-energy dance-off,
or a casual cocktail reception? Whatever you choose, the day's
schedule will determine how your event will play out.*

Your first decision: What kind of party do you want to host? Consider your favorite foods, what the loveliest time of day is to you, and whether dancing is a must-have or a would-be-nice-to-avoid. Also think about convenience; if most guests are coming from out of town, a Saturday morning breakfast or a Sunday bash that goes into the wee hours might be tough for them to attend. Keep in mind how late (or not) your crowd wants to rage. Will your affair be heavy on college friends who want to whoop it up all night? Or will there be lots of family (or guests with long drives home) who will appreciate an earlier start time? Once you've weighed all these factors (as well as, of course, when your chosen venue is available), make the call. Yes, most wedding receptions are dinner. But that's not your only option. You could do a brunch, a lunch, a cake-and-champagne fête, or an entire evening reception that's an extended cocktail party with satisfying appetizers. In most cases, a brunch or lunch will cut down on costs, partly because people tend to drink less during the day, which saves on booze, but also because there is less competition for venues at those times.

PLOT OUT THE FLOW

After you know the type of meal (or nonmeal) you want to serve, you'll want to establish the order of events. That means deciding on how long cocktail hour should last (any longer than an hour and a half and guests may get sloppy), and also determining the length of the meal (and

Brooklyn Bash When our special projects editor Anthony Luscia wed his longtime partner, Russell James, music and revelry fit the Broadway-inspired bill. Martha Stewart shared in the festivities.

of each course, if there's a seated dinner). If there will be dancing, choose when people will get down: between courses or after everyone eats. (One tip: When it comes to seated dinners, most caterers say each course takes about 30 minutes: 10 minutes to serve, 10 to eat, 10 to take away.) Then think about when you want to have your cake-cutting and toasts. Add it all up and make sure that you haven't been overambitious and turned your reception into a marathon: Planners agree that four to five hours is the maximum amount of time guests can enjoy an event and still leave wanting more. Next, let your planner (or, if you don't have one, your caterer) know how you envision the day's timeline. A sample schedule of a typical five-hour reception looks like this:

5:00 *Cocktail hour starts.*

6:00 *The bride and groom enter the reception,
are formally announced, and usually
have their first dance.*

6:30 *If the reception is a sit-down meal,
the first course is served. The host's welcome and
best man's toast kick things off.*

7:30 *The main course is served.*

8:00 *The bride and groom dance
with their parents, and guests join in.*

8:50 *The cake is cut.*

9:00 *Cake and dessert are served.*

9:45 *The bouquet is tossed.*

10:00 *The bride and groom depart.*

Speaking of departures, your event should have a clear ending, rather than slowly petering out. Turn to the "Plan Your Send-off" chapter (page 248) for warm ways to bid your guests adieu, as well as creative favor ideas.

Turn to the "Plan Your Send-off" chapter (page 248)

THE TIMELINE
RECEPTION

10–12 MONTHS AHEAD
Book the caterer (the best ones are often reserved a year in advance).

7-9 MONTHS AHEAD
Book a DJ or band. Book a lighting designer, if using.

4 MONTHS AHEAD
Reserve rentals. Notify the band of special song selections, so they can arrange music for those not in their repertoire. Ask your venue for diagrams to give to the lighting designer so he can draft a proposal for approval.

2 MONTHS–2 WEEKS AHEAD
Plan the menu and taste the food. Print menu cards if using. Have a walk-through of the venue with your lighting designer so he can locate, mark, and test outlets.

1–2 WEEKS AHEAD
Give your caterer a final head count, and supply the band or DJ with a final agenda of the day's events, noting breaks and guest announcements (like the cake-cutting).

Setting the Music

Chances are your favorite weddings had great food and terrific music. Even if you're not having dancing, you'll want the right people to set the best soundtrack for yours.

GOOD TO KNOW

———

There are always additional people beyond your guests who need to be fed, including the musicians. Make sure to give your caterer a list of these people. It should be noted in your contracts, so a simpler meal is prepared for them to eat behind the scenes. (After all, they won't have time to enjoy three courses.)

Music is the least tangible element of a wedding–after all, it won't show up in photos. However, it's a factor that people credit with the success or failure of an event. To get started, think about not only what will be playing but also who will be playing it. How to decide between blues versus big band, or a 10-piece band over two turntables? Begin with your budget: DJs charge a lot less than musicians. And a top-notch DJ may be a better choice than a so-so band; even the most versatile and talented group on earth could never provide the range of songs a DJ can. Still, if the sky's the limit, there's something about hearing live renditions of favorite tunes that can instantly upgrade a nice party into a truly memorable time. Or, there's the DIY route: Firing up your own music player is the most affordable, convenient, and customizable option. And you can play what you want, when you want.

To determine the type of entertainment that's right for you, along with your budget, consider your own personal preference, and your crowd (will they want to hear a huge range of songs exactly as they recognize them, or will they get fired up by live Motown hits or swing dancing all night?). Then factor in your location. It's a lot easier to squeeze a DJ into a tight spot, whereas a vast hall practically begs for a live band. Whatever you choose, make a list of your favorite songs, as well as a don't-play list of forbidden tunes, and you're bound to have a blast.

RESEARCHING ENTERTAINMENT

The easiest way to find a band or DJ is through referrals. Talk to your wedding coordinator, caterer, photographer, florist, or venue manager. Or, use them as a sounding board if you've gotten leads from others. Chances are the most respected DJs and musicians in your area will be known to the other professionals with whom you are working–and those vendors will not want to risk their own reputations by recommending someone who isn't terrific.

If you're marrying on a Saturday in June or September–the busiest times for a wedding–aim to book your entertainment a year in advance. Otherwise, secure a band or DJ with at least six months to spare. The contract should specify the part of the event any performers are booked for (ceremony, cocktails, after-dinner dancing); start and end times; a description of the music (which may include a song list, especially if you're hiring a DJ); what attire the performers will wear; and whether you'll serve them meals. Most contracts cover four to six hours of music; after that, overtime rates apply.

BOOKING A BAND

Ask to hear a live performance of groups you're considering; many invite potential customers to eavesdrop on other events. But keep in mind that at any one occasion, you'll be hearing just a fraction of their repertoire, so ask to listen to clips, watch any videos they may have, and read their song list. In addition, you should get the names of the key band members in writing; groups often resist naming every musician since many use freelancers. This won't matter if you trust the main members to hire others. But if you have your heart set on a certain lead singer, for example, this is where the get-the-names-in-writing comes in handy. Also agree upon the size and type of ensemble, be it a jazz trio or a 30-piece orchestra. The break policy is important, too: Specify how many they will take and for how long, as well as whether the group plays recorded tunes during their off-stage time, and how many band members you'll need to provide meals for. You can also use the same musicians in different combos throughout the day. Not only does it save money–up to thousands of dollars–it means fewer vendors to coordinate with. One of the members of the reception band could play the flute for the ceremony, another the sax for the cocktail hour, for example. Or, you could pair the sax player with the band's pianist to perform as a jazz duo during drinks and appetizers.

———

A Twirl Wind Romance As a live band plays, professional dancers Tiler Peck and Robert Fairchild of the New York City Ballet tear up the floor at their reception in Manhattan's High Line Hotel.

BOOKING A DJ

As with live musicians, see a DJ in action. Either check him out in person or get a sample CD and listen for the vibe, the mix, and the transitions between songs. Inquire about the equipment–he or she should definitely have a microphone, two 15-inch speakers, and turntables or CDJs (disc-juggler players) for mixing. And every good DJ can mix and beat-match, which means blending records together seamlessly. Once you find one you like, your contract should guarantee that the DJ won't leave for another event if you need him or her to stay beyond the scheduled end of the reception. While a DJ's primary function is to play music continuously–unlike bands, disc jockeys don't take breaks, although they, too, need to be fed–he often acts as a kind of host, introducing the bride and groom, announcing the toasts, inviting the guests to come onto the dance floor, and signaling the cake cutting. The best DJ will handle these key moments in a way that accomplishes the mission without calling undue attention to himself. That said, you may prefer to have no formal announcements at all at your reception, instead having the DJ simply play music and fade quietly into the background. Whatever your preferences, down to specific song requests and what he should wear, make sure they're known well before the big day and specified in the contract.

SAVVY SPENDING: MUSIC

When hiring entertainment for your wedding, any one of these clever cost-cutting measures is sure to be music to your ears.

Hire students: Rather than going with a pricey string quartet for your ceremony or cocktails, call a music school and ask them to recommend an experienced student group.

Break up the band: If you're set on a reception band that's out of your price range, inquire if they'll downsize. Large ensembles with lots of members often offer a condensed version at a smaller price tag.

Go for quality over quantity: Secure a four-piece group that sings and plays multiple instruments. That versatility will make them sound like an eight-piece outfit.

Hook up your iPod: With the help of DJ-minded apps, it's easier than ever to program everything you need, from a wedding march to the perfect cocktail-hour playlist, all with professional-sounding results.

LIGHTING IT UP

MUSIC ISN'T THE ONLY WAY TO SET THE MOOD FOR A FABULOUS PARTY. LIGHTING IS AN IMPACTFUL TOOL TO CAMOUFLAGE THINGS YOU WANT TO HIDE, HIGHLIGHT THINGS YOU WANT TO ACCENTUATE, AND CREATE A FESTIVE VIBE. TURN TO A LIGHTING DESIGNER TO TRANSFORM A BARE-BONES VENUE INTO AN UTTERLY WEDDING-WORTHY SPACE.

Do you need a lighting designer? That depends, both on your venue and your budget. However, a good one can turn a spare space with little atmosphere into a warm, inviting, romantic dream come true. The trick is to find someone who specializes in the style you like. If you're aiming for a cozy atmosphere, don't hire someone known for LEDs and holograms. But if you do want to go high-tech, with touches such as neon and strobe lights, search for a professional with that skill set. Ask your planner or venue coordinator for referrals, and when you meet with prospective companies, request pictures of events they've done. While it can be hard to evaluate lighting by looking at photos, it will give you a general sense of a designer's aesthetic.

What type of magic can you expect from these experts? Situating uplights to play up unique architectural details like columns; projecting oversize images, such as a monogram or patterned design, onto blank walls; installing dimmers or putting filters over existing lights for a softer effect; suspending hurricane lamps, vine balls, lanterns, or chandeliers from the top of a tent; and adding washes of color to different areas of the room. Finally, of course, they can make everyone, from the bride and groom to their grandparents, look absolutely smashing.

All Aglow At an alfresco affair on the Greek island of Spetses, dinner was illuminated by twinkling lights strung in the olive trees and candles lining the tables.

Hiring a Caterer

Wedding fare no longer means the easiest food to make for a crowd—namely a choice of beef or chicken. You can serve a downright delicious meal that guests will actually rave about.

Once you have a vague idea of the timing of your event (a lunch? dinner? cocktail reception?), then it's time to figure out who's doing the cooking. Your location may come with a kitchen and chef (and definitely will if it's a restaurant or banquet hall). But in a raw space, or other type of non-food-focused venue, you'll have to find a caterer yourself. In that situation, word of mouth is everything. Ask friends for recommendations. Also, research which companies have exclusive arrangements at notable venues in your area; those are tried-and-true picks. With that list in hand, look at their websites to see their work; each caterer has a niche or style that makes him or her special. Then, set up an appointment and pose the relevant questions: Does your caterer provide his own staff? Will she oversee rentals (tables, china, glasses, linens, etc.)? If you're celebrating in a raw space, is the caterer comfortable working in a makeshift kitchen? Verify that your point person throughout the planning process will be there on the day of, and request a cost breakdown before you sign a contract—one that includes taxes and fees, so there are no surprises in the end.

You'll also want to test-drive the food. Nowadays, most caterers will offer a sampling even before you've hired them, in order to give you a feel for their culinary style. Otherwise, you'll have at least one free tasting after you've signed a contract and have a rough idea of what the menu will be. Keep in mind that if you plan on using seasonal ingredients, your tasting might have to be closer to your wedding day (as little as a few weeks in advance).

After you've signed a contract, many caterers require a deposit of up to 50 percent, with the remaining balance due the day of the event.

Others need 80 or 90 percent of the fee when you provide the final head count. The remaining charges, which may fluctuate based on the length of the party and the amount of liquor consumed, are billed after the wedding. Speaking of liquor, be sure to inquire if your caterer will provide bartenders. If not, see if the caterer works with a bartending vendor who can take on those duties (note: buying your own alcohol and paying a corkage fee will likely be less expensive than serving what your venue offers). One last tip: Request that your caterer pack food for you for after the wedding. A boxed meal will be welcome when it's two in the morning and you realize you've been so busy greeting guests that you haven't eaten in hours.

SPENDING SAVVY: FOOD & DRINK

AN AMAZING MEAL DOESN'T HAVE TO BREAK YOUR BUDGET. HERE, OUR FAVORITE WAYS TO CUT COSTS AND KEEP FLAVOR.

- Go for local ingredients, which are inexpensive and often abundant. Fill up on seasonal produce that can also look bountiful on tables.

- Instead of filet, offer flatiron steaks, which tend to be less pricy.

- Use expensive ingredients, such as lobster, in hors d'oeuvres rather than in a main course.

- Serve prosecco rather than Champagne for toasting.

- Check into wine that's available in magnums (bottles double the size of regular ones). You'll save on two counts: It costs less per ounce, and the corkage fee will go twice as far.

MAKE THE OFFERINGS PERSONAL

Your parents, grandparents, or future in-laws may have outdated ideas of what type of fare adds up to a "nice wedding." ("There has to be prime rib!" "We must offer three choices!" "Two words: carving station.") While it's always thoughtful to take your relatives' opinions into account, the truth is that these days, the "nicest" weddings with the most memorable menus are those that reflect the bride and groom as a couple. Think about basing a meal on childhood favorites, family recipes, or what you ate on your first date or on a special vacation. Or, incorporate a dish from your favorite restaurant. If two cultures are coming together, serve a dish from each as a starter; after all, food is about community and culture as much as it is about taste.

DON'T FORGET GUESTS

Your tastes should be the biggest priority, but remember that your loved ones might have dietary restrictions. In some cases, this will be obvious given the people involved (if the groom's family keeps kosher, nix the raw bar; if the bride's relatives are vegetarian Hindus, re-think the carving station). But in other instances, it comes down to individuals and their food allergies or religious beliefs (which they should let you know on their reply card). As a general rule, for passed hors d'oeuvres, half of the items should be vegetarian or gluten-free. Also, don't go too spicy; have hot sauce available (or on the side) so guests can bring on the heat themselves.

With a Twist Even the waitstaff got into the color scheme during this backyard affair at a Michigan estate, donning custom jackets in the event's robin's-egg, tangerine, and fuchsia palette. They—and the cucumber martinis they offered—made a welcome sight for guests.

Planning the Cocktail Hour

Predinner offerings are a fantastic way to get the party started (even if you're off having photos snapped first). Follow a few of these tips and guests will be enjoying themselves in no time!

THINK AHEAD

What you serve during cocktail hour should feel cohesive with the meal to come—and it's a fun way to share what you love as a couple. Perhaps you prefer a cheese table instead of passed appetizers, or you want to incorporate a theme, like tapas that correspond with dinner and act as a preview for your honeymoon in Spain.

GO BIG TO GO SMALL

Major taste can come in mini packages, and here, it's all about how you pack flavor into a small bite. Cocktail hour is a good time to serve less-familiar dishes, like Grandma's spicy meatballs, which may be too bold a choice for the main course, but are perfect in bite-size form.

FOLLOW THE ONE-BITE RULE

Passed appetizers should be one mouthful's worth, for ease of eating, variety, and to save your guests' party attire from stains. As a general rule, plan on at least four hors d'oeuvres per person. Cheese, antipasti, or other stations are lovely, but having more than two or three can create more crowding than convenience. If you do have stations, set up a few where people can pick up a nibble that doesn't need utensils, like dim sum or sliced filet on toasts.

COCKTAIL-HOUR FLAVORS

Surefire cocktail-hour winners include toast or a cracker with creamy cheese and something sweet (think fruit preserves) as a vegetarian treat; something substantial in mini size (like a slider or crab cake) for hungry guests; a chilled soup served in a shot glass during warm-weather months (or a warm one in cooler months); and french fries in cones to appeal to kids (and grown-up kids, too).

SKIP THE CASH BAR

When you invite people to an event, they shouldn't have to reach for their wallets for any reason. That doesn't

mean you have to offer a top-shelf full bar; a more price-conscious limited selection is just fine. What that may be is up to you (and what you think your guests will like). Note that serving only wine and beer isn't always a cheaper option; it can end up being less economical if you are hosting a crowd that prefers hard alcohol. You only get 5 or 6 drinks per bottle of wine, but 18 to 20 from a bottle of hard liquor (and a veteran vodka soda drinker may have a couple of cocktails in an evening, but several glasses of wine if their preferred tipple isn't available). That said, limiting your bar to beer, wine, and either a signature sipper or a few hard liquors is more affordable than a full bar.

BUY YOUR OWN BOOZE

If your venue allows, purchase alcohol yourself. Even with a corkage fee, it'll save cash. Pick two clear liquors (gin, tequila, or vodka), two brown (bourbon or rye, scotch, or dark rum), add two kinds of beer (one lighter, and one on the fuller side), and at least one red, one white, and one sparkling wine, plus a rosé in summer or hot climates. Also, do your math: one drink per person per hour.

HAVE A SIGNATURE SIP

Offering a drink that defines the day isn't just a fun way to show personality. It can also be a cost-cutter when compared to a full bar, if you offer just beer, wine, and this one cocktail (to please the most people, choose a drink with a vodka base). But be warned: Passing a signature cocktail when there is a full bar available, too, can blow up your budget. It's human nature to take a glass that's offered to you, and many guests will put it down after a sip, then go to the bar to order what they want. For the most affordable cocktail hour, have waiters stationed around the room with trays of wine, champagne, water, and sparkling water, and let guests go to the bar for everything else, including the specialty drink, which can be described on a sign.

IT'S NOT ALL ABOUT THE BOOZE

Be sure to offer nonalcoholic options for guests who don't drink and any kids who attend. One idea: Have your bar service make a virgin version of your signature cocktail.

Cool Idea A booze-free Guava Spritzer (guava juice and sparkling water) is even more refreshing when passed on an ice-filled tray studded with flowers. Each glass has matching ice cubes and a monogrammed stir stick.

Taking a Seat

Creating a guest list is one challenge; making seating arrangements for attendees is quite another. Keep it simple and seamless with these suggestions.

You've got three options: no seating arrangements at all (fine for a cocktail reception, but confusing for seated meals); assigning guests to a specific seat at a particular table; or, a compromise, placing guests at a table and letting them pick their chair. Whichever you choose should depend on the mix of people you have and the style of the party you want to throw (seating guests at an assigned place being the most formal). If you opt for either of the latter two options, here's how to let guests know where to pull up a chair.

1. Seat yourselves first. No matter what style of seating you choose, the bride and groom are the most important people at a wedding, so figure out where you'll sit and go from there. We don't recommend "sweetheart tables" for two, as they can be isolating and discourage guests from coming up to offer congratulations. Decide whether you want to sit with your families (a nice way to spend some time with them on a busy day) or your wedding party (a smart choice if one or both of you has divorced parents, or your folks want to sit with their friends at a table near yours).

2. Focus on relatives. Your friends will probably be the easiest to place; they'll naturally fall into groups who know each other from high school, college, summer camp, work, and the like. Leave them for last and tackle your extended family (and parents' friends) next. Let your folks weigh in on who should be seated with whom, and try to sit people with similar interests together (your dad's business partner might enjoy talking golf with your groom's Uncle Harold). Place children with their parents (it might make everyone's life easier), although if you have a large group of teenagers, they might enjoy a table of their own.

3. Don't single out singletons. When seating your friends, try to strike a balance of letting old pals catch up and introducing people who might get along. Resist the temptation to seat all the unattached guests together in the hopes of forging a love connection; it will make everyone feel pressured. Instead, aim for a mix of couples and singles. And while etiquette recommends splitting up married couples at dinner parties (so everyone can talk to someone they might not otherwise), at a romantic event like this, married pairs want to sit together (and maybe reminisce about their wedding).

4. Take special needs into account. Older guests, who may be more unlikely to dance, don't want to be near the band where they'll get caught in a scrum of youngsters rushing the dance floor. To keep everyone comfortable, don't overcrowd tables, and, if you're having long rectangular tables, split them up with walkways in between so that no one has to hike a long distance to get to an exit or the bathroom.

5. Play with shapes. You can absolutely mix round and square tables to vary the look and seating possibilities at your party. Round tables make it easier for guests to speak to people other than their seatmates and are more flexible when it comes to last-minute adjustments, while rectangular ones feel like a more intimate dinner party.

6. Spread the word. Once you've decided who sits where, you'll need to let them know where to go. Escort cards are practical, because they guide guests to their table, but they can—and should—be pretty, too. And they can even do double duty as favors if you attach a tag with table numbers onto a gift box, potted plant, or some other treat. You can also make an eye-catching display listing names and table numbers (we've seen chalkboards, paintings, even embroidered wall hangings), but whatever you choose, arrange names in alphabetical order so they're easily found; no matter how beautiful a display is, if it's arranged by table, it's time consuming for guests.

Seat Yourself (clockwise from top): Prize-ribbon escort cards made a nice showing at a racetrack-themed event. A modern party featured a mobile composed of gem-shaped "cards" cut from clear lucite. For her outdoor Santa Barbara wedding, the bride made hundreds of paper flowers for the escort cards and table numbers. Magnifying glass paper weights double as escort cards and favors.

Focusing on the Food

Be it brunch, lunch, or dinner, your main meal should feel cohesive, look divine, and taste delicious, no matter how it's served.

PICK A SERVING STYLE

There are a variety of ways to deliver food to your guests, and each one sets a different tone and comes with a different price tag. For example, Food stations can give off a party vibe, sit-down dinners are the most traditional and suited for black-tie events, and family-style affairs can fit a rustic event in a barn or dinner at a farm-to-table or Italian restaurant. Likewise, buffets are a versatile approach that can work any time of day and go upscale or low-key. Each style will also impact the timing of your party in its own way (remember, when it comes to served meals, allot at least a half hour per course). Here, some options to ponder.

Plate Service

A common choice for sit-down meals, this involves offering food in courses presented on individual plates. It's a standard way to serve classic cuisine that appeals to a large audience. The cost of this type of service will be higher than a family-style dinner because a caterer might require as many as ten cooks and three times as much waitstaff to prepare and serve two hundred plates of the same dish. Also, if your venue isn't a restaurant or banquet hall, there are rental costs to factor in; each course comes on a new plate and uses a different utensil, which can add up. Plate service may or may not cost more than a buffet, depending on the selections being offered at each; if you're torn between the two, work out the potential cost per head for each with your caterer before deciding.

French Service

This is a more traditional (as in, dating back to the Middle Ages) version of plate service. The dinner still comes in courses, but it is not brought to the table on individual plates. Instead, each course is arranged on a large serving dish and carried to guests at the table. In the most traditional form of French service, the guests serve themselves from the platter with tongs or a fork and spoon. However, at most weddings these days, the waiter dishes out the food. This service doesn't require as much help in the kitchen because there are fewer plates to put together, but you will need nearly as many servers as with conventional plated service.

Family Style

Another alternative is to have wait staff set food out on each dinner table on big platters and let guests serve themselves. The experience can be as cozy as the name, and "pass the potatoes, please" is always a good conversation starter. While this is a more casual type of service, the food can be as indulgent as you like. It need only hold up over time, which calls for dishes that taste good at room temperature. Comfort foods work well here–think braised ribs, roasted vegetables, and luscious salads of baby greens, soft cheeses, and nuts. Less staff is also needed than with plated service, so family style is usually the most economical choice for a seated dinner.

Buffet

A buffet is a good choice for both finicky eaters and crowds that love to eat. It can include many different dishes and nearly any style of cuisine. Guests can serve themselves (choosing from foods that hold up well over a heat source or at room temperature), or you can have servers offer items that are carved, such as roast turkey, or prepared to order, like omelets or pasta. Though a buffet requires a smaller staff, the cost is often more than plate or French service because the caterer makes more food (and is often saddled with more leftovers). It can also require more rental equipment, such as chafing dishes.

Fine Fare Martha hosted her nephew's wedding, an afternoon picnic-style celebration, on her farm. Guests helped themselves to marinated hanger steak, sliced soppressata, olives, roasted vegetables, and a variety of flatbreads.

Stations

If you want a variety of cuisine, stations set up with particular types of food are a good solution, whether you're having a heavy-appetizers-and-cocktails reception or a seated dinner. A station reception should have four or five tables, and each may offer a different style of cuisine: Japanese noodles, Italian antipasto, and Middle Eastern meze are all fair game. On-the-spot cooking, like grilling, is always interesting. Or, have guests get in on the action, assembling their own tacos or mixing ceviche. The drawbacks? Coordinating stations can be complicated, and with so many options, food and rental costs can be high.

CREATE A MENU

With a delivery style in place, you can focus specifically on what to offer. More so than cocktail bites, the dishes in the main meal should feel like they belong together. For example, fish tacos may not go well with spaghetti carbonara, although each is delectable on its own. For a three-course seated dinner, start with a soup or salad, then go into the main entrée (a protein paired with vegetables), followed by dessert. If the meal is plated, and your main dish is one carefully chosen entrée—say, local lamb raised on the ranch where you're getting hitched, or your favorite paella—have the caterer prepare alternatives for those who might have dietary restrictions, including vegetarians. If you're offering options at a sit-down meal, ask your guests to choose meat (or fish or fowl) or vegetarian on their reply card. (This is also their chance to explain any more complicated dietary restrictions.) And if you're doing a buffet or family-style dinner, offer enough selections for vegetarians, vegans (this option will also please the lactose-intolerant), and carnivores alike. As for more specific food issues, if a guest has a serious allergy, the onus is on him or her to warn you well in advance so you can pass the news on to your caterer ahead of time. On the other hand, if he just happens to hate, say, blue cheese, he can keep that to himself and politely decline any appetizers containing the offending ingredient.

DON'T FORGET DESSERT

Will your caterer provide a dessert in addition to the wedding cake (which may come from a different vendor)? If you're deciding against a cake (or you want a dessert table in addition to one) talk over all the alternative options—an assortment of pies, a cookie or candy bar, or a pastry-filled "Viennese table"—with your caterer and decide who's providing these sweets. For more ideas, see page 222.

THE KIDS' TABLE

CATERING TO THE YOUNGSTERS IN THE CROWD CAN MAKE YOU FEEL AS LIGHTHEARTED AS A KID YOURSELF! DECIDE EARLY IF YOU ARE INCLUDING LITTLES AT YOUR PARTY, AND IF YOU ARE, KEEP THESE THINGS IN MIND.

Adjust the menu: Unless the tykes you know happen to have palates that are refined enough for filet, serve kid-friendly dishes like pasta or chicken tenders to the younger set. Sometimes these can be adapted from your menu—for instance, a pasta dish for the adults can often carry over to the kids. Children 13 and older should be able to eat adult fare, though you may want to ask the parents ahead of time what the child's preference would be (and save yourself the cost of an adult meal if chicken fingers are preferred).

Provide entertainment: Stocking the table with games or crafts is a smart way to keep them happy. Maybe their menus are coloring books, or you provide an "I Spy" game with prompts like, "I Spy a White Dress" or "I Spy a Pair of Sparkly Shoes."

Get sitters: When the youngsters crash (which is bound to happen), it's a good idea to have a sitter on-site to watch the kids while their parents celebrate. The adults will also thank you.

All in the Family Passing dishes and different courses around a table is a nice way for guests to break bread—and get to know one another.

Toasting the Night

When done right, public congratulations can be the most heartfelt and fun element of your party. Ensure that your toasts get "awws" and not "oh mys" with these suggestions.

THE
TRADITION
TOASTING

———

In wedding toasts, the glass is raised with the right hand and held straight out from the shoulder. It's believed that, way back when, this position proved to guests that the person giving the toast had come unarmed and in friend-ship. (This was particularly an issue in Medieval times, when it wasn't unusual to find weapons concealed in the folds of clothing.) The clinking sound of a toast is thought to scare off evil spirits.

TOAST WITH THE MOST

Encourage spur-of-the-moment speeches at the rehearsal dinner so that the reception includes only words from the host, the best man and maid of honor, and the newly-weds. There are two traditional orders of toasting. The best man may start by toasting the couple, followed by the groom toasting the bride and both sets of parents, and the bride toasting the groom and the parents, if she wishes, then the father of the bride, as traditionally the host, toasts the guests. Alternatively, the host welcomes his guests in the first speech of the night. Then the best man (next on the lineup) toasts the happy couple. A toast by the maid of honor might follow, then the groom toasting his bride (who can return the gesture if she so desires).

Whether you stick to a classic order or plan to mix it up, decide ahead of time who will be toasting, and let them know when they'll be doing so. Toasts can be given one after the other during cocktail hour, once everyone has a glass in their hand, or after everyone is seated for dinner, perhaps with one toast per course. You can also wait for the cake-cutting if you like, although, if you're concerned that your designated toasters may overindulge, it's a good idea to schedule toasts to take place early in the festivities. Ask the speakers to keep it brief (no more than four minutes) and, most importantly, sincere. Finally, request a hard copy of each toast after the fact–you'll cherish the souvenirs.

SAY A FEW WORDS

While it's not required that the bride and groom speak at their wedding, it can be a wonderful opportunity to interact with all of your guests–something every couple hopes to do, although, inevitably, someone will skip the receiving line or be in the restroom when you stop by the table to say hello. It's also a great way to slow down the pace of the reception and take in all the love of your friends and family members smiling up at you. What to say? It's easy: Just thank people for coming and let them know how much sharing this day with them means to you (it's always a huge crowd-pleaser if the groom says how lucky he is to be marrying the bride–or vice versa, too). If someone besides yourselves is hosting the wedding, thank them for their graciousness. Other than that, the only rules that apply are always to stand when toasting and sit when being toasted, and to not sip from your glass until the toast is over.

ABOUT THE CHAMPAGNE

Pouring a glass of champagne is often thought of as the norm, but really, any drink will do (guests can even raise a glass of whatever they happen to be drinking at the time). And because it increases your budget when you pour each guest a glass of something whether they want it or not, it can be smarter to serve cost-effective prosecco or cava instead of French champagne, especially if you have a soft spot in your heart for Italy or Spain.

Raise a Glass At a winter wedding at a ski resort in Sundance, Utah, revelers toasted the bride and groom.

CHAPTER
ELEVEN

CREATE YOUR CAKE

THE BEST WEDDING CAKES CAN BOTH LOOK AND TASTE UTTERLY SPECTACULAR.

—Wendy Kromer, *Contributing Editor, Martha Stewart Weddings*

ONLY ONE PART OF THE RECEPTION meal is so important that it gets its own spotlit ritual, and that's the show-stopper of all sweets: the wedding cake. The tradition of cutting it is one of those iconic moments that guests expect and photographers can't miss. It's also been that way for hundreds of years. In England in the Middle Ages, couples used to embrace over a collection of tiny cakes brought to the celebration by guests. Today, newlyweds slice the confection toward the end of their reception to start life together with a sweet taste in their mouth—and to send guests off with the same, as older attendees who aren't interested in dancing often consider the cake-cutting to be the symbolic end of the party. Modern cakes look as good as they taste and can be inspired by fashion (with frosting resembling the lace on your dress), art (an homage to your favorite painter), color (your palette), or anything else that catches your fancy. In dreaming up yours, be as creative as you want. Think of the flavors that thrill you and your soon-to-be-spouse, and the type of frosting and decorative elements that would work best in your setting, season, and location. And if you're just not a cake person, ponder an array of pies, a dessert table featuring cookies, cupcakes, and tarts, or even a candy buffet. There's an infinite number of ways to treat guests and end your night on a delicious note.

THE TRADITION SAVING THE TOP TIER

Back in the day, newlyweds kept the top layer of the cake for the christening of their first child, which was anticipated to be a year or so later. (This worked better when wedding desserts were dense, long-lasting fruit-cakes.) Today, many couples—especially those not planning to become parents right away—put the top tier in the freezer for their first anniversary, or even for their first-month anniversary (decreasing the chance of freezer burn). If you're thinking of doing either, talk to your baker, who will have advice on wrapping and storing the tier.

Imagining Your Cake

You'll want to take into account the weather, location, and style of your wedding as you make your decision. The first step is to dream big, thinking of your favorite flavors, objects, fashions, and customs, with a baker who can make it all a reality.

HIRE A BAKER

Start by talking to your caterer: Some don't bake at all, others require that they provide the dessert, and still others make cakes but will allow you to use an outside baker and charge a cutting fee to plate that vendor's confection. (If you shop around, the latter may even end up being cheaper than ordering from your caterer.) Next, ask your venue manager, photographer, videographer, and any recently married friends for recommendations, as they will likely have tasted a lot of cakes.

Once you have names, see if the candidates are available to make a cake for your date and what the approximate cost would be for a guest list of your size (most bakers charge per slice). Then ask to view a portfolio of their work, and whether you can arrange an appointment for a tasting. (If the answer's no, move on!) While some bakers schedule only group tastings for several couples a few times a year, others will let you try cupcakes or other mini treats that are representative of cake flavors. Whatever the case may be, you should absolutely try something before signing on the dotted line. Tastings may be complimentary, or there may be a charge that goes toward the cost of the cake if you hire the baker. Since everyone's palate is different, attend your tasting together (or if one of you can't make it, bring a friend; you want at least two opinions). Answer any questions the baker has—beyond how many guests you have and the time, date, and locale of your event (location is key as weather will guide the choice of your frosting); a good baker will want to know the colors and theme for your wedding, whether you want a stacked or pillared cake, and what your dress looks like.

After you settle on a professional, the fun part: choosing cake flavors, fillings, frostings, and decorative touches. Ingredients will affect the cost—fondant is slightly more expensive than buttercream as a frosting, and complicated décor techniques will up the price as well. Only once those are agreed upon should you sign a contract (at which point you usually pay a 50 percent deposit). The document should include the design elements you discussed, cost per person, delivery time, directions to the reception, and all contact phone numbers. Make sure you're aware of any extras—some bakers charge a per-mile surcharge after a set distance from their shop.

DREAM IT UP

Maybe you've got a picture of your cake in mind. (White buttercream with real flowers on the top. Or, chocolate painted with gold sheaves of wheat. Or, pale pink fondant to match the roses in your bouquet.) But if you're starting from zero, look for inspiration in your wedding details, such as your palette, flowers, the design on your dress, or even your new married monogram (how pretty would that look piped onto your cake?). If you are still swooning over your invitations, conceive your cake décor around a motif used in your stationery (a flower, a pattern, a knot, a ring—the possibilities are endless).

MAKE IT MOUTHWATERING

Don't just focus on the look of the confection; the taste is just as important. Think of your favorite desserts (yes, your baker can make a cake inspired by caramel apples—or Kit Kats!). If you're sentimental, incorporate flavors that reflect your heritage, such as Mexican *tres leches* cake or traditional British fruitcake.

The Pink of Perfection Snow-white royal icing was hand piped in lacelike patterns onto the pastel frosting of this five-tiered beauty.

THE TIMELINE
CAKE

——

6–12 MONTHS AHEAD
Seek inspiration, research bakers.

3–6 MONTHS AHEAD
Book the baker, have a tasting, and decide on flavors, fillings, and frosting.

1 WEEK AHEAD
Drop off cake topper or any décor elements (except fresh flowers). The remainder of the payment for the cake is often due at this time.

Picking Flavors

In 17th-century France, the first tiered wedding confection was invented when a baker frosted a stack of buns. Today, any look—and certainly any flavor—goes. Here, a primer of tempting options for both the base and fillings of your masterpiece.

1

CHOOSE A CAKE FLAVOR (OR TWO)

Can't decide between red velvet or marble? You don't have to. Since wedding cakes are made up of several tiers, and each tier may be composed of multiple layers, it's possible to mix two or three flavors. You can even put two varieties, like white and chocolate layers, on repeat, or concoct a triple threat with chocolate, yellow, and red velvet. (For recipes, visit marthastewartweddings.com.)

WHITE BUTTER
The most traditional option, this works well with any filling or frosting. We love it with passion-fruit filling or vanilla Swiss meringue buttercream.

YELLOW
Richer than white butter cake, this is another classic choice that tastes great with virtually any pairing.

ALMOND DACQUOISE
A dense, nut-based cake makes an unexpected complement to basic layers like white butter, and is delicious with chocolate fillings. Display the flavors on a menu or card.

LEMON POPPY SEED
A refreshing choice for a summer wedding, it's best when joined with lemon curd, lemon buttercream, or white chocolate buttercream frosting.

CARROT
Spicy, sweet, and sometimes nutty, carrot cake is often coupled with cream cheese icing and is also tasty with fillings like caramel–cream cheese, white chocolate, or vanilla buttercream.

RED VELVET
This flavor relies on cocoa for its chocolaty taste, and red food dye for its dramatic color. Try it with cream cheese frosting, chocolate hazelnut, or caramel buttercream.

MARBLE
Not only does it look cool, but taste-wise, a chocolate-and-yellow option goes with just about everything. It's delectable with fruit flavors, especially raspberry preserves.

CHOCOLATE BUTTER
After white and yellow, chocolate cake is the next most popular wedding flavor. It's typically paired with white or chocolate frosting and makes a nice base for apricot, pistachio, coffee, or caramel fillings.

2 DECIDE ON FILLINGS

Let your taste buds lead the way; fruit, chocolate, or both are common choices, but they're not the only lip-smacking route.

CHOCOLATE GANACHE

This tall, dark, handsome cake filling is fluffy, dense, and oh-so-chocolaty. It makes a nice contrast with white or yellow cake, or ups the ante on an all-chocolate version.

LEMON CURD

Ideal with a light, white cake or a ginger or lemon-poppy base, this thick, creamy, citrusy spread made of lemon juice, egg yolks, and sugar adds a puckery jolt of taste.

CARAMEL SAUCE

Thicker and richer than what's used to top your sundae, the filling version of caramel sauce is suited for flavorful cakes such as chocolate, spice, or pumpkin.

CARAMEL–CREAM CHEESE

A natural partner for apple or chocolate cakes, this sweet, buttery filling also works well with almost any type of butter cake.

CREAM CHEESE ICING

This decadent, creamy filling needs a strongly flavored cake as its base: Think carrot, red velvet, apple spice, or pumpkin.

RASPBERRY PRESERVES

Equal parts tart and sweet, this jellylike filling is great with chocolate, white, yellow, marble, or even almond dacquoise cake.

SWISS MERINGUE BUTTER-CREAM

Fluffy and spreadable, this filling is less sweet than the traditional buttercream on a birthday cake, and works with any cake flavor.

PISTACHIO BUTTER-CREAM

The same great buttercream base, whipped with ground pistachios or canned pistachio paste, has a distinct, nutty flavor and a pretty, pale green color.

APRICOT JAM

A traditional filling for petit fours, apricot jam adds a lip-smacking kick to white, almond, or chocolate cake.

CHOCOLATE BUTTER-CREAM

Butter and cream in one delicious substance? What could be better? Oh, that's right. If chocolate were added.

Choosing the Style

Fondant or buttercream? Piping or painting? Deciding on what you want your cake to look like depends on both the designs you love and which kinds will hold up best—whether your day will be sunny, chilly, or something in between.

FONDANT

The most popular choice for wedding frostings, thanks to its clean finish that's easy to decorate, fondant is incredibly versatile. It's not as flavorful as buttercream, however. Most bakers ice cakes with buttercream before layering on fondant, which makes it a bit pricier than plain buttercream but ups the flavor. If you're celebrating outdoors, consider fondant or marzipan, which won't melt or attract bugs like buttercream, ganache, and cream cheese will. Just bear in mind that fondant can get shiny in humidity.

BUTTERCREAM

A rich and creamy crowd-pleaser that helps keep cakes moist, buttercream can be spread smoothly or piped to create designs. It melts quickly, though, so if you're throwing an outdoor summer wedding, opt for fondant or marzipan instead. Or, if you have your heart set on it, ask your baker to cover a thicker coating of buttercream with a layer of protective fondant. That way, you'll get the taste of buttercream, if not the piped look.

MERINGUE

Made by whipping egg whites with sugar, meringue forms retro-looking peaks and swoops as on a lemon pie. It's light, tasty, and nostalgic, but it does not hold up well in humidity. Italian meringue, while slightly more complicated to make than Swiss, is the most stable version. Even still, leaving it for hours in a hot tent in August is not recommended.

MARZIPAN

This costly almond-paste dough is often used to frost fruitcakes, the traditional wedding dessert in England. Its nutty taste makes it a popular filling, and it can be sculpted into decorative trim and shapes such as fruit, flowers, or animals, but it's not practical for frosting larger cakes, as it tends to tear while being rolled out.

GANACHE

A combination of chocolate and cream, this rich delight works as a filling when whipped, or as a glaze that gets poured over a cake for a glossy finish, though it melts too readily for al fresco affairs. Its color can't be altered; if you love the taste but want a white or colored cake, use it as a filling or to frost a groom's cake.

PIPING

A talented baker wielding a pastry bag can shape royal icing into swirls, flowers, even lace patterns. Elaborate piping requires a strong foundation of marzipan or fondant so the cake holds up through the hours-long decorating process and the party. This labor can be costly.

MOLDING

Ideal for creating architectural designs and ornate details, this technique involves a baker who works with sugar paste or fondant shaped in silicone molds. She may be able to make a new one based on a design you like; otherwise, many pastry chefs use molds that create flowers, leaves, and lacelike patterns.

SCULPTING

Bakers can create individual flowers or fruits that are each unique and gorgeous by sculpting sugar paste by hand. Unlike real flowers, these confections hold up in the heat and taste sweet and delicious. Note that the intense handiwork adds to your cake budget.

PAINTING

The talented artists who hand-paint cakes can be hard to find and costly to hire, but this decorative technique turns a cake into a work of art. They take a brush to a cake (using vodka mixed with petal dust, a food-safe pigment), and the results are breathtaking.

Finding Inspiration

If you learn one thing from us, we hope it's that style ideas for your wedding can be found just about anywhere. For your cake, reflect on what you love and what excites you. Here are some great places to start.

FLAVORS

Love lemons? Crazy about chocolate? Simply mad for s'mores? Tell your cakemaker, who may be able to imagine a flavor profile that will blow your mind, like this lemon-thyme cake alternating with layers of vanilla buttercream, or a zesty Mexican hot chocolate cake, or a giant s'mores cake made from graham cake layers with chocolate ganache, marshmallows, and vanilla buttercream.

CULTURE

Incorporate the wedding dessert
that is customary in your background
(or commonly served in a country you love),
like this Scandinavian kransekake
wreath cake. Italian *millefoglie*, British
fruitcake, or French *croquembouche*
are other options. You can also bring your
personal histories into the cake-cutting
ceremony itself by using an heirloom
cake knife, such as the one
your parents had on their big day.

ART

One great source of inspiration
for your edible masterpiece? A favorite
painting. Whether you like the romantic look
of French impressionism, the retro
whimsy of pop art, or the deep, rich colors
of the Dutch Masters that inspired
this beauty, an artful cake is sure to be
a feast for the eyes.

COLOR

The majority of wedding cakes, like most wedding gowns, are white (and absolutely breathtaking). But there's no reason they have to embrace alabaster. A stunning confection can be gold or hot pink, or covered in chocolate–and sometimes what's on the outside (pale yellow fondant) hints at the beauty within (delicious lemon cake). Behold the pink and peach confections on this page.

TEXTILES

Whether it's your gorgeous gown or Grandma's heirloom hankie, a fabric can serve as a fabulous starting point for cake décor. If there's an element of your dress that you just can't get enough of, such as ruffles, lace, or flowers, have it make a repeat appearance on your cake. Or, draw a design idea from a childhood quilt, vintage curtains, or any beloved pattern. Above left, burlap was pressed into fondant to make it resemble the texture of canvas, and the cake was festooned in fabric flowers. Adornments on the confection at right are made of molded sugar paste to resemble appliqués from a dress.

CHINA

Your cake can also take a cue from your favorite china pattern. These petite cakes, each serving about four people, make an exquisite statement on their Nymphenburg saucers.

SEASONAL

Whatever time of year you marry, it will be extra-special to you from here on out. Celebrate the natural beauty of the season. You might highlight snow in winter, like the marzipan-covered tiers on the opposite page, which are dusted in powdered sugar and adorned with gum paste snowdrops. Or you could play up the leaves, branches, and colors of fall, or the first buds of spring. The *millefoglie* cake (on this page), composed of puff pastry, lemon-flavored pastry cream, and fresh fruit, makes the most of the bounty of summer by overflowing with ripe red currants and juicy raspberries.

Spending Savvy: Cakes

Your cake can enthrall and amaze your guests without shocking and destroying your budget. Consider these ways to save on your sweet scene-stealer.

GOOD TO KNOW

Don't look to cut costs by avoiding delivery fees and picking up your cake yourself (or having a friend with a truck do it). Bakers possess custom-built vehicles and have lots of experience transporting these fragile beauties. Plus, they know how to do repairs should something go wrong. If anyone else transports the cake and damages it, the baker bears no responsibility–and whoever caused the casualty will feel too terrible to enjoy the wedding.

GO SHORT

Building a tall cake is extra work for the baker, so the more height, the higher the price tag. If you want each layer to be the real thing, keep your cake to three tiers or less.

OR FAKE A BIG TALL ONE

If you fancy the look of a four-tier–or higher–confection, ask your baker to decorate a few faux tiers, with only two of them being real so that there's something to cut. Then have the kitchen serve from a sheet cake behind the scenes.

COMMIT TO THE CAKE

Instead of having a cake as well as a separate dessert that your caterer serves (or even a sweets buffet), let your cake be your one and only dessert course. By the time the meal's over, everyone will have eaten their fill, and if you've got a roomful of guests who still crave more sugar, you can always offer candy as a favor.

SERVE AN ALTERNATIVE

It's perfectly okay to skip cake–or to cut a small, ceremonial tier and offer guests a different sweet instead. In fact, it can be exciting (and economical) to serve something else equally stunning and unexpected. Pies, for example, are a delicious and affordable option; set up a buffet with pies displayed on cake stands, including a few eye-catching versions piled high with meringue, and no one will miss the cake. Other crowd-pleasing choices that can make dramatic visual impact without breaking the bank include marshmallows, cupcakes, crispy rice bars, and cotton candy.

DRESS UP DESSERT

While we don't recommend baking your cake–you'll have enough to do in the days leading up to your wedding and you don't want to stress over that–there are a few easy ways to decorate your cake yourself (or ask your caterer to do the honors). Order a plain white cake from a baker, for example, then accessorize it for major impact (this is also a great option if you're getting hitched in a remote area where bakers are scarce, or you simply haven't found one whose work you like). Add a few gorgeous sugar paste flowers, but use them sparingly as they can be pricey. Or opt for inexpensive extras, such as real blooms, candy, or ribbons. (One caveat: When decorating with fresh flowers, make sure they're the edible kind or placed in a cake vase that prevents them from touching the dessert itself.)

TOP IT OFF

Pick a plain cake, then find a fabulous topper and let that become the wow factor. In 1840, Queen Victoria (the original wedding trendsetter) and her groom, Prince Albert, had their lilliputian likenesses placed atop their wedding cake, and the bride and groom cake topper was born. Other classic options include doves–which were thought to foretell a lifetime of bliss if seen in the sky on a wedding day–or bells, used by ancient brides to ward off evil spirits. You could also opt for a snappy saying (like *Just Married* or *Whoopee!*) or your new shared monogram.

Pretty Pleats Sugar paste, royal icing, and fresh flowers aren't the only ways to adorn a cake; this four-tiered geometric wonder is decorated with folded origami paper, which won't wilt, melt, or make a big dent in your budget.

Creating a Dessert Table

If you have a sweet tooth, more is more when it comes to a good finish.
And in that case, a lavish display of small treats instead of (or in addition to) a cake
may appeal to you. Take a look at this eye candy.

Whether you choose to let them have their cake and eat something, too, or to skip the tiers altogether, guests will be tickled at the very sight of a dessert buffet (also known as a "Viennese table," because many European pastries are called "Viennoiserie"). Setting up a sweets table can be easy as pie (or cupcakes, or macarons) if you keep a few tips in mind.

AIM FOR VARIETY

When you're going for pies, cookies, candy, or all of the above, you'll want a range of flavors, ideally six to eight different options.

KEEP IT COHESIVE

It doesn't matter which desserts you choose, as long as the sweets are presented in a similar way. That means the packaging (if needed) and signage should all be in your day's color palette and employ the same fonts.

CREATE A CANDYLAND

A candy bar stirs guests with childlike delight–and can be an impressive but cost-effective array. Plan on six to eight ounces per person.

FILL 'ER UP

Appoint someone on the catering staff to monitor the display and refill when certain areas get low.

ASSIGN DESSERT DOUBLE DUTY

Put out custom bags or boxes and let guests pack up some of the sweets as a to-go treat, turning the goodies into favors as well.

MAKE IT MOVE

A dessert buffet isn't your only option for multiple sweets. You could make dessert a movable feast and have mini ice cream cones passed on trays, for example, or roving carts with doughnuts or Italian ices.

Take Your Pick A color palette (on these pages, think pink!) is what keeps everything on the candy buffet below looking amazing. The same theory applies to the sweets table (opposite), which features raspberry cream cookies, yogurt-covered dried fruit, strawberry tartlets, blackberry gumdrops, fruit-and-poppy-seed pavlovas, raspberry candies, rosé gelée, custom candies, and berry financiers.

Fine Finishes On this page, the sweets table is reimagined with that other divine dessert course: cheese. To set up an appealing array, order a mix of mild and strong flavors, different textures, and cheese made with cow, goat, and sheep's milk (add name tags so guests know what they're diving into). Pair them with breads, stone fruits, and nuts, and display on pedestals of varying heights. **Opposite:** A buffet fits into an outdoor celebration with a marzipan cake stamped with faux-bois finish and a spread of confections covered in green-tinted white chocolate "leaves." Treats include macarons, chocolates, French cannelés, and candied bonbons.

All White Now This dazzling display of snowy treats includes lemon-cream sandwich cookies, ricotta-filled pizzelles, toasted marshmallow milk shakes, coconut macarons, pavlovas topped with cream and white currants, angel food roulade with salted caramel cream, mini panna cotta tarts, *calissons*, mini rum Bundt cakes, and pillow mints.

CHAPTER
TWELVE

PLAN YOUR
SEND-OFF

> **" A THOUGHT-OUT FINISH TO YOUR WEDDING ISN'T JUST A MEMORABLE ENDING TO YOUR PARTY. IT'S ALSO A THRILLING BEGINNING TO YOUR NEXT CHAPTER. "**
>
> — Kate Berry, *Creative Director, Martha Stewart Weddings*

THINK OF YOUR WEDDING as a play, created with love, by you and your groom. You're the stars, but a cast of supporting characters play significant roles as well. There's probably a little drama (naturally), a lot of romance, and likely some comic relief. There's song and dance, and laughter and tears (of the happy variety). And like every proper narrative, there is a beginning, middle, and end. Or, at least, there should be. Many couples focus their creative energy on the first two parts—the ceremony and reception—and forget about the closing chapter. But just like a love story, a wedding deserves a happy ending, too. Giving favors, while not mandatory, is a thoughtful gesture that leaves attendees with a physical reminder of your wedding. These souvenirs don't have to be expensive—many ideas needn't cost more than a few dollars per person—but they can be sweet, either literally or figuratively, and they're a finishing touch to your day. Speaking of finishing touches, make sure to exit your celebration on a high note: You could walk out arm-in-arm under an arch of sparklers held aloft by guests, leave in a horse-drawn carriage with your new spouse by your side, or get behind the wheel of a vintage car decorated with a "Just Married" sign and a garland of tin cans. Whatever you choose, you and your loved ones deserve a memorable conclusion to the party, not just the sight of the house lights going on. And then there's only one thing left to do: Live happily ever after.

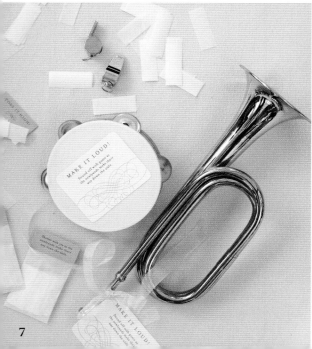

1

2

3

4

5

6

7

8

9

Perfecting the Toss

Love will be thrown at you all day—now consider adding in confetti, petals, or popcorn for a happy toss celebrants can use to mark your walk back up the aisle.

To celebrate the newlyweds' making it official, guests often gather outside the ceremony exit (say, at the front steps to a church) or at the entrance to the reception site and shower the couple with rice, birdseed, flower petals, or confetti while they run past. At a wedding where the ceremony and reception location are one and the same, attendees can get festive as the pair makes their way up the aisle, or at a designated moment when they become man and wife (for example, Greek Orthodox couples are covered in rice or petals as they circle the altar during their vows). Some couples prefer to make their final getaway more dramatic by reserving the toss for their dash from the reception. Whatever you do, delegate the task of passing out what's being tossed to your planner, maid of honor, or another responsible party. Use these ideas for inspiration.

LOOK TO THE SEASON

Spring: Provide fragrant, seasonal, de-stemmed blooms, like cosmos, chamelaucium, or chamomile for a biodegradable, sensational smelling, and package-free option (baskets full of the petals are the simplest vessel).

Summer: Fill small cellophane bags with sunflower seeds and finish them with a rubber stamp for a make-ahead, weather-resistant, and easily transportable option.

Fall: Turn to the surrounding foliage for an autumnal toss that's economical and low-maintenance. Hang leaves packed in paper bags from the back of guests' ceremony chairs or line them up in baskets for a reception toss.

Winter: Escape in a flurry of paper snowflakes in cold-weather shades of white, gray, and silver. Pack handfuls in glassine bags tied with ribbons and marked with monogrammed stickers. While this toss takes a cleanup crew, it's a project that even a rookie crafter can master and calls for only a few simple tools (i.e., paper and scissors).

FIND A FLORAL

Regardless of season, brides love the following buds:

Rose petals: Go traditional by filling paper cones with petals from the flower that's the classic symbol of love (and available year-round). Stand the cones in a tissue paper–lined box that bridesmaids or other delegates can prep on the morning of the wedding.

Dried lavender: The fragrant purple buds package beautifully and infuse the surroundings with a breathtaking scent.

Stephanotis: This white star-shaped bloom is readily available in all seasons and symbolizes good luck and happiness in marriage, making it a wedding floral favorite.

PUT PAPER ON DISPLAY

Paper airplanes: Appeal to guests' childlike sides with an aerodynamic plaything made from colorful vellum.

Confetti blast: Whether sparkly, varicolored, or translucent, these bits-o-fun say, "party!" Go for shredded paper, discs, or geometric shapes to suit the mood of your celebration, whether it's in a backyard or ballroom.

Banner wave: Purchase decorative paper and long, thin dowels to craft wands attendees can wave. Guests keep the memento, and the farewell is completely mess-free!

OPT FOR AN ALTERNATIVE

Make a joyful noise: Give guests tiny bells or other noisemakers to surround you with a cheerful sound.

Let it go: Organize a balloon release, handing adults and children alike a helium filled one attached to a string. When they release it, their good wishes will soar skyward.

Break out the bubbles: The soap kind, that is. Provide invitees with individual bottles and corresponding wands.

Get sparkling: At an evening wedding, invite guests to light sparklers as you exit. To have the festive rods double as a favor, tie a few together and offer them with a keepsake printed matchbox or matchbook.

It's a Toss-Up! 1. A San Francisco bride filled glassine bags with biodegradable confetti. 2. Glassine flowers and tissue dots rained down upon this Tennessee pair. 3. Customized paper bags served as programs and held popcorn to toss at the bride and groom. 4. City regulations prohibit tossing confetti at city hall, so friends showered them at their reception site. 5. Stamped paper packets of rice at a destination celebration in Ireland. 6. As a New York duo left the church, loved ones showered them with on-palette red and white confetti. 7. A New Orleans couple gave attendees at their Caribbean destination affair the tools to make some noise. 8. Oversize circles of confetti announced the arrival of this twosome. 9. At a wedding in Texas, attendees waved homemade pennants.

THE TRADITION THE TOSS

Long popular in the United States, tossing rice is an ancient custom that symbolizes showering the couple with wishes for fertility and prosperity. (Rest assured, rice is safe for birds to eat.) If you don't want to use the grain, borrow these worldly symbols of abundance: In France people throw wheat after the ceremony; in medieval England, it was pieces of cake made of wheat. Italians scatter candy and sugared nuts over newlyweds for a sweet marriage, while ancient Romans and Greeks tossed nuts, dates, and seed-bearing plants.

Gifting Favors

While takeaways are completely optional, they are a gracious gesture that your loved ones will undoubtedly appreciate—and one last chance to personalize your day.

THE
TIMELINE
FAVORS

———

4-6 MONTHS AHEAD

Choose favors; arrange getaway transportation for the wedding day

AT LEAST 1 WEEK AHEAD

Assemble and package favors (if they're not perishable; if they are, delegate day-before or day-of assembly to your caterer or other helpers).

1 DAY AHEAD

Deliver favors to venue

Confirm getaway arrangements

The good news: Favors don't have to be pricey to feel personal. Even dragées—sugar-coated almond candies customarily given at Italian weddings to ensure health, wealth, long life, happiness, and fertility—can feel special when selected in your colors and beautifully wrapped. If you want something less traditional, you're in luck, because these days anything goes. Food (biscuits, preserves, and local delicacies), drinks (think specialty teas, local bottled drinks, or half bottles of wine), and home goods (candles, matches, even soaps) all make great parting gifts. Or, offer a donation to a charity in your guests' honor.

SMART STRATEGIES

In addition to all the ideas in this chapter, consider these tactics when putting together your parting gifts.

Make it: If you have time—and friends willing to roll up their sleeves—cook or bake an edible treat. You'll cut costs, and your guests will (quite literally) eat them up! And who doesn't love Mom's famous brownies, especially when they're accompanied by her recipe? Just be sure to plan time to whip them up a few days before your nuptials; better yet, pick things you can make well in advance, like preserves or flavored olive oils.

Buy in bulk: If cooking's not your thing but shopping is, buy already inexpensive items in bulk (think popcorn, candy, nuts, or dried fruits), then upgrade them with pretty packaging in your day's colors.

Call in the 'maids: Get some wine, invite your bridesmaids over, and make a party out of assembling your favors; schedule the craft night a few days prior to the big event.

Gift a group: When your heart is set on expensive favors, give one to each couple or family (not each guest); just make sure you clearly label the package with the names of the intended recipients.

PERSONALIZE THE PACKAGE

Your favors should look like they belong at your wedding, not like an after-thought. There are several ways to pack, wrap, or box them up in style so they feel special and in keeping with your celebration's aesthetic.

Stick to the text: Use the same font you had on your programs, menus, and other printed goods on the favors (gift tags reading "thank you" or "enjoy!" are fun and festive).

Continue the color scheme: For a completely unified look, make sure your favors hew to your wedding palette.

Play with patterns: Package goodies in wrapping that mimics designs found elsewhere—like the lace of your dress, the chevron of the groomsmen's ties, or the vines on the cake.

Mark it with your motif: Think like a branding expert and use the logo you've designed for your nuptials, such as your shared monogram, or Cupid's arrow, on the favor packaging as well.

Wrap Stars (clockwise from top): Coat plain favor boxes in a layer of glue and dust on metallic glitter. For an even more arresting display, use three different shades of glitter and arrange the boxes in an ombré pattern. Paper pyramids filled with dragées reveal a surprise at the bottom: the couple's initials. Metallic crepe paper, quickstitched into a rosette and secured to a clear container with a dot of glue and monogram sticker, elevates a favor of foil-wrapped chocolates into something to write home about. Instead of slipping dragées into tulle bags, place them in a square box and wrap in loosely woven linen for a twist on tradition.

Tasty Treats

The custom of favors originated in Europe during the Middle Ages, when bonbonnieres, or boxes filled with sugar cubes, were given to guests. Other edible gifts, such as biscuits, fruit, nuts, and spiced buns, soon followed. Nowadays, people still love a takeaway they can nibble or sip.

A wise man once said, "Candy is dandy, but liquor is quicker." To which we'd add, "baked goods are beautiful, chocolate is cheerful, and salt is sensational." Really, any food or drink that's not highly perishable can be packaged cleverly to transform it into a delicious treat guests will savor, whether on the ride home, the next morning, or whenever the mood strikes.

But don't choose something merely tasty; a gift should be thoughtful as well, whether it's a mix of each of your favorite candies, a small reproduction of your wedding cake, or whiskey distilled on the farm where you held your reception. That way each bite comes with a side of sweet memories.

Delightful Delicacies 1. A couple of whiskey aficionados wrapped mini bottles and bitters in paper stamped with their monogram and finished them with a wax seal. 2. Individual-size wedding cakes made a romantic gift for each couple at a black-tie affair. 3. A basket filled with strawberries and scones is a nice next-day breakfast. 4. Salted caramel bars wrapped in wax paper and newsprint adorned with a ribbon, tag, and wax seal are fitting for a laid-back event. 5. Custom chocolate bars split the difference between the bride's beloved salted dark chocolate and groom's pick, caramelized white chocolate. 6. Sourdough pretzels dipped in chocolate, sealed in glassine bags, and stitched closed with on-palette red thread perfectly fit a couple's San Francisco nuptial. 7. Keepsake flasks stamped with the newlyweds' anchor motif and monogram were filled with iced tea and lemonade. 8. This pair chose to give a parfait in either the bride's favorite flavor (peanut butter and chocolate) or the groom's (blueberry with mascarpone). 9. Bags of sea salt in cut bamboo cups, topped with a wooden spoon, are a tropical way to say "mahalo."

2

3

4

5

6

7

9

Green Gifts

What better way to celebrate love in bloom than by giving a takeaway that's blossoming (or fruiting or just gorgeously verdant)? Another bonus: When arranged on a table, they double as reception décor.

In Elizabethan times, wedding guests, both male and female, were presented with corsages upon arrival at the church. Tied with ribbons, they symbolized the tying of the knot and were worn throughout the celebration—and even for a few days afterward. Floral favors are still a great way to commemorate love, while also showcasing the season and location of your event. Evergreens are festive in winter, fresh flowers herald spring, and succulents set a Southwestern scene for a desert affair.

Living Color (this page, clockwise from top): Herbs, available at nurseries, make savory send-offs and guests can cook with them later. Yellow zinnias in on-palette pots act as a centerpiece and, thanks to a "take one" sign, a favor as well. Let guests bring home a mini terrarium; these were fashioned by nesting air plants and succulents in white sand within geometric bud vases. Succulents require very little water, so these can be assembled weeks in advance. Potted African violets, slipped into panettone molds, are charming on their own or when clustered together in a display. **Opposite:** Mini orchids in white-painted terra-cotta pots bear guests' names on the backs of butterfly-shaped tags, making them both escort cards and favors.

Regional Specialties

Bring out the best in your wedding's spot by giving attendees a local delicacy. It makes a thoughtful souvenir, whether you're getting hitched in your hometown or somewhere far, far away.

Unless your wedding is extremely intimate, it's bound to be a destination affair for guests who will travel to attend it—and the place of your nuptials is undoubtedly meaningful for the two of you. Share something that makes it special, whether it's a souvenir or a hometown treat. Another benefit: If you're throwing a wedding outside the U.S., chances are you're not going to be able to transport food across borders, given customs restrictions. Instead, buy presents on-site and package them there, or bring nonperishables like tinned travel candles in destination-inspired scents (think limoncello for Italy, vanilla for Mexico).

Local Flavor 1. Transform a box of store-bought candies by replacing the lid with a band printed with a personal message (leave the shrink wrap intact). 2. For a Texas wedding, favor boxes of pecans feature vintage illustrations of area wildlife; each one represents a different table, turning the favors into escort cards as well. 3. Lobster lollipops are a witty take on a Maine icon. 4. A trio of foil-wrapped chocolate fish (strung together to be hung from a board at the reception) make a whimsical catch for an Alaskan affair. 5. Celebrate your wedding locale by wrapping boxes containing souvenirs in maps of the area, tied with color-coordinated ribbon. 6. Custom print a sticker with your motif and use it to personalize a box of chocolates (here, Ohio buckeyes). 7. Print your own labels to replace the wrappers on local chocolate bars. 8. Glass-topped specimen boxes hold local flora and butterflies. 9. Pecan pralines are a signature New Orleans confection; we dressed up three boxed treats in patterned paper topped with a custom label.

2

3

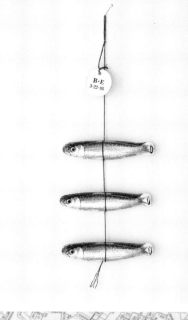

4

6

7

WYOMING

5

9

Two-for-One Takeaways

Great gifts keep on giving—and that's certainly true with multitasking favors, which can save you money by acting as presents, wedding-day décor, and even more.

With your wedding planning duties, you might be feeling as if you've been wearing many hats. And there's no reason your favors shouldn't be as efficient as you are by performing more than one function. A collection of bud vases running down the center of a table acts as a stunning centerpiece that, come night's end, splits apart into takeaway tokens of appreciation. Luggage tags that double as escort cards and favors are especially cute for a destination affair. And then there's the favor equivalent of a quadruple-threat: A photo backdrop manned with a photographer means that (1) a wall at your party is decorated, (2) guests leave with professional portraits of themselves, (3) you get a picture of everyone for your album, and (4) everyone has a blast.

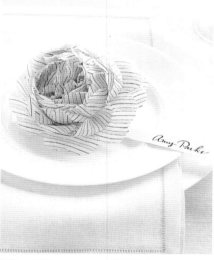

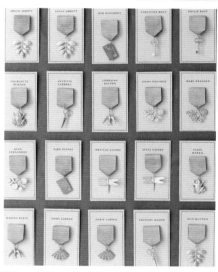

Multitasking Marvels (this page, clockwise from top): Tissue paper, folded in quarters and cut to resemble petals, transforms a cylinder box into a blooming beauty—mass several together to create a centerpiece. A silk millinery flower on a pin is a lovely place card and, post-wedding, a dashing addition to a coat. Table assignments are calligraphed on take-home white pine saplings. Military-inspired medals make four-star escort cards and are charming favors for guests to hang on a chain later.
Opposite: No need to tart up fruit; berries and currants are already irresistible when displayed farm-stand style in wooden pint containers. Add calligraphed name cards on wooden stirrers, and you've got edible escort carts and tasty takeaways.

Making an Exit

*Ancient Greek vases, painted more than two millennia ago, show brides
and grooms galloping away in chariots decorated with flowers. Today, attendees still love a
big finish—and you two deserve a memorable ride off into the sunset.
Here, some inspiration from couples who bid guests a fond—and fabulous—farewell.*

Trail Blazers (this page, clockwise from top left): There's more than one way to hit the road. This pair left their New Year's Eve celebration in Seattle at 2:30 a.m. as guests waved sparklers. Newlyweds at a coastal affair in Maine cruised off on a lobster boat. When this duo wed on her family's farm in Virginia, a neighbor lent them a carriage horse to pull her father's vintage buggy. In New Orleans, the bride and groom rolled away off into the French Quarter in a cart pulled by a miniature horse. **Opposite:** This California couple adorned a 1964 Ford Mustang with paper bells for their grand good-bye.

ACKNOWLEDGMENTS

THIS BOOK REPRESENTS THE hard work, creativity, enthusiasm, and dedication of so many talented individuals over the course of the past 20 years. First, the team who devoted themselves to compiling the best of the best of our wedding content into the volume you hold in your hands: editor in chief Elizabeth Graves, creative director Kate Berry, executive editor Eleni N. Gage, and design director Michael McCormick. They worked tirelessly to create a resource that will help brides today and for many years to come. None of this would be possible without editorial director Darcy Miller, who has worked since the inaugural issue to make Martha Stewart Weddings the highly regarded and inimitable brand that it is today. Over the years, countless other editors, art directors, stylists, hair and makeup artists, florists, designers, planners, crafters, pastry chefs, and caterers have also had a hand in producing beautiful wedding after beautiful wedding. Others on the current Weddings staff who are instrumental in those ongoing efforts are Muzam Agha, Colleen Banks, Lindsay Brown, Jaime Buerger, Katie Covington, Naomi deMañana, Linda Denahan, Elisabeth Engelhart, Erin Furey, Carrie Goldberg, Anthony Luscia, Becky Mickel, Genevieve Panuska, Shira Savada, and Julie Vadnal. And, of course, we are indebted to the many other wedding professionals we have worked with over the years, particularly contributors Peter Callahan, Elizabeth Colling, Cassidy Iwersen, Wendy Kromer, Matthew Robbins, Jason Schreiber, and David Stark.

In putting this book together, the Weddings team was assisted by Susanne Ruppert, Jennifer Wagner, Ellen Morrissey, and Eric A. Pike of *Martha Stewart Living*. Editors Cara Sullivan, Fan Winston, and Michelle Stacey also helped with the voluminous text, and Bryan Gardner, Denise Clappi, John Myers, Duanne Stapp, Alison Vanek Devine, and Daniel Chambers ensured that the photographs are as breathtaking as possible. We are indebted to the many talented photographers whose work graces these pages (a complete list appears on the following page), and especially to Erik Madigan Heck for the stunning chapter openers like artist Maya Lin's outdoor installation "Storm King Wavefield." And special thanks to Liberty View Farm, The Preservation Society of Newport County, and Storm King Art Center for welcoming us onto their awe-inspiring locations.

As always, we are grateful to our longtime partners at Clarkson Potter Publishers for their editorial and creative support and collaboration, chiefly president Maya Mavjee, publisher Aaron Wehner, associate publisher Doris Cooper, editor Ashley Phillips Meyer, art directors Michael Nagin and Stephanie Huntwork, production director Linnea Knollmueller, production editorial director Mark McCauslin, director of marketing and publicity Kate Tyler, assistant director of marketing Carly Gorga, and publicist Sean Boyles.

And finally, we would like to extend our sincere gratitude to all the couples whose inspiring and one-of-a kind weddings appear in the pages of this gorgeous and practical book.

PHOTO CREDITS

William Abranowicz: pages 165, 257 (top left)

Stephen Abry: pages 134 (bottom left), 135 (bottom right), 138 (top left), 139 (bottom left)

Bela Adler & Salvador Fresneda: page 83

Lucas Allen: pages 15, 58 (bottom left), 60-61, 258 (middle left), 262 (middle right)

Allyson Magda Photography: page 170

Sang An: pages 13, 133 (bottom left), 139 (top right), 212

Jessica Antola: pages 28, 30 (middle left), 34 (middle left), 166 (top center), 195 (top right), 215 (top left), 252 (bottom center)

James Baigrie: page 257 (top center)

Christopher Baker: pages 15, 120 (top left), 133 (bottom right), 230 (center)

Paul Barbera: page 15

Kathryn Barnard: page 37 (top)

Harry Bates: illustrations on pages 196-197

Sylvie Becquet: pages 140 (top left), 258 (bottom)

Belathée Photography: pages 36, 103, 160, 187 (bottom left), 264 (top left)

Roland Bello: pages 86-87

Justin Bernhaut: pages 101 (top right), 260 (bottom)

Petra Bindel: pages 2, 236 (left)

Joe Budd: pages 175, 215 (bottom right), 264 (bottom left)

Anita Calero: pages 243, 260 (top), 261 (all except top left and bottom right), 263

Earl Carter: pages 140 (bottom left), 226, 231 (bottom left and bottom right)

Erin Hearts Court: page 192 (top left)

Craig Cutler: page 80 (top center, middle left and right, bottom center)

Andrea D'Agostino: page 179

Joseph De Leo: page 122 (bottom)

Aaron Delesie: pages 31, 33 (middle left), 38 (bottom), 100 (bottom left), 166 (bottom right), 169, 180, 192 (middle left and middle right), 211, 264 (top right)

John Dolan: pages 76, 108 (bottom right), 166 (middle right), 256 (top)

Andrea Fazzari: page 20

Laurie Frankel: pages 126 (middle right), 255 (bottom right)

Don Freeman: page 134 (bottom right)

Douglas Friedman: pages 154, 242

Dana Gallagher: pages 134 (top center), 143, 231 (top left), 235 (top left)

Bryan Gardner: pages 38 (middle left), 58 (top left), 120 (bottom right), 122 (top and middle left), 123, 126 (middle left), 128, 129 (bottom), 153, 258 (top), 262 (middle left)

Gertrude and Mabel: page 125 (top)

Thayer Allyson Gowdy: pages 29 (bottom), 32, 33 (top), 34 (bottom), 37 (bottom), 40, 51-53, 54 (bottom), 55 (top left and middle), 101 (bottom left), 120 (bottom left), 187 (top right), 192 (top center), 203, 204 (all except bottom center), 252 (top center), 262 (bottom)

Corbin Gurkin: page 192 (top right)

Patricia Heal: page 136 (top right and bottom center)

Erik Madigan Heck: pages 10-11, 22-23, 46-47, 62-63, 90-91, 112-113, 146-147, 162-163, 172-173, 200-201, 222-223, 248-249

Raymond Hom: pages 15, 140 (top right), 159

Troy House: pages 44, 77 (top left), 176

Jen Huang: page 166 (middle left)

Lisa Hubbard: pages 133 (top right), 234, 235 (right)

Collin Hughes: page 208

Ingalls Photography: pages 30 (top), 37 (middle left), 108 (top right), 166 (bottom left), 195 (top left), 257 (middle left)

Ditte Isager: page 135 (bottom left)

Addie Juell: pages 233, 239

Jonathan Kantor: page 258 (middle right)

Stephen Karlisch: page 33 (bottom)

John Kernick: pages 16, 244

Yunhee Kim: pages 56 (top left, center, bottom right), 57, 58 (center), 100 (top right), 115, 124, 137 (top left), 261 (bottom right)

Ken Kochey: page 189

Anna Rosa Krau: page 25

Erin Kunkel: pages 30 (bottom), 38 (middle right), 100 (top left), 127, 166 (top left), 257 (bottom left)

Franceso Lagnese: page 251

Lauren and Abby Ross Weddings: page 39

Laura Letinsky: pages 134 (top left), 139 (top left)

Rick Lew: pages 30 (middle right), 133 (top left), 199, 252 (middle right)

Sivan Lewin: pages 93, 98

Charlotte Jenks Lewis: page 207

Stephen Lewis: pages 137 (top right)

Love Life Images: page 204 (bottom center)

MaeMae & Co.: page 149

Sarah Maingot: pages 35, 151, 246-247, 255 (bottom left)

Amanda Marsalis: pages 29 (middle right), 264 (bottom right)

Kate Mathis: pages 49, 97, 116

David Meredith: page 136 (top left)

James Merrell: page 192 (middle center)

Elizabeth Messina: pages 19, 29 (middle left), 65, 166 (middle center), 185, 192 (bottom right), 195 (bottom right), 252 (middle center)

Michéle M. Waite Photography: page 34 (top)

Johnny Miller: pages 6, 15, 33 (middle right), 84, 100 (bottom right), 122 (middle right), 126 (bottom), 129 (top), 134 (top right), 135 (top left and right, bottom center), 137 (bottom left), 138 (bottom left and right), 192 (bottom left), 217, 218, 228-229, 231 (top right), 236 (right), 252 (top left), 257 (top right and middle center), 262 (top)

Emily Nathan: pages 108 (bottom left), 192 (bottom center), 252 (middle left)

N. Barrett Photography: page 252 (bottom right)

Amy Neunsinger: page 261 (top left)

Ngoc Minh Ngo: pages 4-5, 59, 125 (bottom), 126 (top), 136 (bottom right)

Marcus Nilsson: pages 34 (middle right), 107, 108 (top left), 110, 119 (top left), 256 (bottom)

Kate Osborne: page 221

Christian Oth: page 120 (top right)

Our Labor of Love: page 183

Anna Palma: page 77 (bottom row third from left and right)

Carrie Patterson: page 187 (bottom right)

Victoria Pearson: pages 132, 255 (top right), 259

Jose Picayo: pages 77 (top row second from left and right, bottom row left), 215 (bottom left), 237, 245

Con Poulos: pages 54 (top), 55 (all except top left and middle) 230 (right), 231 (top center), 235 (bottom left), 255 (top left)

Frank Rainer: page 77 (bottom second from left)

James Ransom: page 139 (bottom right)

Ryan Ray: pages 191, 195 (bottom left)

Maria Robledo: pages 75, 140 (bottom right)

Alexandra Rowley: pages 15, 58 (top right)

Lucy Schaeffer: page 37 (middle right)

Tamara Schlesinger: pages 80 (top left and right, bottom left and right), 89

Scott and Zoe: page 56 (top right and bottom left)

Courtesy of Martha Stewart: page 9

Thomas Straub: pages 77 (top third from left), 119 (all except top left), 215 (top right)

Sandra Suy: illustrations on pages 72-73, 130-131

Marie Taillefer: page 68

Paulette Tavormina: pages 15, 136 (bottom left)

Holger Thoss: page 29 (top)

Rachel Thurston: page 265

Thuss and Farrell: pages 137 (bottom right), 138 (top right and bottom center), 144, 241

Elisabeth Toll: pages 79, 80 (middle center)

Jonny Valiant: pages 15, 58 (bottom right), 101 (bottom right), 156

Mikkel Vang: pages 38 (top), 94, 252 (bottom left)

Jose Villa: pages 101 (top left), 166 (bottom center), 187 (top left), 252 (top right), 257 (bottom right)

Liz Von Hoene: pages 67, 70-71

Max Wanger: page 166 (top right)

Anna Williams: pages 225, 230 (left), 231 (bottom center), 238

Romulo Yanes: page 232

Roey Yohai: page 42

INDEX

Note: Page numbers in *italics*
      indicate photo captions.

A

Accessories
    for bride, 74–75
    for bridesmaids, 88–89
    for groom and attendants, 86
Accommodations card, 95
Addressing
    envelopes, 106–107
    escort cards, 214
Alcohol, cocktail hour and, 213
A-line dresses, 72
Amaryllises, *126, 129, 135*
Anemones, *117, 132, 137, 145*
Announcements, wedding, 109
Announcing engagement, 14
Apple branches, *122*
Art, inspiring cake design, 234
Attire. *See also* Dress; Styling your look
    bridesmaids, 88–89
    groom and attendants, 86–87
Autumn flowers, 126–127

B

Baby's breath, meaning of, 142
Bachelorette/bachelor party, 158–159
Ballerina veil, 77
Ball gowns, 72
Balloon release, 253
Bands, choosing. *See* Rings
Bateau dresses, 73, 74
Beauty tips. *See* Dress; Styling your
    look
Berries, with flowers, *60, 125, 126,
    134, 136, 137, 139,* 141
Berry, Kate, 64, 250
Best man. *See also* Groomsmen
    choosing, 190
    responsibilities, 190
    toasts by, 190, 205, 220
Birdcage veil, 77
Bittersweet branches, 126
Bleeding hearts, *52, 139*
Bloat, banishing, 85
Blusher veil, 77
Book overview, 12
Bouquets. *See also specific flowers*
    about, 118
    for bride, 118, 190
    for bridesmaids, 118
    bride tossing, 205
    carrying/holding, 131
    ceremony, 118
    classic, *132*

color palette and, *52, 60*
    for flower girls, 188
    graphic, *137*
    modern, *135*
    needs determination, 117
    romantic, *138, 139*
    rustic, *134*
    seasonal examples, *122, 125, 126, 129*
    shapes, 130–131. *See also specific
        shapes*
    spending savvy, 145
    symbolic meaning by flower type, 142
    theme-based examples, *17*
    tropical, *136*
Boutonnieres, 118, 141, *142,* 188
Branches, flowering/flowers with, 126,
    129, 135, 141, *141*
Branches, fruit, *54, 122, 125*
Bridesmaids. *See also* Maid of honor
    assembling favors, 252, 253
    bachelorette party and, 158
    bouquets, 118
    bridal dress selection and, 66
    bridal shower and, 152
    choosing, 190–191
    color palette and, *54,* 56, 88
    day-of kit and, 82
    dressing, 88–89
    hairstyles, 81
    junior, 18, 158, 188
    paying for own dresses, 88
    processional order, 196
    receiving line and, 189
    recessional order, 197
    rehearsal dinner and, 161
    responsibilities, 190
    shoes for, 88–89
    substitutes, 188
    table for, at reception, 145
    throwing bridal shower, 152
Brows, shaping, 78
Brunch, day-after, 171
Bubbles, for celebrating couple, 253
Budget, 14–17
    about: overview of considerations, 14
    break-out by category, 17
    cake, 240
    caterer, 210
    dress/fashion, 17, 66, 69
    engagement party, 150
    fees and taxes, 17, 41, 117, 168
    floral, 17, 145
    food, 17
    guest list and, 18
    managing, 167
    music, 17, 209
    photography/video, 17
    planner, 21
    season impacting, 17
    stationery, 17
    timing impacting, 17
    tipping and, 17, 21
    transportation, 17
    venue, 41, 45
    venue funding special touches
        and, *17*
    who pays for what, 14

Buffet, 216–217
Buttercream
    about, 230
    cake examples, *30,* 227
    cake flavors compatible with, 228
    fillings, 229
    flavor inspiration and, 232
    fondant vs., 230

C

Cake, 224–247. *See also* Buttercream
    about: overview of considerations,
        224
    budget considerations, 240
    choosing/imagining, 227. *See also
        Cake, inspiration sources*
    color palette and, *56, 58, 60*
    cutting, 205, 209
    desserts in addition to, *17, 54,* 219,
        240, 242–247
    filling options, 229
    flavors. *See* Cake flavors
    flowers on, *34,* 121
    fondant, *58,* 227, 230, 231, 235, 236
    ganache, 229, 231
    general guidelines, 121
    hiring baker for, 227
    icings and creams, 229
    individual-size, as favors, 256
    lollipops, *60*
    marzipan, 231, 239
    meringue, 230
    molding, 231
    painting, 231
    piping, 231
    reflecting theme, *30, 37*
    royal icing, 227, 231, *240*
    saving top tier, 226
    sculpting, 231
    silver-leaf-covered, *37*
    spending savvy, 240
    style selection, 230–231
    timeline, 227
Cake flavors
    almond dacquoise, 228
    carrot, 228
    chocolate, 228
    choosing, 228
    lemon poppy seed, 228
    marble, 228
    red velvet, 228
    summary of options, 228
    white butter, 228
    yellow, 228
Cake, inspiration sources, 232–239
    art, 234
    china patterns, 237
    color, 235
    culture, 233
    flavor, 232
    seasonal themes/ingredients, 239
    textiles, 236

Callahan, Peter, 202
Calla lilies, *126, 132, 135, 136*
Calligraphy
    escort cards with, *30,* 56, 109, *109*
    invitations with, *29, 99,* 102, *106*
Candles, 145, 182, 188, *209,* 260
Carnations, 128, *132,* 142, 145
Cascade bouquets, 131, *132, 136*
Casual attire, 86
Catering
    coordinating cake with, 227, 240
    feeding more than guests, 206
    food delivery, 219
    hiring caterer, 210–211
    to kids, 219
    reception schedule and, 205
    spending savvy, 210
    tipping and, 21
    venue providing, 41, 45
Cathedral hemline, 71
Cathedral veil, 77
Centerpieces. *See also specific flowers*
    adding unexpected elements to, 141
    budget considerations, 145
    color palette and, *52, 58,* 145, *258*
    as favors (takeaways), *258, 262*
    fragrance importance, 121
    general guidelines, 121
    seasonal examples, *126*
    style examples. *See* Flowers, styles of
    theme-based examples, *29, 33,* 35, *38*
    vessels for, 141
Ceremony, 172–201. *See also* Officiant
    about: overview of considerations,
        174
    basic sketches by type, 178
    blessing of rings, 182
    Christian, 178, 196, 197
    combining religions and cultures, 181
    composing, 178–179
    décor, 118–119
    explaining rituals to guests, 181
    flowers. *See* Flowers
    friendship circle ritual, 182
    handfasting at, 182
    Hindu, 178
    including family, 188–189
    Jewish, 178, 196, 197
    keeping everyone comfortable, 194
    kids in, 188
    music, 186–187
    Muslim, 178
    non-denominational, 178
    personalizing, 27, 182–183
    photographer/videographer for, 17,
        198–199
    prepping people before, 194–195
    processional order, 196
    program for. *See* Programs
    readings, 186
    recessional order, 197
    same-sex weddings, 197
    staying calm for, 194
    tents for, 43
    timeline, 177
    tree planting commemoration, 182

unity candle ritual, 182
water cleansing ritual, 182
welcoming committee, 194
writing vows, 184–185
Chamomile, *134*, *138*, 253
Chapel hemline, 71
Children. *See* Kids
China, inspiring cake design, 237
Chocolate cake, 228
Chocolate fillings, 229
Chocolate ganache, 229, 231
Chocolates, *245*, *252*, *256*, *260*
Christian ceremony, 178, 196, 197
Chrysanthemums, 121, *137*, 145
Classic flowers, 132–133
Classic invitations, 101
Classic wedding, 29
Clematis, *122*, *125*, *126*, *135*, *136*, *139*
Coast, weddings on, 30–31, 38–39
Cocktail hour, 213
Collections, with flowers, 141
Color palette, 46–61
    about: overview of, 48
    bridesmaid attire, 88
    choosing, 50–51
    complementary colors, 48
    examples. *See* Color palette examples
    importance of, 48
    inspiring cake design, 235
    invitations and, *52*, *54*, *56*, *60*, 99
    physical examples to confirm, 50
    seasonal considerations, 54–55
    selecting one only, 56–57
    sticking to, 50
    testing, 50
    venue coordination, 52–53
    working together to pick, 50
Color palette examples
    aqua, white, chartreuse, *52*
    blue and nude, 60
    blues, 56–57
    mustard, rust shades, *50*
    neutrals (shades of brown, taupe,
        gray, nude), 60–61
    pink and white, *54*
    taupes and browns, *60*
    white, 58–59
Confetti, *102*, 253
Congratulating the couple, 253
Coral bells, *139*
Corsages, 118, *142*, 188, 258
Cosmos, *122*, *126*
Cover-ups, 74
Coworkers, 18
Creams and icings, for cake, 229
Crescent bouquets, 130
Crocus, meaning of, 142
Culture(s)
    combining religions and, 181
    inspiring cake design, 233

D

Daffodils, 122
Dahlias, *60*, *117*, *125*, *126*, *139*
Daisy, meaning of, 142
Day-after brunch, 171
Day-of planners, 21
Desserts/dessert table, *17*, *54*, 219,
    240, 242–247
Destination weddings. *See also* Guests
    ceremony booklet aiding guests, *193*
    congratulating the couple, 253

considerations for, 38, 41
guest list and, 18
guest timeline and, 167
invitations for, 95, 99
maps for, 95
save-the-dates for, 95
transportation for guests, 168–169
tropical wedding, 38–39
welcome bags for guests, *167*
Diet and nutrition, 85
Dogs, as ring bearers, 27, 190
Dogwood, *17*, *52*, *134*, *142*
Dress
    about: overview of considerations, 64
    accessories to complement, 74–75
    appointments to source, 66
    budget, *17*, 66, 69
    color palette examples, *50*, *52*, *54*
    cover-ups for, 74
    entourage for finding, 66
    extras to accentuate, 74–75
    finding/selecting, 66–73
    foundation for trying on, 69
    hemline options, 71
    jewelry to complement, 74
    planning ahead, 66
    purchase contract, 69
    researching, 66
    shoes to complement, 74
    shopping tips, 66–69
    silhouette options, 72–73
    size of, 69
    timeline, 66
    tracking contenders, 69
    type of wedding and. *See* Themes
    veils with, 76–77
Drinks, cocktail hour, 213

E

Elbow veil, 77
Empire dresses, 72
Engagement, announcing, 14
Engagement party, 150–151
Engraving, *95*, 96, 97, 99, 102
Envelopes
    addressing (titles/other
        considerations), 106–107
    inner, 95
    for invitations, 95
    liners, 99, 102
    postage considerations, 106
    special touches, 102–103. *See also*
        Stationery printing processes and
        special touches
    wax seals, 102
Escort cards
    about, 109
    addressing, 214
    calligraphed examples, *30*, *56*, *109*
    examples, *38*, *54*, *109*, *214*
    as favors (takeaways), *56*, 109, 155,
        214, *258*
    flowers and, 141, 145
    programs doubling as, *193*
    seating arrangements and, 214–215
    table for, 188
    theme-based, 38
    tradition of, 109
Event designers, 21
Exercise, 85

F

Fall flowers, 126–127
Family. *See also* Parents
    grandparents, 18, 118, 178, 188, 196
    guest list, 18
    involving in ceremony, 181, 188–189
    seating arrangements, 214
Family style meal, 216
Favors (takeaways), 254–255, 256–263
    about: giving, 250, 254
    for bridal showers, 155
    candy/treats as, 240, 242, *254*,
        256–257, *262*
    color palette and, 50, *50*, *54*, *56*, *58*
    coordinating invitations with, 95
    custom origin, 256
    escort cards as, *56*, 109, 155, 214, *258*
    flowers/plants as, 45, *45*, 117, 121,
        141, 145, 258–259
    multitasking, 262–263
    packaging examples, *254*
    personalizing, 254
    questions to help identify, 26–27
    regional specialties as, 260–261
    shower, 155
    timeline, 252
Ferns
    adding to arrangements, 141
    arrangements with, *29*, *52*, *126*, *132*,
        134, *135*, *136*, 141
    symbolic meaning of, 142
Fillings, cake, 229
Fingertip veil, 77
Flat printing, 96, 97
Flavors, cake. *See* Cake flavors
Floor-length dresses, 71
Flower girls, *54*, 188, 196, 197
Flowers, 112–145. *See also* Bouquets;
    Centerpieces; *specific flowers*
    about: overview of considerations,
        114
    adding unexpected elements to, 141
    boutonnieres, 118, 141, *142*, 188
    budget considerations, 17, 145
    candles with/instead of, 145
    ceremony, 118–119, 145
    color palette and, *56*
    corsages, 118, *142*, 188, 258
    creating look, 117
    décor, 121
    fall season, 126–127
    farmer's markets for, 145
    as favors (takeaways), 45, *45*, 117, 121,
        141, 145, 258–259
    hiring florist, 117
    jewelry compatibility, 74
    needs determination, 117
    reception, 120–121
    repurposing ceremony, 145
    seasonal considerations, 122–129, 145
    spring season, 122–123
    styles. *See* Flowers, styles of
    summer season, 124–125
    symbolic meaning by flower, 142
    timeline, 117
    tossing in celebration, 253
    vessels for, 141
    winter season, 128–129
    wreaths, *125*, *126*
Flowers, styles of, 132–139
    classic, 132–133
    graphic, 137
    modern, 134

romantic, 138–139
rustic, 134
tropical, 136
Foil stamping, *34*, *56*, 102
Food. *See also* Catering; Favors (take-
        aways); Menus; Parties
    budget, 17
    buffet, 216–217
    day-after brunch, 171
    delivery of, 219
    extra, to food bank, 216
    family style, 216
    French service, 216
    hiring caterer, 210–211
    main course, 216–219
    making offerings personal, 210
    for more than guests, 206
    nutrition, self-care and, 85
    plate service, 216
    serving styles, 216–219
    stations, 219
    theme-based touches, *34*
    welcome drinks or opening dinner,
        171
Forget-me-nots, *138*, 142
Formal attire, 86
Formal invitations, 99
Freesia, 125, 142
French service, 216
Friendship circle, 182
Fruit branches, *54*, *122*, *122*, *125*
Fruit, with flowers, 141
Fuchsia, *136*, 142

G

Gage, Eleni N., 174
Gardenias, *29*, *58*, 126
Garden wedding, 33
Geraniums, 142
Getaway ideas, 264–265
Gifts. *See also* Favors (takeaways)
    engagement party, 151
    registry for, 157
    shower, 152, 155, 190
    thank-you notes for, 110–111, 155, 157
    who pays for what, 14
Grandparents, 18, 118, 178, 188, 196
Graphic flowers, 137
Grasses, with flowers, *126*, 141
Graves, Elizabeth, 48
Groom
    attire and extras for, 86–87
    at bridal shower, 155
Groomsmen. *See also* Best man
    attire and extras for, 86
    boutonnieres for, 118, 141, *142*
    choosing, 190
    junior, 18, 158, 188
    processional order, 196
    receiving line and, 189
    recessional order, 197
    rehearsal dinner and, 161
    responsibilities, 190
    ushers and, 194
Guest list, 17, 18
Guests, 162–171. *See also* Destination
        weddings
    about: planning for and welcoming,
        164
    entertaining, 169
    getting them around, 168–169

Guests (*continued*)
    managing logistics for, 167, 171
    maps for, 95, 99, 167, 171, *260*
    timeline, 167
    weekend activities and schedule, 170–171
    welcome bag examples, *167*
    who pays for what, 171

H

Hair
    best hairspray for, 81
    bridesmaids, 81
    cutting, coloring, 78
    hiring stylist, 78
    location considerations, 81
    secret weapon, 81
    selecting style, 80–81
    timeless look, 81
    timeline, 78
    trial run, 81
    updo update, 81
    washing, 78
    wearing down, 81
Halter dresses, 73
Handfasting, 182
Hellebores, *58*, 129, *134*, *135*, *139*, *141*, 142
Hemline options, for dress, 71. *See also* Silhouette options
Hindu ceremony, 178
Holidays, 17, 37, 45
Honeymoon, newlyweds leaving for, 264–265
Hyacinths, 129, *138*, 142
Hydrangeas, *52*, *125*, *132*, *137*, *139*, *141*

I

Icings and creams, for cake, 229
Invitations, 95–107. *See also* Envelopes; Stationery printing processes and special touches
    about: overview of considerations, 92
    accommodations card, 95
    budget, 17, 102
    calligraphed, *29*, 99, 102, *106*
    choosing design, 99
    classic, 101
    color palette and, *52*, *54*, *56*, *60*, 99
    destination, 95, 99
    feline-inspired, *99*
    formal, 99
    hiring stationer, 95
    maps to accompany, 95
    minimalist, 101
    modern, 99, 100
    nature-inspired, 99, 101
    nautical, 101
    postage considerations, 106
    reception card, 95
    reflecting theme, *29*, *30*, *33*, 33, *34*, *37*
    reply card, 95, 99
    romantic, 100
    rustic, 99, 100
    save-the-dates and, 95
    shower, 152
    special touches, 102–103. *See also* Stationery printing processes and special touches

    stamps reflecting theme, *34*
    suite elements, 95
    suite examples, *29*, *30*, *38*, *56*, *60*, *95*, *102*
    timeline, 95
    tropical, 100
    wording, 104–105
Irises, *122*, *139*
Ivy, meaning of, 142

J

Japanese anemones, 126
Jasmine, pink, meaning of, 142
Jasmine, white, meaning of, 142
Jewelry, by gown style, 74. *See also* Rings
Jewish ceremony, 178, 196, 197

K

Kale, ornamental, *126*
Kids
    in ceremony, 188. *See also* Bridesmaids, junior; Flower girls; Groomsmen, junior; Ring bearers
    envelope addresses and, 106
    table/menu, 219
    wedding party of only, *29*
    who to invite, 18
Knee-length dresses, 71
Kromer, Wendy, 224

L

Lady's mantle, meaning of, 142
Lakefront weddings, 30–31
Lavender, *126*, 253
Lemonade, *194*
Letterpress print form, *34*, 96, 97, *99*, *102*, *193*
Lighting, 209
Lilacs, *122*, *132*, *136*, 142
Lilies, white, 142
Lily of the valley, *132*, 142

M

Maid of honor, 190. *See also* Bridesmaids
    choosing, 190
    responsibilities, 190
    toasts by, 190, 220
Makeup
    choosing, 82–83
    day-of kit, 82
    dress selection and, *82*
    elevating skin and, 78
    flushing cheeks, 82
    playing up eyes/lips, 82
    scheduling artist, 78
    shaping brows, 78
    skin luminosity, 82
Mañana, Naomi de, 114
Manicure, 78
Mantilla veil, 77

Maps, for guests, 95, 99, 167, 171, *260*
Marriage license, 17, 177
Menus
    calligraphed, 102, *109*
    cards with, 109
    caterer and, 210
    creating, 219
    examples, *14*, *52*, *109*
    for kids, 219
    planning ahead, 205
    timeline, 95, 205
Mermaid dresses, 72
Midcalf dresses, 71
Miller, Darcy, 24, 148
Mini dresses, 71
Minimalist invitations, 101
Mint, meaning of, 142
Modern flowers, 134
Modern invitations, 99, 100
Modern soirée, 37
Music
    booking band, 206
    booking DJ, 209
    budget, 17, 209
    ceremony, 186–187
    DJs, 205, 206, 209
    lighting and, 209, *209*
    reception, 206–209
    researching, 206
Muslim ceremony, 178

N

Narcissus, 129
Nature-inspired invitations, 99, 101
Nautical invitations, 101
New Year's Eve fête, *37*
Noisemakers, 253
Non-denominational service, 178
Nutrition and diet, 85

O

Oak branches and leaves, *126*
Officiant
    budget considerations, 14
    ceremony timeline, 177
    combining religions/cultures and, 181
    hiring, 177, 181
    honoring parents, 188
    personalizing your ceremony, 182–183
    processional order, 196
    rehearsal dinner and, 161
    showing gratitude to, 182
Orchids, *38*, *58*, 128, *135*, *136*, *138*, *141*, 142, *258*
Organic bouquets, 131, *132*, *134*
Outdoor weddings
    coastal/lakefront site, 30–31, 38
    garden affair, 33
    rustic setting, 34–35
Oval bouquets, 130

P

Pages, 188
Pansies, *138*, 142
Paperwhites, 129

Parents
    announcing engagement to, 14
    divorced, 214
    flowers for. *See* Boutonnieres; Corsages
    guest list and, 18
    honoring, 188
    hosting engagement party, 150
    hosting farewell brunch, 171
    hosting rehearsal dinner, 161
    invitation wording and, 104–105
    processional order, 196
    recessional order, 197
    seating, 214
    stepmother and/or stepfather, 188
    toasting, 220
    toasts by, 161
    unity candle ritual and, 182
    on welcoming committee, 194
    welcoming guests to reception, 220
Parties, 147–161. *See also* Gifts; Reception
    about: overview of, 148
    bachelorette/bachelor, 158–159
    coed showers, 155
    engagement, 150–151
    rehearsal dinner, 160–161
    shower, 152–155
    timeline, 150
    who throws/who pays/whom to invite/how to celebrate. *See specific party types*
Pedicure, 78, 158
Peonies, *54*, *58*, *117*, *122*, 131, *132*, *137*, *139*, 142
Personalizing wedding, questions to consider, 26–27
Pets, as ring bearers, 27, 190
Photography/videography, 17, 198–199
Place cards, *60*, 95, *141*, *145*, *262*. *See also* Escort cards
Planners, 21
Planning, 12
Plate service, 216
Plus-ones, 18
Poppies, *125*, *136*
Postage, for invitations, 106
Processional order, 196
Programs
    creating, 193
    distributing, 190, 193, 194
    examples, *193*, *253*
    printing, 109, 177
    timeline, 95, 177

Q

Queen Anne's lace, 125
Quince, *129*
Quince branches, *54*

R

Ranunculus, *54*, *58*, *60*, *117*, *122*, *125*, *126*, *135*, *136*, *138*, *139*, 142
Readings, 186
Receiving line, 189, 197
Reception, 200–221. *See also* Cake; Catering; Favors (takeaways); Food; Menus

about: overview of considerations, 202
ceremony flowers to, 118
cocktail hour plans, 213
colors. *See* Color palette
décor, 121
desserts/dessert table, *17*, *54*, 219, 240, 242–247
flowers. *See* Flowers
kids' table/menu, 219
lighting, 209, *209*
music, 206–209
personalizing, questions to consider, 26–27
photographer/videographer for, 17, 198–199
place cards/settings, 109
planning schedule, 205
seating arrangements, 214–215
timelines, 43, 205
Reception card, 95
Recessional order, 197
Registry, 157
Reply card, 95, 99
Ring bearers, 18, 27, 188, 190, 196, 197
Rings
band selection, 74
blessing of, 182
Romantic flowers, 138–139
Romantic invitations, 100
Rose hips, 126
Rosemary, 141, 142
Rose petals
in aisle, *135*
tossing in celebration, 253
Roses
bouquets with, *17*, *122*, *126*, *132*, *134*, *136*, *138*, *139*
centerpieces with, *52*, *54*, *58*, *60*, *125*, *126*, *135*
as classic staple, 128
color palette and, *52*, *54*, *58*, *60*
spill of flowers with, *117*
symbolic meaning of, 142
wreath with, *125*
Round bouquets, 130, *132*
Rustic flowers, 134
Rustic invitations, 99, 100
Rustic theme, 34–35

S

Same-sex weddings, 197
Sauces and fillings, cake, 229
Savada, Shira, 92
Save-the-date cards, 95
Scabiosa, *129*, *134*, *139*
Season
budget impacted by, 17
color palette and, 54–55
flowers by, 122–129, 145
hairstyle and, 81
inspiring cake design, 239
tossing congratulatory items at couple and, 253
Seating arrangements, 214–215
Semicathedral hemline, 71
Semiformal attire, 86
Send-off, 250–265. *See also* Favors (takeaways)
about: overview of, 250
congratulating the couple, 253
newlyweds departing, 264–265

Sheath bouquets, 131, *132*, *134*, *135*
Sheath dresses, 73
Shoes
for bride, 74
for bridesmaids, 88–89
for guys, 86
Shower, bridal, 152–155, 190
Signage, 109
Silhouette options, for dress, 72–73
Skin care, 78
Sleep, importance of, 85
Smile, brightening, 78
Snowdrops, 129, *134*, *135*, 142, 239
Sparklers, 253, *264*
Spirea, *52*, *129*, *139*
Spring flowers, 122–123
Stamps, thematic, 102
Stationery, 90–111. *See also* Escort cards; Invitations
about: overview of considerations, 92
budget, 17, 102
choosing printing process, 96–97
place cards, *60*, 95, *141*, *145*, *262*. *See also* Escort cards
programs, 109
signage and, 109
special touches, 102–103
thank-you notes, 95, 110–111, 150, 155
timeline, 95, 96
wedding announcements, 109
Stationery printing processes and special touches. *See also* Calligraphy
blind embossing, 102
deckled edges, 102
die-cutting, 102
edging, 102
engraving, 95, 96, 97, 99, 102
flat printing, 96
Flat printing, 97
foil stamping, *34*, *56*, 102
letterpress, *34*, 96, 97, *99*, *102*, *193*
liners, 99, 102
printing process options, 96–97
special touches, 102–103
thematic stamps, 102
thermography, 96, 97, 102
wax seal, 102, 106
Stations, food, 219
Stephanotis, *58*, *132*, *136*, 142, 253
Stepmother and/or stepfather, 188
Strapless dress, jewelry with, 74
Styling your look, 62–89. *See also* Attire; Dress
about: overview of, 64
beauty rehearsal, 78
bloat banished, 85
brightening smile, 78
cutting, coloring hair, 78
diet, nutrition and, 85
exercise and, 85
final appointments, 78
hairstyle, 78, 80–81
makeup, 78, 82–83
manicure and pedicure, 78
pacing yourself, 78
self-care and, 85
skin care, 78
sleep and, 85
tanning skin, 78
timeline, 78
Succulents, 141, *141*, *258*
Summer flowers, 124–125
Sweet peas, *54*, *122*, *125*, *132*, *134*, *136*, *138*, 142

T

Tablesettings, color palette and, *58*
Takeaways. *See* Favors (takeaways)
Tanning skin, 78
Tea-length dresses, 71
Teeth, whitening, 78
Tent, renting, 43
Textiles, inspiring cake design, 236
Thank-you gifts, 150, 155
Thank-you notes, 95, 110–111, 150, 155
Themes, 22–43
classic wedding, 29
coastal celebration, 30–31
garden affair, 33
modern soirée, 37
personalizing, 26–27
rustic party, 34–35
stamps reflecting, 102
tropical, 38–39
Thermography, 96, 97, 102
Three-piece veil, 77
Timelines
cake, 227
ceremony, 177
dress, 66
favors, 252
flowers, 117
guests, 167
photographer/videographer, 198
planner orchestrating, 21
prewedding parties, 150
reception, 43, 205
registry, 157
stationery, 95, 96
tent, 43
transportation, 168
venue, 41
wedding-ready makeover, 78
Tipping, 17, 21
Toasting, 220
by best man, 190, 205, 220
Champagne for, 210, 220
at engagement party, 150
guidelines for, 220
honoring parents, 188, 220
by maid of honor, 190, 220
at reception, 190, 205, 209, 220
at rehearsal dinner, 161
tradition of, 220
at wedding weekend, 171
Topiaries and trees, 141
Tossing bouquet, 205
Tossing congratulatory rice, petals, etc., *198*, 252–253
Traditional wedding, 29
Traditions
choosing wedding party, 190
Christian ceremony, 178
cutting cake, 224
decorating getaway car, 265
engagement party, 150–151
escort cards, 109
Hindu ceremony, 178
Jewish ceremony, 178
Muslim ceremony, 178
non-denominational service, 178
photography, 198
rehearsal dinner, 161
reply card, 99
saving cake top tier, 226
sending shower invitations, 152
toasting, 220

tossing rice, 253
wearing a veil, 76
writing vows and, 184
Transportation
assessing needs, 168
budget, 17
as entertainment, 169
getting guests around, 168–169
making deal, getting in writing, 168
newlywed getaway, 264–265
timeline, 168
valet parking and, 168
Tree planting, 182
Tropical flowers, 136
Tropical invitations, 100
Tropical wedding, 38–39
Tulips, *58*, *117*, *122*, *129*, *136*, *139*, 142

U

Unity candles, 182, 188
Ushers, 188, 190, 193, 194, 196, 197

V

Valets, 168
Veils, 76–77
Venue
budget considerations, 41, 45
coastal/lakefront, 30, 38
color palette and, 52–53
comparing options, 41
factors affecting cost, 45
garden affair, 33
having plan B, 43
hotel/club pros and cons, 29
modern metro soirée, 37
questions to ask, 41
selecting, 41
timeline, 41
visiting locations, 41
Viburnums, *125*, *137*, *139*
Videography/photography, 17, 198–199
V-neck dresses, 73, 74
Vows, writing, 184–185

W

Water cleansing, 182
Wax seals, on envelopes, 102, 106
Wedding announcements, 109
Wedding party, choosing, 190–191. *See also* Best man; Bridesmaids; Groomsmen; Maid of honor; Ushers
Weekend activities and schedule, 170–171
Weekend weddings
budget and, 17
planning meals and activities, 171
Welcome bags, *167*
Welcoming committee, 194
White jasmine, meaning of, 142
White lilies, meaning of, 142
White roses, meaning of, 142
Winter flowers, 128–129
Workouts, 85
Wreaths, *125*, *126*

271
INDEX

ABOUT THE AUTHOR

Martha Stewart, founder of Martha Stewart Living Omnimedia, is America's most trusted lifestyle expert and teacher. Her first book, *Entertaining*, was published in 1982, and since then she has authored dozens of bestselling books on cooking, gardening, weddings, homekeeping, and decorating, including *Martha Stewart's Baking Handbook*, *Martha Stewart's Wedding Cakes*, *Martha Stewart's Cooking School*, *Martha's American Food*, *One Pot*, *Clean Slate*, *Martha Stewart's Appetizers*, and many more. MSLO publishes two award-winning magazines, *Martha Stewart Weddings* and *Martha Stewart Living*; designs branded merchandise for a broad group of retailers; and provides a wealth of inspired ideas and practical information at marthastewart.com.